POLITICAL LIFE WRITING
in the Pacific
Reflections on Practice

POLITICAL LIFE WRITING
in the Pacific
Reflections on Practice

Edited by
JACK CORBETT
AND BRIJ V. LAL

PRESS

Published by ANU Press
The Australian National University
Acton ACT 2601, Australia
Email: anupress@anu.edu.au
This title is also available online at http://press.anu.edu.au

---

National Library of Australia Cataloguing-in-Publication entry

Title: Political life writing in the Pacific : reflections on practice / Jack Corbett, Brij V. Lal, editors.

ISBN: 9781925022605 (paperback) 9781925022612 (ebook)

Subjects: Politicians--Islands of the Pacific--Biography.
Authorship--Social aspects.
Political science--Social aspects.
Research--Moral and ethical aspects.
Islands of the Pacific--Politics and government--Biography.

Other Creators/Contributors:
Corbett, Jack, editor.
Lal, Brij V., editor.

Dewey Number: 324.2092

All rights reserved. No part of this publication may be reproduced, stored in a retrieval system or transmitted in any form or by any means, electronic, mechanical, photocopying or otherwise, without the prior permission of the publisher.

Cover design and layout by ANU Press

Revised edition © August 2015 ANU Press

Contents

List of Tables vii
Preface ix
Contributors xi

1. Practising Political Life Writing in the Pacific 1
   Jack Corbett

2. Political Life Writing in Papua New Guinea 13
   Jonathan Ritchie

3. Understanding Solomon 33
   Christopher Chevalier

4. The 'Pawa Meri' Project 47
   Ceridwen Spark

5. 'End of a Phase of History' 59
   Brij V. Lal

6. Random Thoughts of an Occasional Practitioner 75
   Deryck Scarr

7. Walking the Line between *Anga Fakatonga* and
   Anga Fakapalangi 87
   Areti Metuamate

8. Writing Influential Lives 99
   Nicole Haley

9. Celebrating My Journey 111
   Sethy Regenvanu

10. Reflections on *A Remarkable Journey* 121
    Carol Kidu

11. Solomon Islands' Biography 129
    Clive Moore

12. Biographies of Post-1900 New Zealand Prime Ministers . . . 145
    Doug Munro

List of Tables

Table 1: Biographical works about, or by, Papua New Guineans 29

Table 2: The life and career of Solomon Mamaloni – a synopsis 33

Table 3: Summary of interviews conducted by Christopher Chevalier (to March 2013) 42

Table 4: Newspapers and magazines relating to the Solomon Islands 43

Table 5: New Zealand prime ministers (since 1900) and their biographies. . .147

Table 6: Edited collections on New Zealand prime ministers. 150

Table 7: Sales figures for political biographies published by Auckland University Press 165

Preface

This book emerged from a workshop symposium on political life writing held at The Australian National University (ANU) in October 2012. The inspiration for the workshop came over a cup of tea we shared with Chris Chevalier in the Coombs Tea Room earlier that year where we discussed the practice of life writing and the issues and challenges that one faces while writing political biography. Chris is currently writing a life of Solomon Mamaloni. Some of the themes we explored related to life writing in general; the ambiguous place of the genre within the academy, its 'great person in history' tendencies, the relationship between writer and subject, and the big question that faces us all when we produce our manuscripts: what to leave in and out.

As we began to dig deeper we also touched on aspects of the life writing art that seemed particularly pertinent to political figures: public perception and ideology, identifying political successes and important policy initiatives, grappling with issues like corruption and age-old political science questions about political leadership and 'dirty hands'. We also explored the nature of certain source materials: Hansard, political speeches, interviews, and the divergent perspectives offered by supporters and opponents.

Some of these themes seemed to be of particular significance in a Pacific context, including patterns of colonisation and the memory of independence, issues elliptically captured by terms like 'culture' and 'tradition', the nature of 'self' presented in Pacific life writing, and the tendency for many of these texts to have been written by 'outsiders', or at least the increasingly contested nature of what that term means.

With this broad canvas in mind, we sought to bring together, for the first time, a community of scholars writing 'political lives' in the Pacific. Specifically, we wanted to explore the practice of life writing according to the people involved: the practitioners. Our aim was to reflect on the experiential side of life writing and to consider what this meant for the texts we produce. The workshop exceeded even our expectations in the quality and range of papers. This collection is the product of that discussion.

Not all of the presenters were able to write for this volume but we are nevertheless grateful for their comments and careful suggestions throughout the workshop. In keeping with the conversational nature of the proceedings, we have only very lightly edited the papers so as to preserve the familiar tone. This is, we believe, particularly important given that we hope this volume will be of use to practitioners working outside of the academy and its self-referential vernacular.

The invitation to participate in the workshop was open-ended and papers were invited that explored any or all of the themes outlined above in relation to the unique aspects of writing political life history in the Pacific region. The workshop was generously funded by the ANU School of Culture, History and Language's Research Committee and the School of International, Political and Strategic Studies' State, Society and Governance in Melanesia Program. We are particularly grateful to James Holman for his assistance with logistics and to Nicholas Halter for editing the manuscript.

Jack Corbett and Brij V. Lal
Canberra

Contributors

Christopher Chevalier is a PhD scholar in the School of Sociology at The Australian National University.

Jack Corbett is a Research Fellow on a joint appointment with Griffith University's Centre for Governance and Public Policy and the Griffith Asia Institute.

Nicole Haley is the convenor of The Australian National University's State, Society and Governance in Melanesia Program.

Carol Kidu is a former Minister and Leader of the Opposition in Papua New Guinea.

Brij V. Lal is Professor of Pacific and Asian History in the School of Culture, History and Language, College of Asia and the Pacific, at The Australian National University.

Areti Metuamate is a PhD scholar in Pacific Studies at The Australian National University.

Clive Moore is Professor of Pacific and Australian History and Head of the School of History, Philosophy, Religion and Classics at the University of Queensland.

Doug Munro is a Wellington-based biographer and historian and an Adjunct Professor at the University of Queensland.

Sethy Regenvanu is a former Deputy Prime Minister of Vanuatu.

Jonathan Ritchie is a Senior Research Fellow at Deakin University's Alfred Deakin Research Institute.

Deryck Scarr is a member of the Emeritus Faculty at The Australian National University.

Ceridwen Spark is a Fellow at the State, Society and Governance in Melanesia Program at The Australian National University.

1. Practising Political Life Writing in the Pacific

Jack Corbett

> … biography is not solely a quest to imagine and transform the other. No. It is also a quest to understand and transform the self through a journey mediated by feeling and self-discovery.[1]

The state of life writing in the Pacific presents us with something of a paradox. On the one hand, on a country-by-country basis, there seem to be numerous gaps, with academics the primary authors of the few lives that have been written. On the other hand, as Doug Munro has remarked, when taken as a group, the corpus of life writing in the Pacific is one of the most substantial bodies of work about the politics and history of the region.[2] Certainly, when it comes to the study of leadership and political leadership in particular, nothing from the mainstream academic disciplines rivals its breadth and depth, which is especially remarkable given that much of this writing is of recent – that is, post-colonial – origin. This point is argued most persuasively by Jonathan Ritchie's contribution to this volume, which focuses specifically on the state of the life writing art in Papua New Guinea, but it is of more general relevance. Academic and popular commentators in the Pacific regularly observe that politics tends to be heavily personalised, highlighting the ways that governments and coalitions rise and fall on the strength of their leaders. In this context, the individual life takes on added significance than it might elsewhere. Despite this, life writing generally, and life writing about political figures in particular, is a recent development and as such tends not to be based on a wide reading of the available literature. There is comparatively little reflexive analysis about how these texts have been created and what they contribute to mainstream disciplinary approaches.

Reflecting this discrepancy, a number of edited collections dedicated to the art of life writing have recently attempted to fill the void. The Stewart and Strathern volume *Identity Work: Constructing Pacific Lives* addresses several life writing themes of immediate concern to anthropologists and debates about Melanesian ethnography, including the nature of personhood, self, and sense of place and gender.[3] A year later, Lal and Hempenstall edited the *Pacific Lives,*

---

1 R. Morley, 'Fighting Feeling: Re-thinking Biographical Praxis', *Life Writing*, 9: 1 (2012), 79.
2 D. Munro, 'Would the Biographers Please Stand up', in B. Lal and P. Hempenstall (eds), *Pacific Lives, Pacific Places: Bursting Boundaries in Pacific History* (Canberra 2001).
3 P.J. Stewart and A. Strathern, *Identity Work: Constructing Pacific Lives* (Pittsburgh 2000).

Pacific Places: Bursting Boundaries in Pacific History collection which, in many respects, provided an historian's perspective on these same themes – although the answers each discipline delivered were very different.[4] Where anthropologists have tended to see autobiography and biography as presuming a 'western' understanding of the individual subject that is alien to Pacific cultures, the Lal and Hempenstall volume sees life writing as a counterpoint to this characterisation of Islanders as acting solely through a cultural template.[5] Instead, they recognise the capacity of life history to provide a sense of human agency often missing from structuralist accounts. These tensions are deeply embedded in the scholarly literature more generally, but life writing has been one avenue where these debates have surfaced in the Pacific context.

The most recent addition is the Lal and Luker volume *Telling Pacific Lives: Prisms of Process*.[6] An explicitly multidisciplinary and wide-ranging endeavour, this book takes on the existing debate between historians and anthropologists about the place of culture and world view in Pacific life writing – although it does not resolve it. Where it differs from previous attempts, aside from being significantly longer with more contributors, is in its focus on life writing practice. We learn more about the process of conducting research – about how relationships are negotiated and information is accessed, verified and interpreted. That is not to say the two previous volumes ignored this topic – ethnographic reflexivity is a core theme in Stewart and Strathern's book, for example – but the Lal and Luker volume puts the issue front of stage.[7] They conclude that '"Telling [l]ives" is an intricate and contested exercise' that is complicated 'in cross-cultural and non-literate contexts where notions of time, space, history, myth, the role and obligations of individuals in society differ greatly and where, moreover, historical memory is not archived.'[8] They ask: 'How, in these situations, do we construct lives?' The answer, they contend, 'varies enormously depending on the teller's discipline as well as the subject's circumstance and context. If "making bare the poor dead secrets of the heart" is the task, it is not easy, never was.'[9]

As something of a successor to the *Telling Pacific Lives* project, this volume takes its cue from their description of the complexity and negotiation embedded in the practice of life writing. The contributions assembled here vary significantly in terms of circumstance and discipline, aim and method. This is a collection of authorial reflections about how they have gone about writing a life, what the experience was like, and what they have learnt through the process. Axiomatically, by looking across these accounts we appreciate that

---

4   B. Lal and P. Hempenstall (eds), *Pacific Lives, Pacific Places*.
5   Ibid.
6   B. Lal and V. Luker (eds), *Telling Pacific Lives: Prisms of Process* (Canberra 2008).
7   Stewart and Strathen, *Identity Work*.
8   Lal and Luker, *Telling Pacific Lives*, xiii–xiv.
9   Ibid., xiv.

there is no set formula for writing a life, political or otherwise. Rather, we see how each author has, in their own way, negotiated the myriad of overlapping issues and tensions that Lal and Luker describe. However, while each instance is unique, there are patterns, themes and lessons that offer guidance to future practitioners. Accordingly, while this book does not provide a theoretical or practical road map on how to write a political life, it contains numerous insights about the types of obstacles that authors encounter along the way, and offers some reflections on how they went about overcoming them.

The obvious point of departure from the Lal and Luker volume is the emphasis on writing 'political' lives. So, let me begin by getting the definitional questions out of the way. Defining what constitutes a 'political' life is fraught and all such attempts are necessarily porous in practice. More than any of the conventional disciplines, life writing muddies attempts to distinguish between personal and political. Consequently, in conceptualising our initial workshop, Brij and I left the 'what is and is not political' question open, allowing authors to self-identify their work. However, like all categorisations, we had in mind a group of texts that we felt formed the core of a genre. This group comprised more than 40 autobiographies, biographies, and collections of writings and speeches written by or about politicians in the Pacific Islands.[10] This is in many respects an unwieldy group that, as evidenced by the chapters in this book on new projects, is growing yearly. The earliest example is an autobiographical book written by Sir Tom Davis – who later became Prime Minister of the Cook Islands – and his first wife Lydia,[11] while the latest is David Hanlon's life of Tosiwo Nakayama.[12] In a broader sense, if we begin to include other political figures – colonial governors, chiefs and prominent clergy for example – the list gets longer and the dates older.

A similar point can be made about the organisation of this book around a geographic location. The life stories of politicians mentioned above all come from the 14 independent and self-governing political entities in the Pacific region. However, they are not spread evenly as there is a greater concentration of works from Fiji, Papua New Guinea and Solomon Islands relative to other parts of the Pacific. That is, the bulk of the writing, political and otherwise, has focused on the Melanesian region. This book includes chapters from outside the Melanesian region which, while adding a contrasting perspective, also highlight some of the distinctive aspects of life writing in Melanesia. For example, Munro's chapter on life writing about New Zealand's prime ministers brings the relative newness of the Pacific literature into sharp focus. The genre in New Zealand is

---

10   For review, see J. Corbett, '"Two Worlds?" Interpreting Leadership Narratives in the 20th Century Pacific', *Journal of Pacific History*, 47: 1 (2012), 69–91.
11   T. Davis and L. Davis, *Doctor to the Islands* (London 1955).
12   D. Hanlon, *Making Micronesia: A Political Biography of Tosiwo Nakayama* (Honolulu 2014).

well established and forms part of a larger intellectual discourse. By contrast, life writing in the Pacific Islands has tended to be an occasional art practised by academics – for nearly all of the contributors to this volume, life writing makes up only a small portion of their principal work – and other enthusiasts, all of whom have tended to be outsiders.

Without labouring the point, the term 'life history' raises the same issues. As above, it is predominantly employed in this book to capture a variety of materials, the bulk of which fall into the conventional categories of autobiography and biography, along with edited collections of speeches and diaries. However, there are many other ways to record a life, including via film, which is the subject of Ceridwen Spark's chapter. Indeed, some of the most famous life histories written about political figures in the Pacific region – for example, the Ulli Beier assisted life of former Deputy Prime Minister of Papua New Guinea, Albert Maori Kiki;[13] the Roger Keesing edited book on former Solomon Islands Minister Jonathan Fifi'i;[14] or the Judith Bennett and Khyla Russell edited life of the former Speaker of the Solomon Islands parliament, Lloyd Maepeza Gina[15] – were initially recorded as interviews before they became substantive texts. There have also been several attempts at writing a collection of lives. The Davidson and Scarr edited *Pacific Islands Portraits*[16] and Deryck Scarr's *More Pacific Islands Portraits*,[17] contain short biographical works in the mould of Plutarch's famous *Lives,* as does the Firth and Tarte edited *20th Century Fiji: People Who Shaped This Nation*[18] and the Pollard and Waring collection *Being the First: Storis Blong Oloketa Mere lo Solomon Aelan.*[19]

Having outlined the limits of the terms that define the essential parameters of this collection, it is important to say that all three nevertheless serve as a useful shorthand which, while contentious, captures a sense of the people we are talking about, the places they come from, and the ways in which their stories have been recorded and made accessible to a range of audiences. In other words, while all categorisations are somewhat arbitrary, this does not mean they serve no function – quite the opposite. In the context of this book, their usefulness stems from the sense of an ideological Pacific community that, in many respects, has been created by the people we call political leaders and sustained through their writings.

---

13 A.M. Kiki, *Kiki: Ten Thousand Years in a Lifetime, a New Guinea Autobiography* (Melbourne 1968).
14 J. Fifi'i, *From Pig-Theft to Parliament: My Life Between Two Worlds* (Suva 1989).
15 L.M. Gina, *Journeys in a Small Canoe: The Life and Times of a Solomon Islander* (Canberra 2003).
16 J.W. Davidson and D. Scarr (eds), *Pacific Islands Portraits* (Canberra 1970).
17 D. Scarr (ed.), *More Pacific Islands Portraits* (Canberra 1979).
18 S. Firth and S. Tarte, *20th Century Fiji: People Who Shaped This Nation* (Suva 2001).
19 A.A. Pollard and M. Waring, *Being the First: Storis Blong Oloketa Mere lo Solomon Aelan* (Auckland 2009).

Largely, political life writing in the Pacific has taken on literary and empirical rather than theoretical forms. This partly reflects the nature of the genre which is why it occupies such a contentious place within political studies, both historical and contemporary. Critics of life writing argue that the genre is overly subjective, is not explanatory in orientation, and does not articulate a rigorous methodology.[20] In particular, the strong relationship between the author and their subject is the source of some ambivalence for scholars concerned with objectivity and scientific rigour. Certainly, the 'great person in history' tendency of the single person narrative sits in stark contrast to conventional disciplinary approaches that portray leaders as products of social, economic and political forces or as responding rationally to institutionally structured incentives.[21] However, this type of approach has limits, not the least of which is the inability to consider the human dimension of political life. This takes on particular significance in the Pacific where writers grapple with topics that tend to fall outside the purview of biographical scholarship. Both Nicole Haley and Clive Moore's subjects, for example, emphasise the importance of spirituality, including dreams and premonitions, in the lives they consider.

In addition to the overarching rationale for this book – to reflect on how writers have gone about constructing political life histories – it also serves as a response to the ambiguity with which the genre is treated by mainstream disciplines. Political life writing, as David Hanlon outlines, provides a 'critical focal lens' through which we can examine a host of key themes and debates pertinent to the contemporary Pacific in particular, and the study of politics in general.[22] However, to support the veracity of these claims we need to understand how political lives are written and consider how each author leaves their own imprint on the text. This is true of all life writing but takes on added significance in the context of political figures.

Political life histories are more than mere stories about politicians or influential men and women – they focalise wider ideals, values and aspirations and, in the case of independence leaders, embody the story of a nation.[23] The importance of retelling the story of Vanuatu's independence struggle is central to former Deputy Prime Minister, Reverend Sethy Regenvanu's chapter in this collection. Regenvanu describes his motivation for writing autobiography as stemming

---

20   T. Arklay, J. Nethercote and J. Wanna, 'Preface', in T. Arklay, J. Nethercote and J. Wanna (eds), *Australian Political Lives* (Canberra 2006), xi.
21   T. Arklay et al., *Australian Political Lives*; R.A.W. Rhodes, 'Theory, Method and British Political History', *Political Science Review*, 10: 2 (2012), 161–76.
22   D. Hanlon, '"You Did What, Mr President!?!?" Trying to Write a Biography of Tosiwo Nakayama', in B. Lal and V. Luker (eds), *Telling Pacific Lives* (Canberra 2008), 167.
23   P. Holden, 'A Man and an Island: Gender and Nation in Lee Kuan Yew's the Singapore Story', *Biography*, 24: 2 (2001), 401–24; D. Morais, 'Malaysia: The Writing of Lives and the Constructing of Nation', *Biography*, 33: 1 (2010), 84–109.

in part from anger at how his political career ended but also, as one of the founding fathers of the nation, out of a sense of duty to record the past for future generations.[24] His chapter, like his book, presents a passionate case for why autobiography, which often attracts even greater suspicion than biography in the eyes of many mainstream scholars, is an important medium for recording memories. Specifically, he argues that it provides an account of events as seen through the eyes of somebody who lived it, experienced it, and who knows what the burdens and pressures of holding public office are like.

In a distinct but similar vein, Brij Lal's chapter addresses the same question. Daunted by the prospect of turning all of his carefully collected data into a substantive text, Lal describes receiving the impetus to finish his biographical manuscript from a group of high school students who, despite his considerable significance to Fiji's contemporary history, did not know who former Leader of the Opposition Jai Ram Reddy was. Like Regenvanu, Lal describes how he approached writing with a sense of fury that stemmed from a desire to not only capture the essence of his subject's public persona, but to set the record straight and ensure that Reddy and the party he represented was not expunged from the historical record: 'I write because I have to, to bear witness to the time in which I have lived. I see writing as an act of revenge against a culture of indifference and forgetfulness, an act of revenge against historical amnesia' (Chapter 5). In contrast, Christopher Chevalier outlines in his contribution how he writes about former Prime Minister of Solomon Islands, Solomon Mamaloni, 'to repay a debt to Solomon Islands for having given me an adopted daughter and more than 20 years of fascinating work, travel and study' (Chapter 3).

The strong relationship between author and subject is particularly apparent in Nicole Haley's chapter about Sane Noma, a ritual leader, land mediator and visionary from Lake Kopiago District, Papua New Guinea. She writes 'to honour the life and memory of Sane Noma' (Chapter 8). Haley describes how Noma has informed or inspired almost every piece of academic writing she has ever written. More significantly, his prophecies are of great importance to her life and that of her daughter Aliria. However, despite the significance of Noma's life, and the window it offers into a century of dramatic change in Papua New Guinea, Haley relates struggling with one question in particular: how to tell his story. She wonders how her relationship with Noma will be received and describes a sense of trepidation at the potential ridicule the type of personal account, which would do justice to her subject, might attract in the academy. Nonetheless, she is prepared to brave the odds and defy scholarly conventions to give us her account of a sensitive engagement with a world beyond the realm of traditional scholarship.

---

24 S.J. Regenvanu, *Laef Blong Mi: From Village to Nation: An Autobiography* (Port Vila 2004).

As Doug Munro's chapter poignantly illustrates, the connection between an author and their subject is central to any theoretical or practical conceptualisation of biographical writing. It is normally assumed that for one person to dedicate so much of their time to the study of somebody else's life there must be an important bond that links these two people. Sometimes there is, as in the case of Lal and Reddy or Haley and Noma. In other instances, as Deryck Scarr's chapter illustrates, chance and fortune play a significant role in pairing an author and their subject. Like many life writers, serendipity, Scarr recalls, brought him to the Pacific and had a hand in his decision to write a two-volume biography of Sir John Bates Thurston, Governor of Fiji, which imposed itself on him during his work in the Western Pacific High Commission archives. Similarly, Scarr describes being approached unawares by the selection committee tasked with finding a biographer to write the life of Fijian statesman Ratu Sir Lala Sukuna. Based on the success of the Sukuna book, he further explains how he felt that a life of Sukuna's onetime protégé, inaugural Prime Minister and former President of Fiji, Ratu Sir Kamisese Mara, 'was rather expected of me' (Chapter 6). That is not to say Scarr wrote on a whim – the interest of the subject, the availability of materials and the political significance of the latter two subjects, we can infer, were key considerations – but that writing biography is often something people stumble upon rather than set out to do.

Somewhat scarcer than reflection on the relationship between author and subject, but of great significance in the Pacific where nearly all political autobiographies have been compiled with some assistance, is consideration of the role of editing a life or a collection of lives. This is the subject that Clive Moore tackles and his thoughts reveal several interrelated themes. The first concerns recognition. Editing a life or a collection of lives requires the investment of an enormous amount of time and yet this commitment remains largely undervalued by those who judge academic outputs. This quandary, Moore relates, is often under-appreciated by his subjects. One solution he explores is the possibility of becoming a co-author of his latest project, the life of former Minister and Governor-General of Solomon Islands, Sir Nathaniel Waena, thus side-stepping the bureaucratic requirements of the academy. But, as he concedes, it also entails greater ownership of the content – creating new problems and questions about historical veracity and authorial integrity.

The Moore chapter raises several themes that are taken up by other contributors to this book, including the nature of source materials used to compile political lives. Each author, as Munro highlights, solves this problem differently depending on their subject and the type of life they want to write. In the case of his current subject, Moore grapples with how to interpret and incorporate the significance of premonitions and dreams in early drafts. As he relates, there is something refreshing about the way these private experiences are related but he wonders how a book is to be made from such material. He, and several others, make a similar point about Christianity. A Christian faith is central to how most Pacific Islanders understand and give meaning to their lives and yet this spiritual commitment is often foreign to the academics that assist with editing or writing their life stories. None of the chapters resolves this dilemma but all concede that, in some way, this disjuncture has had some impact on the final product.

Locating and accessing the information required to write a life is a common challenge for all practitioners. However, there is something about securing interviews that is both distinctively demanding and uniquely rewarding. This point is made with particular force in Areti Metuamate's chapter on writing the life of the late Tupou V, King of Tonga. Where all interviewers have to confront questions of permission and access, Metuamate also describes learning and observing the protocols that surround a subject like the King of Tonga. What's more, many of the King's friends – Sir Michael Hill the jeweller, Lord Glenarthur of Britain and the King of Bhutan – who could talk with some authority on the nature of the man, are not easily accessible. Despite acknowledging inevitable mistakes and the providential hand of Facebook, Metuamate expresses gratitude for the generosity of his interviewees.

The willingness of informants is also a theme that Christopher Chevalier addresses when reflecting on writing a life of Mamaloni. Interviews, says Chevalier (Chapter 3), 'provided original and fascinating insights not available from the public record'. Where Chevalier and Metuamate disagree is with respect to how far a biographer should probe the life of their subject. Chevalier, perhaps conscious of the complexity of Mamaloni's private life – he had four wives in a highly Christianised country – stands true to the adage that a biographer 'should go up to the bedroom door but do[es] not go beyond'. But Metuamate, whose subject had a much-commented-upon private life, disagrees and argues instead that public figures forgo a certain amount of privacy by virtue of the office they hold. This discussion is particularly pertinent to political life writing in the Pacific as it forces us to consider what public office means in this context, and what types of norms and standards govern how public roles are understood and reinterpreted, both by biographers and constituents.

While every situation is unique, retrieving and interpreting written or oral data is nevertheless a well-trodden path in scholarly work. Certainly, even if insights come in the form of dreams and premonitions, the mode of delivery, be it oral or written, is not alien to most researchers, even if certain disciplines privilege different sources. Film, on the other hand, is relatively unique and certainly, as a medium for political biography, its use is less common in the Pacific. However, as Ceridwen Spark argues in her chapter about the 'Pawa Meri' project in Papua New Guinea, film can be an incredibly powerful way of telling a life story. Significantly, Spark argues, unmediated by the academy, many Pacific filmmakers are documenting their own stories and those of their relatives and fellow villagers, and communicating them to audiences all over the world via the internet. Like Moore, Spark has sought to be a facilitator rather than the primary author of these works with the six documentaries all directed by Papua New Guinean women. Cooperation and compromise are the corner stone of her approach. Spark aims to preserve a narrative that the people themselves will recognise. Metuamate also makes this point: any assessment of individuals must be seen in the context of wider roles and relationship in society, necessitating modification of the genre's conventions.

This type of life history raises many interesting and exciting possibilities. In the context of this book, one of the most important questions Spark raises is: who is the audience? Audience is a theme that runs through former Minister and Leader of the Opposition in Papua New Guinea, Dame Carol Kidu's chapter. Kidu describes how personally rewarding she found the positive reaction to her autobiography *A Remarkable Journey*,[25] and relates that a number of people have asked her to write a sequel that covers her three terms in parliament. But how would readers want to access this chapter in her life, she wonders aloud? Humorous anecdotes and personal insights would satisfy a larger audience but, she worries, they might seem superficial or frivolous to serious scholars. Certainly, she concedes, a detailed life and times approach would require time and resources that she does not have. Accordingly, the Kidu chapter illustrates some of the barriers that political leaders in the Pacific Islands face in writing their own life stories, not the least of which is that life writing does not pay the bills.

In addressing the audience question with regards to film, Spark argues that Papua New Guineans want to represent and watch themselves. In theory, books also provide an avenue for Pacific Islanders to write and read about themselves. Indeed, as Jonathan Ritchie outlines in his chapter, the need to provide future generations of Pacific Islanders with role models from the past was a central reason for his biography of Ebia Olewale. The assumption, however, as the Lal chapter argues, is that the younger generation are reading. There is a proverbial chicken and egg problem here because, as Regenvanu highlights explicitly but nearly all the authors touch on implicitly, since the closure of the Institute of Pacific Studies at the University of the South Pacific, there are few local avenues through which Pacific scholars can publish their writing. Film and the internet provide new possibilities that may circumvent this problem. However, as the continued reliance of the genre on the input of scholars from Australia, New Zealand and Hawaii in particular highlights, there are considerable inequalities that underpin who writes Pacific lives and who the audience is for these works.

---

25 C. Kiku, *A Remarkable Journey* (South Melbourne 2002).

Both editors know from personal experience of the desire for Pacific Islanders to write their stories – of parents, pastors and places – but they often lack the skills and resources to do so. The relative absence of non-academic publishers, and the size of the market, presents significant barriers. Outsiders step in to fill this void but, as Moore asks, how much influence should they have?

Beyond writing about political figures, the Spark chapter also asks us to consider the *politics* of writing political lives. She raises two questions: who are considered leaders or role models worth writing about and who can represent them? As outlined, questions about representation are longstanding in disciplinary scholarship on the Pacific but, as Peter Hempenstall argues, they bite hardest in life writing as it seeks to 'reach across cultures and deal with multi-ethnic senses of the self and the person in the Pacific'.[26] However, Spark illustrates that they take on additional significance as donors in particular have become interested in Pacific leadership. The six Pawa Meri films, while directed by Papua New Guinean women, were funded by the Australian aid program and so reflected a particular leadership image they wanted to extol. In some respects, the tendency to celebrate remarkable achievements is an indelible feature of all political life writing. Certainly most of the existing works have been written by or about leaders of some stature who were usually highly educated – often overseas – and who held numerous senior positions in both government and business. However, beyond the general point that life writing tends to attract a certain type of subject, and the warning that donor influence presents a two-edged sword for life writers, Spark's chapter also highlights one of the most obvious features of the genre in the Pacific: it is almost entirely dominated by men.

Given the considerable push to increase women's representation in parliament, Spark asks how we should treat these women as biographical subjects. Should their lives be subjected to less scrutiny in the service of the broader feminist agenda? As the Kidu chapter highlights, there is considerable scope for life writing about women political leaders to reveal the gendered practice of politics in the Pacific and provide inspirational examples of how female politicians make a substantial impact in this predominantly male domain. But, when does biography become hagiography? The answer, Spark concedes, is complicated. By recording the lives of young educated women who are atypical in Papua New Guinea we risk, she argues, misrepresenting who these leaders are while setting up a standard to which most young women in Papua New Guinea cannot aspire. On the other hand 'the exploration of exceptional lives can reveal a privileged person's very ordinariness and humanity' (Chapter 4).

---

26 P. Hempenstall, 'Introduction, in B.V. Lal and P. Hempenstall (eds), *Pacific Lives, Pacific Places* (Canberra 2001), 4.

At the beginning of this chapter I argued that political life writing in the Pacific has predominantly taken a literary and empirical rather than theoretical focus. While largely true – the genre rarely deals with the theoretical questions that occupy biography journals for example – it is also somewhat misleading as it overlooks the dominant metaphor or theme used to describe the way Pacific leaders navigate and define their lives: that they live 'between worlds'. Steeped in modernist precepts, as Ritchie (Chapter 2) illustrates, the use of the metaphor is both pervasive and revealing: 'ten thousand years in a lifetime', 'the stone age to the space age', 'man of two worlds', 'one woman, two cultures'. Despite its appeal, Ritchie points to the limits of this 'obvious and easily adopted' trope, and asks whether it remains useful for understanding leaders into the future, if it ever did in the past.

The use of the 'two worlds' metaphor is, as I have argued elsewhere, an overly simplistic and even unhelpful analytic device for understanding political leadership in the Pacific.[27] The task then for aspiring political life writers is to find new ways of conceptualising the social setting in which their subjects act. The subtitle of Ritchie's life of Ebia Olewale, *A Life of Service*, offers one solution here. Indeed, 'service' is not an unpopular metaphor used in Pacific political life writing. *He Served* is the title of Robert Kiste's (1998) biography of former Fijian Senator Macu Salato,[28] while former Governor-General of Papua New Guinea, Sir Paulias Matane's autobiography goes by the name *To Serve With Love*.[29] In contrast to the stale tradition versus modern dichotomy, what it means to serve a community and a nation via public office, the demands and rewards of acting out political roles, and how the endeavours of leaders are received by the people they represent offers, to borrow Ritchie's words, 'a more nuanced and sophisticated' way into the human dimension of political life. Rather than mimicking the interpretations that dominate mainstream disciplines, life writing has the unique capacity to capture this humanity, but to do so it requires concepts and questions that coherently align with its aims. Exploring the nature of public service in the Pacific Islands offers one such avenue by which life writers can set a new theoretical and empirical research agenda.

This volume then is about political life writing practice in the Pacific Islands. It is not a theoretical treatise but rather a collection of authorial reflections from a variety of disciplinary and personal perspectives, which does not conform to a dictated template, but rather explores how they have gone about writing a life, what the experience was like, and what they have learnt through the process. This is the first step in a long journey, not the last word. There are questions hinted at in this volume that remain unresolved (and are perhaps

---

27 Corbett, '"Two Worlds?"'.
28 R. Kiste, *He Served: A Biography of Macu Salato* (Suva 1998).
29 P. Matane, *To Serve with Love* (Victoria 1992).

beyond resolution). These include more general reflections about power and culture, and the interpretation of Pacific Island values. But, for now, we leave detailed investigation of these themes for another day. We seek instead to record the experiential side of life writing and to consider what this means for the texts we produce. What emerges is a series of patterns, themes and lessons that will be of benefit to those contemplating writing a life, or merely to those interested in understanding more about the lives that have been written.

2. Political Life Writing in Papua New Guinea

What, Who, Why?

Jonathan Ritchie

Political life writing in Papua New Guinea (PNG) raises themes and issues which resonate across much of Melanesia. Like elsewhere, the individual lived life provides a convenient prism through which to view the larger patterns and processes of society. In this chapter, I write about the pleasure of researching and writing the biography of one of Papua New Guinea's independence leaders and a 'founding father' of the nation, the late Sir Ebia Olewale, and reflect on how my book relates to other efforts.[1] I worked on this project between 2009 and 2012.

This most rewarding exercise has led me to think about the context in which it was undertaken. When I started researching for the book I was under the impression that, by and large, it would be one of the very few works of biography or autobiography about or by Papua New Guineans who played a part in PNG's journey to independence. It would join the small group that includes, among a handful of other works, Michael Somare's *Sana*, Maori Kiki's *Ten Thousand Years in a Lifetime*, and Josephine Abaijah's *A Thousand Coloured Dreams*.

As the project developed, however, I began to wonder more and more about this. Why was it that so little had been written, either by or about Papua New Guineans and their almost unique experience – of moving, to borrow Kiki's often-repeated title, 'ten thousand years in a lifetime'? This apparent dearth is even more pronounced when compared with the flourishing genre of writing about PNG by Australians, as Hank Nelson explored in his contribution to the 'Telling Pacific Lives' symposium at The Australian National University: Nelson listed 207 books published between 1980 and 2008 'primarily by or about Australians who went to Papua New Guinea'.[2] Was it that, after the efflorescence of the late 1960s and early 1970s, the idea of a Papua New Guinean historiography – writing by or about Papua New Guineans rather than Australians in PNG – had withered, a victim like so much else of the turning off of the money tap? Was it that, as Stephen Pokawin told the 2008 Waigani Seminar at the University of

---

1 J. Ritchie, *Ebia Olewale: a Life of Service* (Port Moresby 2012).
2 H. Nelson, 'Lives Told: Australians in Papua and New Guinea', in B. Lal and V. Luker (eds), *Telling Pacific Lives: Prisms of Process* (Canberra 2008), 264.

Papua New Guinea (UPNG), 'Papua New Guinea is a speaking culture', in which the written word takes second place to the primacy of orally handed-down tradition? Why was it?

In fact, at that same Waigani Seminar I became aware of the possibility that there might be more to PNG life writing than the 'usual suspects' of Somare, Kiki, Abaijah and others. Specifically, the workshop on PNG writing and publishing that preceded the seminar ('Buk2Book', organised by Dr John Evans of the UPNG Press and Bookshop) revealed that there was a significant number of writers toiling away, telling the stories of their villages, their people, and their own lives – publishing, if at all, via the medium of the A4 sheet of paper, the printer, and the ring binder. Since then, the growth of internet use and social networking has provided an even more available avenue for publishing life stories.

So, when the opportunity arose to contribute to a symposium on political life writing in the Pacific, I thought that it might be helpful to dig into this a little more, to try to find out what the real situation might be. What has been, or is being, written in the way of life stories by or about Papua New Guineans? What is the status of political – or any – biography and autobiography in that country? Are *Sana*, *Ten Thousand Years*, and *A Thousand Coloured Dreams* more or less it, or is an entire undercurrent of self-published writing going on in offices, schools, and missions? In what follows, I hope to be able to address these questions, and attempt some analysis of not only the question of what has been written, but also why it has been written. As part of this survey, I will subject my own experience with the biography of one Papua New Guinean, Ebia Olewale, to a closer analysis: what motivated me to take on this task, what I learned during the exercise, and what I hope the outcomes will be.

Before beginning to examine what life writing has been written in PNG, by or about Papua New Guineans, it might be helpful to devote a few sentences to the question of how much of Papua New Guinean life writing can be called 'political'. By this I mean the extent to which biography or autobiography in PNG can be considered political, or whether it is life writing of another variety – set for example in the context of a sporting or religious life. This distinction need not delay us much, however. On reflection, I am persuaded by the assessment made by Philip Selth at a symposium on political biography held at The Australian National University in 2005. 'Trying to define a political biography', Selth concluded, 'is a sterile debate'.[3] I concur; it is very difficult and, by and large, unnecessary to try to separate the political from any other filter that one might attempt to place on a life. To borrow a catchcry popular in late

---

3 P. Selth, 'Political Biographies and Administrative Memoirs: Some Concluding Comments', in T. Arklay et al. (eds), *Australian Political Lives: Chronicling Political Careers and Administrative Histories* (Canberra 2006), 103, available online at press.anu.edu.au/anzsog/auspol/html/frames.php.

1960s second-wave feminism, in PNG 'the personal is political'.[4] Any account of a life must encompass the social context in which that life has been lived: after all, man is by nature a political animal, as Aristotle famously expressed it.[5] Especially in a new state like PNG, meaning and influence can be attached to the life experiences of any member of the community who – through their lives being recorded in some way – automatically becomes part of the politics of the community or nation. Furthermore, as Tracey Arklay has expressed it, political biography:

> … provides one set of tools by which to explore history and events from within the temporal and historical context of one life. It allows exploration of the events of history – from a micro perspective – looking at them through the eyes of someone who lived, breathed and was part of that history.[6]

Returning to the question of what has been, or is being, written, I consider that using this broader definition is the best way to look at PNG political life writing. While the most well-known works by players like Somare, Kiki or Abaijah are clearly books of political biography, it is possible to see a political aspect to many others. I hope that this will become obvious in the necessarily brief overview that follows.

The most immediate conclusion is that, despite my original perception, PNG biography and autobiography is – while not exactly well – far from moribund. There have been many books of life writing and a large number of shorter pieces that together form a body of literature about the lives of men and women in PNG. While many were produced in the brief period of efflorescence from the late 1960s to the early 1980s, they continue to be written to this day.

This paper will focus on books published and will not devote a great deal of space to the collection of shorter biographical works, apart from one vital mention: the outstanding record of the lives of many hundreds of Papua New Guineans in the journal *Oral History* published since 1972 by the Institute of PNG Studies. The articles in *Oral History*, collected by students of UPNG and others, often with the aid of small cassette recorders, are indelible reminders of the power of life story telling and really deserve special attention by themselves.

---

4 C. Hanisch, 'The Personal is Political', *Women of the World, Unite! Writings by Carol Hanisch* (1969) available online at www.carolhanisch.org/CHwritings/PIP.html.
5 Aristotle, *Politics*, 1.1253a, available online at www.perseus.tufts.edu/hopper/text?doc=Perseus:abo:tlg, 0086,035:1:1253a.
6 T. Arklay, 'Political Biography: Its Contribution to Political Science', in T. Arklay et al. (eds), *Australian Political Lives: Chronicling Political Careers and Administrative Histories* (Canberra 2006), 21.

The collections open a window into a time in which the world for many Papua New Guineans had begun to change, and they deserve fuller exposition in their own right as records of lives lived very much in a political context.

Outside of the pages of *Oral History*, there are four chief locations for this shorter type of life story writing. In each case, the purpose for recording and retelling carries a different emphasis.

The first of these are the biographical accounts provided in official and semi-official publications, mainly with the purpose of assisting the program of political education in late colonial and early independent PNG. The most prominent of these are three publications about the structure and membership of PNG's legislative body, the House of Assembly, during the last years of the colonial era. Included here are brief descriptive profiles of every Member of the House from 1964 to 1976, set out in as objective and dispassionate a manner as the (unknown) writers were able to achieve. Typically these would list sketchy details of birth, education, and employment, and where applicable some information concerning the subject's parliamentary record. There are 182 individual records of elected Members of the House of Assembly from 1964 to 1976, including nine who won their seats in each of the first three consecutive elections in 1964, 1968 and 1972: Tei Abal, Kaibelt Diria, Sinake Giregire, John Guise, Paul Lapun, Pita Lus, Ronald Neville, Pangial Momei, and Matthias Toliman.[7] Other short descriptions of a biographical nature are in the Australian Government publication *Australian External Territories*, from 1968 to 1971. As well, they appear in the files of the Australian administration and other overseas governments; these, however, were usually not intended for public consumption.[8]

Moving away from the officially recorded biographical portraits, there have been a number of short articles in journals such as *New Guinea and Australia*, *The Pacific and South-east Asia*, *The Journal of the Papua and New Guinea Society*, and *Yagl-Ambu*; usually these encompassed biographical sketches of prominent Papua New Guineans such as Josephine Abaijah, John Momis, Julius Chan, and Kondom Agaundo. In some cases, they were compiled by other Papua New Guineans: one example is the detailed and informed exposition of the 1974 leader of the United Party, Tei Abal, by Utula Samana, then a student of UPNG.[9]

---

7   *The Members of the House of Assembly 1964*, Port Moresby: Department of Information and Extension Services, (1964); *1968–1972 Members of the Second House of Assembly: Territory of Papua and New Guinea*, Port Moresby: Department of Information and Extension Services, (1968); *1972–1976 Members of the Third House of Assembly: Papua New Guinea*, Port Moresby: Department of Information and Extension Services, (1972).
8   See, for example, the British Government file 'Leading personalities in Papua New Guinea 1978', National Archives of the United Kingdom, Commonwealth Office, Far East and Pacific Department and Foreign and Commonwealth Office, South West Pacific Department: Registered Files (H and FW Series), FCO 24/2489.
9   U. Samana, 'Tei Abal', *Yagl-Ambu*, 3: 1 (1974), 219–29.

A third avenue for publishing short biographical profiles of Papua New Guinean subjects comes in the form of specific anthologies of life stories. Two prominent examples of this are *Shaping the Future: Papua New Guinea Personalities* and *Niugini Lives*, both published in 1974 and both with an overtly political message. *Shaping the Future*, edited by the German missionary and lecturer Friedrich Steinbauer, comprises mostly autobiographical portraits by a diverse group of Papua New Guineans active in public life during the early 1970s; subjects range from leading political personalities such as Michael Somare, Paulias Matane and Oala Oala-Rarua to less well-known figures whom Steinbauer considered to represent the emerging character of the new nation. As he explained:

> I have chosen some less famous people to make clear that the development of a country depends not only on Government decisions at high levels, but also on the many trends and influences which flow from ordinary men and women in their everyday life.[10]

Prepared at the same time, and similarly selective in its choice of subjects, but with an even more pronounced sense of the alliance between literature and political consciousness, is *Niugini Lives*, the collection of mainly autobiographical sketches edited by Ulli Beier. As Beier explained in the introduction to the collection, interest in autobiography arose in response to the 'flood of mission memoirs, *kiap* [patrol officer] tales, anthropological treatises and sensational coffee table books'. He continued: 'It was clearly felt that by talking about their own lives, Papua New Guineans could be authentic and authoritative in destroying the intricate maze of myth woven by white writers'.[11] The accounts in *Niugini Lives*, with one exception (by Ligeremaluoga Osea, explored below), were included because of the light they shed on a people discovering their potential after the preceding decades of repressive and paternalist colonialism.

Last in this brief overview of the shorter pieces of life story writing are the biographical entries included in two general reference collections: Ann Turner's *Historical Dictionary of Papua New Guinea* and the *Australian Dictionary of Biography*. Turner's monumental work includes brief descriptions of 63 Papua New Guineans, ranging from the Highlands leader Ningi Kama (c. 1893–1963) to John Pundari (1967–), the Minister for Environment and Conservation in the PNG National Government. It is an essential reference for anyone interested in PNG, not only in its biographical entries but also in its scope of the many factors which have contributed to the composition and character of the contemporary nation.[12]

---

10 F. Steinbauer, *Shaping the Future: Papua New Guinea Personalities* (Madang 1975), ix–x.
11 U. Beier, (ed.) *Niugini Lives* (Milton 1974), 3.
12 A. Turner, *Historical Dictionary of Papua New Guinea* (Lanham 1994).

Finally in this overview of the shorter pieces of political life writing on or by Papua New Guineans are the – admittedly few – entries in the *Australian Dictionary of Biography*. As Hank Nelson observed, the criteria for inclusion in the *Dictionary* are somewhat blurred for Papua New Guineans, with their complicated historical relationship with Australia (Papuans as 'less than citizens of Australia', and New Guineans as Australian protected persons).[13] Nevertheless, there are 15 Papua New Guineans included in the online version of the *Dictionary* (up to 2012): Kondom Agaundo, Paulus Arek, Francis Hagai, Tommy Kabu, Gabriel Ehava Karava, Oala Oala-Rarua, Ahiua Ova, Pita Simogun, Simoi, Sumsuma, Matthias Toliman, Peter ToRot, Louis Vangeke, Alice Wedega, and Yali.[14]

Turning to published books, most observers have concluded that PNG's biographical output has been moderate, if not meagre. At the 'Telling Pacific Lives' symposium, the anthropologist Michael Goddard began his discussion of Motu-Koita personal narratives by asserting that 'since the late colonial period, there have been a significant number of publications which could be roughly classified as Melanesian autobiography'.[15] He includes in this number Michael Somare's *Sana*, Maori Kiki's *Ten Thousand Years in a Lifetime*, Josephine Abaijah's *A Thousand Coloured Dreams*, the autobiographies of two Western Highlands Big Men, Ongka and Ru, and Virginia Watson's *Anyan's Story*.[16] While each of these books is without doubt significant, if this represents all there is by way of PNG life writing then there is a problem. The situation, however, is substantially more positive than would perhaps appear.

In fact, over the 80 years between 1932 and 2012, 37 biographical or autobiographical books have been published by, or about, Papua New Guineans. Sixteen have been autobiographies and 21 biographies. Eighteen have been written either completely or primarily by Papua New Guineans – not surprisingly, this includes all the autobiographies but also two of the biographies. It is probable that many more have been written, and either self-published or produced in such a way that they are not easily sourced outside their immediate locality.

---

13   Nelson, 'Lives Told', 254.
14   These are all available in the *Australian Dictionary of Biography* online, Canberra: National Centre for Biography, The Australian National University, available online at adb.anu.edu.au.
15   M. Goddard, 'From "My Story" to "The Story of Myself" – Colonial Transformations of Personal Narratives among the Motu-Koita of Papua New Guinea', in B. Lal and V. Luker (eds), *Telling Pacific Lives: Prisms of Process* (Canberra 2008), 35.
16   J. Abaijah and E. Wright (eds), *A Thousand Coloured Dreams: The Story of a Young Girl Growing Up in Papua* (Mount Waverley 1991); A.M. Kiki, *Kiki: Ten Thousand Years in a Lifetime; a New Guinea Autobiography* (Melbourne 1968); Ongka, *Ongka: a Self-account by a New Guinea Big Man* (London 1979); Ru, *Ru, Biography of a Western Highlander*, (Boroko 1993); M. Somare, *Sana: an Autobiography of Michael Somare* (Port Moresby 1975); and V. Watson, *Anyan's story: a New Guinea Woman in Two Worlds* (Seattle 1997).

Beginning in 1932, the earliest attempt at either biography or autobiography is that of Ligeremaluoga Osea. Ligeremaluoga, born in the 1890s in New Ireland, was an early convert to Christianity who became a teacher in the 1920s. Using his baptismal name of Hosea or Osea, he became an instructor at George Brown College at Watnabara in New Britain, marrying Anasain Pisig whose death in 1930 left him depressed and desolate. On the advice of the Australian missionary Ella Collins, who gave him 'the only help he received from a white person being a slip of paper with half-a-dozen headings written on it as a guide',[17] Ligeremaluoga wrote his life story until that time; it was published in 1932 as *Erstwhile Savage*. The Papua New Guinean writer and academic Steven Winduo, at least, considers this book to be 'by all accounts the first written account by a South Pacific Islander'.[18]

In later life, Ligeremaluoga continued to be an elder, becoming second in charge of George Brown College in 1946. Retiring in 1961, he 'left a large footprint in the sand for his children and others to follow' in Winduo's assessment, and indeed his son David Linge became the first Papua New Guinean to gain a doctorate in biological sciences. In 2013 he was a member of the School of Medicine and Health Sciences at UPNG.

That this pioneering writer has not received the plaudits he should have, is in no small part due to the criticism of his writing by the late Ulli Beier. Beier, who sadly passed away in 2011, was a hugely influential figure in both Nigeria and PNG, considered by many to be 'the father of modern literature' in both nations.[19] On his arrival at UPNG in 1967, after a groundbreaking period in Nigeria, Beier set about the task of introducing creative writing to a group of Papua New Guineans: '… some of the brightest and certainly the most politically conscious students … aware that they were the first generation of Papuans and New Guineans who could talk back to the white man'.[20]

Many of those first students, anti-colonialists all, went on to prominence in post-independence PNG. In relation to *Erstwhile Savage*, however, Beier was unimpressed. A man of strong ideas and judgement, he was dismissive of Ligeremaluoga's book which, while he included an excerpt from it in his *Niugini Lives*, he nonetheless considered 'a book without literary merit',[21] written by a man who, as 'the first Christian convert in his village … was therefore

---

17   E. Collins, 'Preface', in L Osea (ed.), *An Account of The Life of Ligeremaluoga (Osea)* (Melbourne 1932), 6.
18   S. Winduo, 'The first PNG Writer: Hosea Linge', *Steven's Window*, available online at stevenswindow.blogspot.com.au/2012/03/first-png-writer-hosea-linge.html.
19   W.H. Chong, 'Death of a Giant (blak soul white skin: Ulli Beier)', *Crikey*, 5 April 2011, available online at blogs.crikey.com.au/culture-mulcher/2011/04/05/death-of-a-giant-ulli-beier/.
20   U. Beier, *Decolonising the Mind: the impact of the university on culture and identity in Papua New Guinea, 1971–74* (Canberra 2005), 56.
21   —— 'Literature in New Guinea', *The Hudson Review*, 24: 1 (1971), 119.

anxious to prove himself a good disciple'.[22] While remaining deeply critical, Beier permitted a part of the book to be included with the other contributions to *Niugini Lives,* not for its literary (or indeed political) merit but as 'an interesting historical document' that sheds light on the 'objectionable' paternalism of the missionaries.[23]

But does Ligeremaluoga warrant such condemnation? The fact that Beier dismissed his book shows much about the context of the times in which the criticism was made, when authentic literature was considered the handmaiden of political consciousness, and reading between the lines about indigenous responses to colonialism was not practised as often as it has been more recently. But Ligeremaluoga was himself writing in such a context, and a more nuanced understanding of his work and his place in the small pool that is Papua New Guinean historiography is required. As Steven Winduo points out, Ligeremaluoga was a significant and influential leader in his church and society until his death in 1975 (he lived long enough to read Beier's criticism of his groundbreaking work). He was a role model for many young Papua New Guineans who, one way or another, would need some way of successfully managing the transition to nationhood. As such, and as the writer of what was certainly PNG's first autobiography (if not the entire South Pacific's), he deserves his place in this brief exposition.

At the other end of the 80 years, two books of biography were published in 2012. One was the biography of the late Sir Ebia Olewale, one of the founders of Papua New Guinean independence and an influential figure in the shaping of the modern PNG nation, of which more will be said later.

The other is *Nameless Warriors: the Ben Moide Story* by the Papua New Guinean diplomat Lahui Ako. Both books were published by UPNG Press, and although – as its author – I am able to discuss the Olewale book in some detail, unfortunately Ako's book has remained elusive for the non-Papua New Guinean resident; and the following brief exploration relies on a presentation by Ako in Port Moresby in November 2012, and a slightly less recent (August 2012) review by the Papua New Guinean journalist, Malum Nalu.[24]

Ben Moide was not a politician – at least not in the sense that is often understood. In 1940, aged 16, Moide ran away from home to join the Papuan Infantry Battalion, with whom he fought alongside his Papuan and New Guinean comrades throughout the Kokoda campaign and until 1945. Ako's biography addresses both his war service and the challenges that faced him and other Papuans and

---

22 —— 'Introduction', in U. Beier (ed.), *Niugini Lives,* 1.
23 —— 'Literature in New Guinea', in U. Beier (ed.), *Niugini Lives,* 119.
24 M. Nalu, 'New book tells of the nameless warriors of PNG', *Malum Nalu* (blog), available online at malumnalu.blogspot.com.au/2012/08/new-book-tells-story-of-nameless.html.

New Guineans who returned to paternalism and racism following the war as they tried to make a living for their families. Moide's experience as a soldier and instructor led the Australian administration to entrust him with the job of driver for senior public servants, including the Administrator, J.K. Murray, and the Director of Health and Assistant Administrator, Dr John Gunther. Nevertheless, and despite his position of apparent powerlessness compared with Olewale, Moide has been a person of some influence in his modelling of behaviour and community leadership, including his representational role internationally that reminds us – or educates us – about the vital part played by Papuans and New Guineans in the war.[25]

Ebia Olewale was very much a politician; or at least he believed in the importance of public service and his own role in attempting to make positive differences in the lives of his fellow Papua New Guineans. He related how, when he was a boy at school in Daru in PNG's Western District, the teacher scolded the class for misbehaviour, telling them that nothing would come of them. Olewale's response was life changing:

> I thought about those words and I said 'well, I think one day I'm going to really work hard and show him that I'm going to do something for my own people'. So that's where I really set my mind on politics.[26]

The vow that he made that day took him to further education at the influential Sogeri High School (at the time PNG's only government secondary school) and Port Moresby Teachers' College, where his interest in anti-colonialism grew, fed by the ham-fisted policies of the Australian Administration on public service pay issues and poor conditions for local (that is, Papua New Guinean) officers. Stimulated by the late night discussions with other like-minded young Papua New Guineans, and informed by the rapidly unfolding decolonisation process in Africa – in particular as expounded by people like Kenya's Tom Mboya – Olewale became a key member of the small pro-independence group that led eventually to the founding of the nationalist Pangu Pati.

After being elected to the House of Assembly, he was a Minister in the Somare government from 1972 to 1980, in which capacity he drove initiatives in education, small business, and justice, as well as helping to shape the new nation's foreign policy as Minister for Foreign Affairs, following Maori Kiki in that role. After electoral loss in 1982, he spent more than a decade searching

---

25 A recent example being his interview on ABC Local Radio on 20 April 2012, available online at blogs.abc. net.au/queensland/2012/04/ben-moide-and-the-fuzzy-wuzzy-angels.html.
26 Ritchie, *Ebia Olewale: a Life of Service*, 33.

for ways to further his political involvement, before re-entering the arena as an 'elder statesman' in the 1990s, continuing into this century as a board member of the PNG Sustainable Development Program Ltd. Olewale died, aged 68, in 2009.

The opportunity to research and write Olewale's biography is something that I have valued enormously. Funding for the project was provided by the Sustainable Development Program, the company set up in 2002 following the withdrawal of the transnational mining giant BHP Billiton. The project was intended to form part of Olewale's legacy, the other main parts of which were his strong interest in economic regeneration for Daru and the development of the mining town of Tabubil to ensure continued commercial activity following the eventual retirement of the Ok Tedi mine which it serviced. The project has inherited much from the approach taken by Ulli Beier four decades earlier in that it has facilitated seeing the process of colonial demise and new nation formation, not from the perspective of the expatriate specialist but through the eyes of someone who was there and whose life was influenced – profoundly – by the process, and who in turn was able to influence it. The main problem – that it is still me, an expatriate and not a Papua New Guinean writer who has taken the project on – is partially countered by my own connection with PNG (I was born there, with both my parents and grandparents having lived and worked there since the 1920s) and by the fact that Olewale had taken the trouble to record some of his early life experiences and so, in a sense, had influenced the way his story – his legacy – would be told.

Despite this problem, however, I am proud to have been associated with the project – however flawed it has been. Olewale lived through times that were more momentous than possibly any that had gone before, with the most profound effects on all inhabitants of the islands we now call Papua New Guinea. His experiences – and those of his contemporaries – need to be recorded for the benefit of the many generations of Papua New Guineans to come, and it has been a privilege to be part of this project. I hope that there will be many more such biographies.

Among the accounts of these three key figures – Ligeremaluoga and Olewale and Moide – lie some 34 other books that can be categorised as political life writing. With the broad definition in mind of what political life writing entails, there are a few ways in which these can be further classified.

To begin with, there are the books that are openly and avowedly political in scope and purpose. Leading the way is Sir Michael Somare and his autobiography *Sana*, curiously perhaps published in 1975 when he was still a young man (he turned 40 the following year). Sir Maori Kiki's book *Kiki: Ten Thousand Years in a Lifetime* (published in 1968 while the author was 37 years old) has a similar purpose. As Beier – with whom he collaborated closely on the book –

has noted, at a time when 'Papua New Guineans felt they were being reduced to the status of guinea pigs … Kiki showed them that they could recreate their own image'.[27] He and others place Kiki's book at the forefront of the renaissance (or should it be the 'naissance') of Papua New Guinean literature.

Beier was also influential in the preparation of Somare's autobiography, *Sana*, a book with an avowedly political purpose (he worked with interviews taped with Somare and – jointly with Tony Voutas – edited the outcome).[28] Indeed both books were intricately caught up in the politics of nationalism and anti-colonialism, and it is significant that they appeared when Ulli Beier's influence through his work at UPNG and, later, the Institute of PNG Studies was at its zenith. They appeared amid the explosion of indigenous Papua New Guinean creativity that characterised this period, including in the visual arts (Akis, Kauage and others), theatre (Arthur Jawodimbari, Kumalau Tawali), poetry (the *Papua Pocket Poets* series), and fiction (Vincent Eri's *The Crocodile* being the leading example of this genre).

While Somare's book and Kiki's are the most prominent examples of the political autobiography genre, others deserve a mention in this discussion of books of life writing in PNG. One of these is Dame Josephine Abaijah's *A Thousand Coloured Dreams: The Story of a Young Girl Growing Up in Papua*, which she wrote with her advisor and friend Dr Eric Wright. Although ostensibly a work of fiction – she insisted that it was 'based on my life but … all of the characters in this work are fictitious' – *A Thousand Coloured Dreams* nonetheless can be considered in this survey of political life writing in PNG. Abaijah, as the public face of Papua Besena (the movement agitating for separate development of Papua from New Guinea), was a significant feature of the PNG landscape in the 1970s and *A Thousand Coloured Dreams*, although published some time afterwards, recorded her encounters with colonialism and her own political journey. In the words of Jeffrey R.J. Dickens' introduction to the book, Abaijah 'has devoted her life to the People and the country she loves and in so doing has provided the inspiration the National women of Papua New Guinea needed'.[29]

Other books have been written by Papua New Guineans who also had prominent roles in public affairs spanning the late colonial and early independence era. The former Governor-General, Sir Paulias Matane, has been quite prolific in more recent times, and among his 27 books there are two in particular that can be counted in this overview of political biography: *My Childhood in New Guinea* (1972) and *To Serve With Love* (1992). Born in 1931 in a village in

---

27 Beier, 'Introduction', 3.
28 T. Lipp, *The Hunter Thinks the Monkey is Wise, But He Has His Own Logic: A Bibliography of Writings by Ulli Beier, Obotunde Ijimere & Co.*, (rev. edn), Clin D'Oeil, (Bayreuth 1986), available online at www.thorolf-lipp.de/publications/documents/TheHunterthinksthemonkeyisnotwise.pdf.
29 R.J. Dickens, 'Tribute to Josephine', in J. Abaijah and E. Wright (eds), *A Thousand Coloured Dreams*, iii.

East New Britain, Matane's life has taken him through the ranks of teaching and other public service roles, culminating in ambassadorial postings in the United States, Mexico, Canada and the United Nations, and, finally, as Governor-General from 2004 to 2010. His two books of autobiography (leaving aside the accounts of travels) tell the story of, as he described it in *My Childhood in New Guinea*, a journey which 'began with the stone age and has entered the space age'.[30]

Two autobiographies by leading Papua New Guinean women can also be considered in this survey: Dame Alice Wedega's *Listen My Country* (1981), and Dame Carol Kidu's *A Remarkable Journey* (2002). Wedega's life story spanned a large part of the twentieth century, from her birth in 1905 to her death at the age of 82 in 1987; she witnessed many of PNG's most important moments, from missionising to war, to the growing movement for self-determination and independence. The book emphasises her experiences as a Christian and as a woman; and indeed the political purpose she had in mind in writing it was laid out in its concluding chapter:

> The real need of Papua New Guinea is for unity. Unity in families, unity between tribes and different areas of the country. If women see this need and care for everyone they work with, they can show others how this can be done. Meeting the needs of people is the aim we must have.[31]

Kidu's career in PNG politics formally ended with her retirement at the 2012 elections, although she remains an enormously significant figure in PNG public affairs. In *A Remarkable Journey*, she chose to write about her journey from Brisbane schoolgirl to that of a Member of Papua New Guinea's National Parliament.[32] It is, as Regis Stella describes, 'a narrative about her mental and physical struggles, pains and perseverance to adjust and adapt into a culturally different society'.[33] Although born an Australian, Kidu features in this survey because of her choice to identify with the nation of her husband, the late Sir Buri Kidu, and as a Motuan woman. The first part of her autobiography was published as *A Remarkable Journey*. She is now contemplating a second part which would detail her life in politics including her years as a Minister and Opposition Leader (see Kidu, Chapter 10).

All of these books reflect the excitement and optimism of the nation, a people in transition to a future that was unknowable but which would, without doubt, be drastically different to what had gone before. In the words of John Momis at the time of independence, '… we really did not know where we were going.

---

30 P. Matane, *My Childhood in New Guinea* (Melbourne 1972), 112.
31 A. Wedega, *Listen, My Country* (Sydney 1981), 107.
32 C. Kidu, *A Remarkable Journey* (Sydney 2002).
33 R. Stella, '*A Remarkable Journey* (review)', *The Contemporary Pacific*, 15: 1(2003), 222.

We were like Abraham, called to a destination which he didn't know.'[34] As Ted Wolfers wrote in the introduction to Matane's second volume of autobiography, '… the experiences depicted … are, in their essentials, those of an entire generation of Papua New Guinean pioneers'[35] and the stories that each of these books tells are important reminders of the great hopes and expectations of that era.

Before moving on from books that are clearly political in their scope – dealing with subjects who have been intricately connected with the political landscape of PNG – there are two 'honourable mentions' that should be included here. They are not counted as books as such because they have not been published, but are certainly book-like in their scope and structure. These are the doctoral dissertations by Basil Shaw on Michael Somare, submitted in 1991, and Lisabeth Lee Ryder on Iambakey Okuk, submitted in 1992. Both are detailed and scholarly examinations of their subject's lives, in Ryder's case from a close personal relationship with her subject, while Shaw's was more archive-based.

Shaw approached his subject by looking at concepts of leadership in traditional Papua New Guinean societies, and how these played out in the contemporary political world; in particular, how Somare and his colleagues were confronted with challenges arising from this process. Although limited by the timeframe – concluding his examination of Somare in 1985 when he left office – and the lack of interview material, Shaw's dissertation effectively addressed its central question of 'whether the style of political leadership in PNG has expressed itself in a different set of behaviours from what is traditional among leaders in the Westminster Parliament and its associated executive form of government'.[36]

Ryder, on the other hand, chose to examine the life of the Chimbu leader Sir Iambakey Palma Okuk, who came close to becoming Prime Minister before his untimely death in 1986. An anthropologist, Ryder explained how her dissertation's aim was 'both to supplement the interpretations of Papua New Guinean history, and to contribute to the investigation and evaluation of life histories as an anthropological methodology'.[37] Her recognition that too often in Western literary accounts, 'Papua New Guineans … are dealt with as a

---

34 J. Momis, 'Transcript of Discussion by Constitution-Makers, Port Moresby, 28 March 1996', in A.J. Regan, O. Jessep and E.L. Kwa (eds), *Twenty Years of the Papua New Guinea Constitution* (Sydney 2001), 357.
35 T. Wolfers, 'Introduction', in P. Matane (ed.), *To Serve with Love* (Mount Waverley 1992), viii.
36 B. Shaw, *Somare: a Political Biography of the First Prime Minister of Papua New Guinea* (Nathan 1991), 545.
37 L.L. Ryder, *Iambakey Okuk: Interpretations of a Lifetime of Change in Papua New Guinea*, PhD thesis (Los Angeles 1992), ix.

mass phenomena' led her to the conclusion that 'Papua New Guinea's past was populated with extraordinary people, people with names'.[38] This is a conclusion with which this paper is in complete agreement.

Many books articulate the same story of progression from 'the stone age to the space age', as Matane described it, or 'ten thousand years in a lifetime', in Kiki's words, whether the book has been written by a Papua New Guinean or by an expatriate. Sometimes a duality, a sense of existence in two worlds that conveys a similar meaning, is also expressed. Thus, we have Elin Johnston's biography of the Anglican Bishop George Ambo, subtitled *Man of Two Worlds*: someone who exists in the traditional and the modern worlds at the same time. Johnston describes him as 'a transitional man, [whose] life stretches from the end of the Stone Age, through the Colonial Period and into the modern Technological Era'.[39] Other examples are *Mama Kuma*, Deborah Carlyon's biography of her grandmother, Kuma Kelage. *One Woman, Two Cultures*, its subtitle, conveys the duality of Kelage's world between her Sina people and those of the man she married, Malcolm Warrick.[40] Audrey McCollum's account of her friend Pirip Kuru, *Two Women, Two Worlds: Friendship Swept by Winds of Change*,[41] similarly addresses this duality, marvelling at the paradox where 'a feminist activist from an ancient culture that included the subjugation of women could preserve that endangered culture and organize women to achieve greater equality and power'.[42]

Life story telling is an approach deployed by anthropology as well as history and political science, as Geoffrey M. White has noted: 'the study of life history' he wrote in 2000, 'continues to be put forward as an effective, even innovative way to approach issues of agency, meaning, and representation', an outcome he ascribes to the fact that 'life histories and associated issues of individual agency have in theoretical terms been a marginal and largely unexamined element of a discipline otherwise preoccupied with analyzing the collective'.[43] Andrew Strathern has explained this in a more specific reference to his relationship with the Western Highlands Big Men Ongka and Ru. The point of using life histories in anthropological research, he argues, is 'to relate local ideas about personhood and individuality, in a broad sense, to local cases of life experience, especially when these cases are narrated by the people themselves'.[44]

---

38 Ibid., 4.
39 E.E. Johnston, *Bishop George: Man of Two Worlds*, self-published (2003), x.
40 D. Carlyon, *Mama Kuma: One Woman, Two Cultures* (St Lucia 2002).
41 A. McCollum, *Two Women, Two Worlds: Friendship Swept by Winds of Change* (New Hampshire 1999).
42 ——— 'Two Women Two Worlds', *Whole Earth*, Winter (2002), 80.
43 G.M. White, 'Afterword: Lives and Histories', in P.J. Stewart and A. Strathern (eds), *Identity Work: Constructing Pacific Lives* (Pittsburgh 2000), 172.
44 A. Strathern, 'A twist of the rope', in V. Keck (ed.), *Common Worlds and Single Lives: Constituting Knowledge in Pacific Societies* (Oxford 1998), 119.

2. Political Life Writing in Papua New Guinea

So here is another contributor to the corpus of autobiographical and biographical literature of PNG and one, moreover, that is again overtly political, if on a sub-national scale.

Three final mentions of books remain to be added to this list (although much has been passed over – as the list of published works of a biographical nature at the end of this chapter indicates).

The first is Amirah Inglis's *Karo: the Life and Fate of a Papuan*, which retells the story of a Kerema man, Karo Araua, whose life began in the village and spanned the arbitrary divide of colonial Port Moresby. Like Chief Roi Mata in Vanuatu, Araua has acquired a legendary and mythic reality, not least through the songs Inglis recorded, including on how his fame grew:

> The fame of his daring deed spread to his Auavavu land,
> The story of his reckless exploit reached his Mukosore place;
> It spread to his Auavavu-Mukosore land.
>
> His Savoripi clansmen's ears heard the fame of his daring deed,
> His Savoripi clanswomen's ears learned the story of his reckless exploit,
> The fame of his daring deed.[45]

As Inglis noted:

> Even though Papuans are now Papua New Guineans and the government is no longer a colonial one, they still sing and enjoy to hear the story of 'white foreigners' brought down or at least made to sit up and take notice of a Papuan man.[46]

Without a doubt, Inglis has written a biography of a political figure who lived and died many years before the idea of PNG as a nation began.

The second is perhaps something that may seem out of place in a survey of political life writing: the sporting autobiography, a genre often passed over by academic observers but usually enormously popular with the general public. The autobiography that is included here belongs to a prominent player and coach of rugby league, the sport of which most Papua New Guineans are passionate devotees. Stanley Gene's *Daydream Believer* – edited, if not exactly ghostwritten, by Stuart Wilkin – tells of his journey from a squatter settlement in Goroka to rugby league stardom in the United Kingdom with Hull Kingston Rovers, and several Test caps with PNG's national rugby league team, the Kumuls, whom he then moved on to coach following his eventual retirement as

---

45   A. Inglis, *Karo: the Life and Fate of a Papuan* (Canberra 1982), 125.
46   Ibid., 120.

a player.⁴⁷ Gene's book, with its strong message of self-betterment and service, is a political work in its promotion of an activist and change-oriented outlook, particularly among PNG's mostly disenfranchised young people. In a country as rugby league mad as PNG, the power of a book such as *Daydream Believer* to influence political outcomes is evident.

Final in this partial exposition of the books of political life writing in PNG are the many short books written by Eric Johns, intended for schools and published by Pearson Education. Johns' work has been largely unreported in academic or literary circles. This is a great shame as he has researched meticulously and the books he has produced provide a valuable aid for young Papua New Guineans to understand their own history.

So, to conclude. Far from being moribund, there are signs of healthy life in Papua New Guinean biographical historiography, especially if a wider interpretation is taken of what constitutes a publication. There are, however, too few works of serious biography of contemporary political or otherwise national leaders. What is needed is to move away from the trope that is perhaps the most obvious and easily adopted – that of the progressive journey from the village to the nation, the stone age to the space age, ten thousand years in a lifetime – to a more nuanced and sophisticated treatment of the impact modernity has had on PNG's people. Studies of how the nation's leaders manipulated and were affected by the arrival of a global marketplace of commodities and ideas are important avenues to increasing our understanding of the ways of articulation, action, and response. While biography has sometimes been disparaged as being 'not quite kosher', and the standard of scholarship which might even be considered 'suspect',⁴⁸ it has the ability to 'provide students of politics with another perspective of how power is shared, how leaders are made not born, and how circumstances can catapult ordinary people into extraordinary situations'.⁴⁹ In the context of PNG, these are all worthy aims.

---

47 S. Gene and S. Wilkin, *Daydream Believer* (Derbyshire 2007).
48 T. Arklay, J. Nethercote and J. Wanna, 'Preface', in T. Arklay et al. (eds), *Australian Political Lives*, xi.
49 Selth, 'Political Biographies and Administrative Memoirs', 101.

Table 1: Biographical works about, or by, Papua New Guineans

Published books				
Subject	**Title**	**Author(s)**	**Publisher**	**Date**
Josephine Abaijah	*A Thousand Coloured Dreams*	Josephine Abaijah and the late Dr Eric Wright	Dellasta Pacific	1991
Lahui Ako	*Upstream Through Endless Sands of Blessings*	Lahui Ako	CBS Publishers & Distributors	2007
George Ambo	*Bishop George: Man of Two Worlds*	Elin Johnston	self-published	2003
Anyan	*Anyan's Story: A New Guinea Woman in Two Worlds*	Virginia Drew Watson	University of Washington Press	1997
Karo Araua	*Karo: the Life and Fate of a Papuan*	Amirah Inglis	Institute of Papua New Guinea Studies in association with Australian National University Press	1982
Pipi Gari	*Pipi Gari of Elevala*	Eric Johns	Pearson Education Australia	2003
Stanley Gene	*Daydream Believer*	Stanley Gene with Stuart Wilkin	TH Media	2007
Kei Geno	*Beyond the Untrod Road: Biography of Major Kei Geno, the First Papua New Guinean Salvationist*	Ruth Raimo and Anja Marie Bray	self-published	2006
Golpak	*Sir Simogun Pita and Paramount Luluai Golpak*	Eric Johns	Pearson Education Australia	2004
Ravu Henao	*Ravu Henao of Papua*	Marcus L Loane	S. John Bacon	1945
Rose Kekedo	*Dame Rose Kekedo*	Eric Johns	Pearson Education Australia	2002
Kuma Kelage	*Mama Kuma: One Woman, Two Cultures*	Deborah Carlyon	University of Queensland Press	2002
Limbie Kelly Kelegai	*Through the Eye of the Storm: Every Step, Every Heartbeat, in God's Grace*	Limbie Kelly Kelegai	BookPal	2009
Carol Kidu	*A Remarkable Journey*	Carol Kidu	Longman	2002
Carol Kidu	*Lady Carol Kidu*	Eric Johns	Pearson Education Australia	2005
Albert Maori Kiki	*Kiki: Ten Thousand Years in a Lifetime: A New Guinea Autobiography*	Albert Maori Kiki	Cheshire	1968

Published books				
Subject	Title	Author(s)	Publisher	Date
Pirip Kuru	*Two Women Two Worlds: Friendship Swept by Winds of Change*	Audrey T McCollum	Hillwinds Press	1999
Osea Ligeremaluoga	*An Account of the Life of Ligermaluoga (Osea): An Autobiography*	Osea Ligeremaluoga (trans. Ella Collins)	FW Cheshire	1932
Hosea Ligeremaluoga	*An Offering Fit for a King: the Life and Work of the Rev. Hosea Linge*	Hosea Linge (trans. Neville Threlfall)	Toksave Buk	1978
Hosea Ligeremaluoga	*Ligeremaluoga of Kono*	Eric Johns	Pearson Education Australia	2002
Maino	*Maino of Moatta and the Explorers of the Fly River*	Eric Johns	Pearson Education Australia	2002
Paulias Matane	*My Childhood in New Guinea*	Paulias Matane	Oxford University Press	1972
Paulias Matane	*To Serve with Love*	Paulias Matane	Dellasta Pacific	1992
Ben Moide	*Nameless Warriors: The Ben Moide Story*	Lahui Ako	UPNG Press	2012
Ebia Olewale	*Ebia Olewale: a Life of Service*	Jonathan Ritchie	UPNG Press	2012
Ongka	*Ongka: a Self-account by a New Guinea Big Man*	Ongka with Andrew Strathern	Duckworth	1979
Ongka	*Collaborations and Conflicts: a Leader Through Time*	Ongka with Andrew Strathern and Pamela J Stewart	Thomson	2006
Madi Roua	*The Past Years: the Autobiography of Madi Roua*	Madi Roua	self-published	2005
Ru	*Ru: Biography of a Western Highlander*	Ru, translated by Andrew Strathern	National Research Institute	1993
Pita Simogun	*Sir Simogun Pita and Paramount Luluai Golpak*	Eric Johns	Pearson Education Australia	2004
Michael Somare	*Sana*	Michael Somare	The Jacaranda Press	1975
Peter ToRot	*The Life of Peter ToRot Catechist Church Leader and Martyr*	Caspar G. Tovaninara	Missionaries of the Sacred Heart	n.d.

2. Political Life Writing in Papua New Guinea

Published books				
Subject	**Title**	**Author(s)**	**Publisher**	**Date**
Benedict To Varpin	*Tubuan and Tabernacle, the Life Stories of Two Priests of Papua New Guinea: the Most Reverened Benedict To Varpin, CBE Archbishop Emeritus: Reverend Father Bernard Franke MSC, CBE Missionary in New Britain*	Mary R Mennis	Lalong Enterprises	2007
Tui	*Tui of Gorendu*	Eric Johns	Pearson Education Australia	2003
Louis Vangeke	*Bishop Sir Louis Vangeke*	Eric Johns	Pearson Education Australia	2002
Alice Wedega	*Listen My Country*	Alice Wedega	Pacific Publications	1981
Alice Wedega	*Dame Alice Wedega*	Eric Johns	Pearson Education Australia	2002
Theses				
Michael Somare	*Somare: A Political Biography of the First Prime Minister of Papua New Guinea*	Basil Shaw	Griffith University	1991
Iambakey Okuk	*Iambakey Okuk: Interpretations of a Lifetime of Change in Papua New Guinea*	Lisabeth Lee Ryder	University of California, Los Angeles	1992

Source: Author's compilation.

3. Understanding Solomon

Writing the life of Solomon Mamaloni, an account of the social organisation, magic and religion of the people of San Cristoval in the Solomon Islands

Christopher Chevalier

The life of Solomon Sunaone Mamaloni – the first Chief Minister and three-time Prime Minister of Solomon Islands – sheds light on the social, cultural, economic, political and historical forces that have shaped that country leading up to and beyond independence. Like other figures discussed in this volume, Mamaloni was a significant actor in some of the most crucial events in his country's transition up to and beyond independence. His memory remains deeply cherished by many of those whom he led. He was a mercurial yet human leader, with both vices and endearing qualities, who took on the herculean task of attempting to bind a fragmented country, only lightly touched by the institutions and values of the Westminster tradition, into a nation. In the first part of the chapter, I summarise the life, career and legacy of the Solomon Islands' most significant and controversial politician; in the second part, I reflect on writing his life story and what I have learned in the process.

Table 2: The life and career of Solomon Mamaloni – a synopsis

Born 23 January 1943 at Rumahui, Arosi (West Makira)
Brought up in a Maasina Rule stronghold, 1946–50
Attended Church of Melanesia schools 1952–59, King George VI school 1960–63 and Te Aute College, New Zealand 1964–65
Junior public servant 1966–1968, Assistant Clerk to Legislative Council 1968–70
Elected to seat of Makira in 1970, aged 27
Elected first Chief Minister in 1974, aged 31
Resigned from Parliament 1977
Re-elected to Parliament 1980 for the seat of West Makira, which he held for the next 20 years
Prime Minister three times: 1981–84, 1989–93, and 1994–97
Died aged 56 years on 11 January 2000 from end-stage kidney disease

Source: Author's compilation.

Mamaloni was born during World War II at Rumahui on the west coast of Makira. He had links to South Malaita through his grandmother and to Guadalcanal through his father's side, connections he used to his political advantage years later.¹ His grandfather Suharahu had been executed in 1892 by a Royal Navy Australia Station firing squad for the murder of a white trader in 1889.² His father, Joash Sunaone, was born nearby in 1911 and his mother, Bethseda Irageni, was born in Rumahui in 1920. Both were teachers with the South Sea Evangelical Mission (SSEM) and opened a SSEM boarding school at Rumahui; they married in 1939 and their first son was born in 1940.

With the arrival of Allied forces on the neighbouring island of Guadalcanal, Islanders fled to the hills and bush, where Mamaloni was born on 21 January 1943 as the Battle of Guadalcanal reached its climax and the Japanese were repulsed. Two more siblings were born in 1945 and 1946 but Mamaloni was raised separately by his grandmother because he had severe yaws.³ His parents separated around 1945 and both remarried quickly; Mamaloni himself did not realise who his real parents were until he was five or six years old.⁴ From 1947 to 1950, Mamaloni lived at Rumahui, which became a collective stronghold under Maasina Rule, the proto-nationalist movement which protested against British colonial rule between 1946 and 1952. Mamaloni was exposed to anti-colonial propaganda and paramilitary rituals, as well as renewed interest in customary ways.⁵ When he was six or seven years old, Mamaloni ran away to live with his father, Sunaone, who managed a copra plantation belonging to Frederick Campbell, a former Commandant of the Native Constabulary who became the first District Officer in Makira (or San Cristoval as it was then known) in 1918.

---

1   In parliament Mamaloni said, '… in actual fact I am not a Makira man. I am 'Are'are, from South Malaita, I am from the Guadalcanal Weather Coast.' *Proceedings of the Governing Council*, 9th meeting, 3 April 1973, 163.
2   For sources regarding the execution of his grandfather Suharahu see *Records of the WPHC Secretariat 1875–1914*, Series 4, Inwards Correspondence General, 191/89 (in Auckland); and United Kingdom, Royal Navy, Commander-in-Chief, Australian Station, *RNAS 23 Printed Reports of Islands Cases 1888–92* (in Wellington).
3   Mamaloni had secondary yaws – a severe tertiary infection causing sores in his mouth, face, limbs and back. After World War II, it could be cured by a single dose of penicillin, which became available in mass health campaigns from the 1950s onwards.
4   Different family members attribute his parents' divorce to infidelity on both sides. Divorce was surprisingly common and casual among the Arosi, even amongst fundamentalist Christians like the SSEM. Mamaloni was raised by his grandparents and thought they were his real parents until he was five or six years old. While it is tempting to speculate on the psychological impact of this situation, intra-family adoption was and still is common throughout the Pacific.
5   Inspired by American fraternity and frustrated by British colonial arrogance, the Maasina Ruru (MR) movement was started in 1945 by the predominantly Malaitan Solomon Islands Labour Corps. They demanded better pay, political representation, and the revival of local custom and laws. They refused to pay head taxes, provide labour, or take part in censuses. Collective Maasina 'towns' were established, mainly on Malaita but also on Makira, including Rumahui. The threat to British authority led to outlawing of the movement and mass imprisonment but the movement showed remarkable resilience despite such adversity. Prisoners were eventually released in 1950 and long-overdue reforms were introduced in 1952, including Island Councils. These were viewed as a victory by MR supporters. Although MR was regarded as a failure by the authorities, it was to prove very influential in the minds of Independence leaders. See H. Laracy, *Pacific Protest: The Maasina Rule Movement Solomon Islands 1944–52* (Suva 1983); R. Keesing, 'Politico-Religious Movements and Anticolonialism on Malaita: Maasina Rule in Historical Perspective', *Oceania*, Part 1, 18: 4 (1978), 241–61 and Part 2, 18: 5 (1978), 46–73; M. Scott, *The Severed Snake: Matrilineages, Making Place, and a Melanesian Christianity in Southeast Solomon Islands* (Durham 2007), Chapter 3.

Thanks to his father's career and an Anglican education, Mamaloni was in the right places at the right times. In 1950 Sunaone moved to manage another plantation for Campbell on the north coast. This provided the opportunity for Mamaloni to attend Anglican schools and get a far better education than at SSEM schools, which taught bible studies and literacy. Mamaloni attended Anglican junior and senior primary schools from 1952 to 1959, including Pawa, 'the Eton of the Pacific', where he forged lifelong connections. He then went to the new government secondary school, King George VI on Malaita from 1960 to 1963, where he was educated with a cohort of future leaders, including Peter Kenilorea. Mamaloni was small, fast, and a gifted soccer player. Popular at school as a prankster, orator, and actor, he was a smart but lazy student who failed his 'O' level exams. Nevertheless, he won a scholarship to Te Aute College, another prestigious Anglican school in New Zealand founded in 1854, famous for its tradition of training Maori leaders and restoring self-reliance and cultural pride.[6] He sat for university entrance exams in 1964 and 1965 but failed these too.[7]

Mamaloni entered the colonial administration as an Executive Officer for Central District from 1966 to 1968.[8] His work was criticised by his superiors and he received probationary reports from 1966 to 1967 until his transfer to the Government Secretariat as Assistant Clerk to the Legislative Council in 1968. This was a lucky break because it gave him knowledge of parliamentary procedures, a great advantage when he was elected to the newly established Governing Council in 1970. In Makira, he traded on his father's name and reputation as a Makira Big Man. Sunaone had been elected to the Makira Council in 1955 and was Council President from 1958 to 1962. He was an appointed member of the Advisory Council from 1958 to 1959 and the Legislative Council from 1960 to 1962. These councils were the first opportunities for political representation allowed after the war.

The youngest member of a new 17-member Governing Council, Mamaloni was 'the 31-year-old firebrand … humble and vain, penetrating and yet blind … [and] an engaging personality.'[9] Mamaloni described himself as a 'rather young radical politician' and 'a very strong nationalist'.[10] He repeatedly berated the colonial administration and the racism of white officials, especially 'the Africa

---

6 J. Wehipeihana, *Te Aute College: Koiri 1854–2004, Celebrating 150 years* (Palmerston North 2005).
7 Failing external exams such as 'O' levels and university entrance exams was not uncommon for Maori and Islander students, many of whom struggled and were significantly disadvantaged in written English.
8 Others who passed matriculation and university entrance exams entered the colonial administration at higher levels and became Administrative Officers and District Officers, which gave them competence and experience that Mamaloni lacked. He worked in Central District administration, primarily in Guadalcanal and the Russell Islands, one of the four Districts – Western, Central, Malaita, and Eastern.
9 *Pacific Islands Monthly*, February (1973), 8.
10 'I am a radical politician' and 'strong nationalist', said Mamaloni during two speeches to the first and second meetings of the Governing Council on 20 July and 27 November 1970.

Club'. He spoke fearlessly and provocatively, deploring colonial ignorance and parsimony. In 1973, he was one of only six members re-elected and was catapulted into leadership; and the poacher turned gamekeeper. He formed the People's Progressive Party and become the country's first Chief Minister from 1974 to 1976 when the Legislative Assembly and ministerial system began. In 1975 he led talks in London on the timetable for self-government and independence.

Mamaloni's first administration was undermined by personal hostilities and labour unrest. He reshuffled his Cabinet three times in two years, a hallmark of his administrations. His leadership was tainted by the Letcher Mint scandal in 1975 over plans to mint commemorative coins with his head on one side; he was forced to resign over his *lèse majesté* but was soon reappointed. He led the country to self-government in January 1976, which was greeted by strikes led by Bart Ulufa'alu.[11] Mamaloni was re-elected in West Makira in June 1976 but his reputation was sufficiently damaged that he narrowly lost the ballot for Chief Minister to newcomer Peter Kenilorea and also the poll for Opposition Leader to Ulufa'alu. His star had truly fallen and he resigned his seat in January 1977.

During his absence, Kenilorea led constitutional talks in London, a task that he was temperamentally much better suited to than Mamaloni, who was averse to formality and monarchy. He returned to politics in 1980, winning back his West Makira seat by a landslide but again losing the ballot for Prime Minister to Kenilorea, but he did become Opposition Leader. He used his political cunning and mastery of parliamentary procedure to undermine Kenilorea and took over as Prime Minister in August 1981, promising a radical agenda. His second administration introduced some notable changes, including a provincial government system, a pro-Asia policy, and diplomatic recognition of Taiwan.

Always a trenchant anti-colonialist, he was also critical of Australia and New Zealand in Pacific Forum and Commonwealth meetings. He loathed protocol, red carpet, and 'sugar diplomacy', preferring the relaxed style and brotherhood of the Melanesian Alliance. His independent foreign policy was exemplified when the *Jeanette Diana*, a US purse seiner, was caught fishing illegally and confiscated. The Reagan government imposed an embargo on Solomons goods and Mamaloni showed courage taking on a superpower; the rewards were improved fishing returns and surveillance for Pacific Island countries.

Domestically, Mamaloni pulled levers but very little happened. His hobby-horse was decentralisation but his experimental provincial super-ministries failed. Motivated by hostility towards foreign advisers and the belief that Solomon

---

11   Bart Ulufa'alu was a University of PNG economics graduate and student leader who became the new firebrand of Solomons politics. He was elected in the 1976 elections prior to independence in 1978. He was Mamaloni's Finance Minister (1981–84) and became Prime Minister (1997–2000) until he was deposed in an armed coup. He died from complications of diabetes in 2007 aged 56, the same age as Mamaloni.

Islanders should control their own country, his plans for localising the public service were more successful but the quality and discipline declined significantly. He introduced legislation to allow logging on customary land that opened the door to unsustainable logging and corrupt Asian loggers. Mamaloni again showed poor judgment in pursuing overseas loans from dubious sources that were fortunately stopped by an independent Monetary Authority. Ministerial disloyalty, multiple reshuffles and resignations were again trademarks, moving Mamaloni to say: 'I do not enjoy being a Prime Minister because there are no funs [sic] in being one … to clean up someone else's droppings is not my idea of "a good time"'.[12]

In 1984 he again lost to Kenilorea in the ballot for Prime Minister for a third time; he could now enjoy the luxury of opposition and allow Kenilorea and his successor, Ezekiel Alebua, to struggle with increasingly difficult economic circumstances.[13] Mamaloni pursued his agenda of decentralisation as Chairman of the Constitution Review Committee in 1987 but implemented none of its recommendations when he was in power between 1989 and 1997, more proof that he preferred the talk to the walk.

He won a resounding victory in the 1989 elections but the hubris was short-lived. Many of his Cabinet were directors of logging companies and the government became increasingly reliant on revenue from unsustainable logging, despite pricing rorts. Two more loans scandals were again only averted by the due diligence of the Central Bank. His government was chaotic and shambolic with lax financial discipline and declining public services. The poor behaviour of Mamaloni and his ministers led his own party, the People's Alliance Party (PAP), to move against him in November 1990 but he acted swiftly to sack five of his ministers and brought in five opposition members, including the prize catch of Sir Peter Kenilorea. Hailed as a masterstroke, the political coup led to further political intrigue and ministerial horse-trading. During the Bougainville civil war of 1989 to 1998, Bougainvillean militants and civilians were allowed to use the Solomon Islands to evade a blockade imposed by Papua New Guinea. Relations between the two countries became very tense, especially after PNG Defence Forces killed Solomon Islander civilians at the border with Bougainville.

Re-elected in Makira in June 1993, Mamaloni lost the poll for Prime Minister by one vote to Francis Billy Hilly, who led a fragile coalition with a reform agenda to restore government finances and control logging. Mamaloni used his customary cunning, charisma and logging funds to lure cabinet members to

---

12   'Being Prime Minister is no funs', letter to the *Solomon Star*, 15 March 1984.
13   Kenilorea was forced to step down as Prime Minister in 1986 over alleged misuse of aid funds for his own village after Cyclone Namu. He became Deputy to Ezekiel Alebua who took over as Prime Minister until the 1989 election.

his side. He also started his own company, SOMMA, to log large areas of Arosi with a Malaysian Chinese contractor. Eventually, the Hilly government fell and Mamaloni began his fourth administration in October 1994. His was the loggers' government, removing restrictions and increasing duty exemptions for logging companies. The country slid further downhill due to high inflation, razor-thin foreign reserves, rising corruption and declining services.

Mamaloni became increasingly erratic and reclusive as his health declined. Despite pleas from his family to retire, he retained his seat in the 1997 election but not the leadership. Voters were sick of corruption and declining services and Ulufa'alu, leading a 'Coalition for Change', won the poll for Prime Minister. For the first time since 1980, Mamaloni was neither leader of the government nor the opposition. However, he became Opposition Leader again in 1999 as long-standing tensions between Guadalcanal and Malaita turned to violence and armed struggle. Mamaloni had implicit faith in traditional reconciliation mechanisms and begged the Ulufa'alu government to resolve tensions with compensation as both he and Kenilorea had done in their administrations.

After 30 years of stress, heavy smoking, alcohol and prodigious betel nut chewing, Mamaloni succumbed to kidney disease. Refusing dialysis in Australia, he went home in November 1999, clearly very ill and tired. He spent his last Christmas at home and then returned reluctantly to Honiara for treatment; he died in a public ward at Central Hospital in January 2000, aged only 56.[14] His death shocked the whole nation and saddened even his opponents. Mourned as 'Solo, Father of the Nation', thousands came to his funeral, the largest ever seen in Solomon Islands. Six months later, the Malaita Eagle Force, an armed coup, overthrew Ulufa'alu and the country descended into civil war and chaos. His family lost many assets due to the tensions after 2000 and the SOMMA logging business fell apart due to family infighting.

A common question or opinion is whether Mamaloni could have prevented the coup in 2000 had he lived. He made strenuous efforts, even on his deathbed in hospital, to get Prime Minister Ulufa'alu to use customary compensation to pay for Guadalcanal demands, then only a matter SI$2 million. Had Ulufa'alu done so, especially earlier, the armed coup may well not have happened. Had Mamaloni been in office, he would certainly have used compensation, as he had done three times in the 1990s. And had he lived to see the armed coup, he would probably

---

14 Mamaloni's early death at 56, while not unusual in Solomon Islands, was premature and due to the stress of high office, his unhealthy habits, and refusal to obey doctors and comply with treatment. It is interesting to speculate how Winston Churchill, another small rotund man with prodigious appetites, would be remembered and regarded had he died at the same age. Had Churchill died in 1930, ten years before he became Prime Minister, he would perhaps be remembered as an orator, arrogant maverick, and a repeated failure who presided over the Battle of Gallipoli and the British economy from 1925 to 1929 up to the Great Depression.

have secured the ballot for Prime Minister based on his experience and links to Malaita and Guadalcanal. But Mamaloni was dead and Kenilorea, the only other statesman capable of national unity, was no longer in politics.

Mamaloni soon became part of legend, his memory kept alive by people in Makira who want to retain the prestige and status of their most famous son and spokesman. Rumours started after his death that he was alive and was part of a secret Makira army preparing to save Makira from the threat of Malaita.[15] Mamaloni's legacy was divisive and contested. He was populist and had great charisma so he was much loved on the street. He was admired for his wit, political savvy, his independence and patriotism, and refusing to kowtow to foreigners, especially Europeans and Australians. Despite his jocular style, he took himself and his name very seriously, regarding himself as synonymous with the country. He was both admired and detested for his Machiavellian politics. His dislike of colonialism led him to ignore sound administration, which led to erratic and inept governance. He presided over a rising tide of corruption and destruction from logging. A former High Commissioner to Solomon Islands assessed his contribution thus:

> His legacies had a devastating impact … [they] fostered a climate of corruption that paved the way for criminal groups to hold the country to ransom … a culture of corruption in the public arena arose and increased.[16]

His detractors were, and still are, many. He was described by a former Member of Parliament as 'grossly corrupt and inept' and by the Australian government in a leaked document as 'an obstacle to responsible government for as long as he is in power.' A former colonial administrator described him as 'a nasty little shit, a wicked man, a shrewd operator, brilliantly manipulative, amoral since day one, a godfather, a shyster'. But many of his old opponents admired him and remained friends. Ulufa'alu described him as 'distinguished and respected', while Sir Peter Kenilorea said: 'Mamaloni did not lose his casual approach. He blended informality with officialdom. He carried no political grudges. He is worthy of regard as a great political leader.'[17]

---

15 While conducting fieldwork at Makira, I was often asked whether I thought or knew that Mamaloni was living underground at the western end of Makira. Michael Scott has analysed the motives for these beliefs about Mamaloni in the afterlife. See M. Scott, 'The Makiran Underground Army: Kastom Mysticism and Ontology Politics in Southeast Solomon Islands, in E. Hviding and K. Rio (eds), *Made in Oceania: Social Movements, Cultural Heritage and the State in the Pacific* (Wantage 2011), Chapter 6.
16 Detractors' quotes were often provided anonymously. The unflattering Australian government assessment was contained in a briefing dossier for Australian delegates at a Pacific Forum meeting in Honiara in 1994. It was picked up by a journalist and circulated, much to the embarrassment of the Australian Government.
17 Kenilorea gave a very touching funeral oration, *Solomon Star*, 18 January 2000.

Researching and writing the biography

Over the past four years, I have often been asked and have asked myself, 'Why write the life of Mamaloni?' The idea of writing his life first occurred to me in 2005 as a possible PhD topic but it was the publication of Sir Peter Kenilorea's autobiography that spurred me to action.[18] Mamaloni clearly merited a biography and, having sought permission from both sides of his family, I decided to take up the task. Writing this biography is a 'labour of love', not of the man but of his country. I am also motivated by desire to repay a debt to the Solomon Islands for having given me an adopted daughter and more than 20 years of fascinating work, travel and study. A controversial maverick like Mamaloni is a much better subject for biography than a dull worthy one. Mamaloni was a very engaging character whom I knew personally, having played in his cricket team in Honiara in the early 1990s before gout forced him to give up the game. He would stand at mid-off smoking, relaxing from politics – he much preferred a green wicket to a red carpet. Mamaloni was a wily leg spinner who bamboozled batsmen with high flight and bounce on synthetic wickets, an apt metaphor for his political skills. According to Neil Gunson:

> Biography can only be an approximation of a life … Usually a good biographer goes beyond the life and attempts to illustrate the age in which his or her subject lived.[19]

Researching this biography has provided the opportunity to study the fascinating, complex and diverse history of Solomon Islands in the 19th and 20th centuries. I have called the biography *Understanding Solomon* because Mamaloni provides a fascinating prism through which to understand the country and the history of the islands. His origins and life story provide fascinating insights into the historical, sociocultural, economic and political forces that have shaped the country. His upbringing and rise to power is the story of Solomon Islands from a backwater of British colonialism to independent country and, arguably, a failed state.

Understanding Mamaloni combines conventional narrative life with social biography, particularly his life up to 1970 when he entered politics. Social biography combines biography with social and world history to understand the lives, especially those of ordinary men and women, for which there are fragmentary or non-existent sources.[20] Prior to 1970, interviews with his

---

18 P. Kenilorea and C. Moore, *Tell It As It Is: Autobiography of Rt. Hon. Sir Peter Kenilorea, KBE, PC, Solomon Islands' First Prime Minister* (Taipei 2008).
19 N. Gunson, 'Telling Pacific Lives: From Archetype to Icon', in B. Lal and V. Luker (eds), *Telling Pacific Lives: Prisms of Process* (Canberra 2008), 1.
20 E. Burke, *How to Write a Social Biography*, available online at www.cwh.ucsc.edu.

family and peers were the primary source of information, supplemented with secondary sources on Anglican schools from the *Southern Cross Log*, *Melanesian Messenger* (with the assistance of Dr Terry Brown), and the SSEM.[21] The Eastern District annual reports in the Solomon Islands National Archives provide details on Makira going back to 1918. The National Archives in Honiara also contain Mamaloni's public service and confidential files.

The history of Makira is superbly annotated in a Master's thesis, 'An Ethnohistory of Arosi', which documents virtually all written references to Makira from the arrival of Mendana in 1567 to the 1970s.[22] The anthropology of Makira is well described, first by Charles Fox in 1924 and recently by Michael Scott's ethnography of the Arosi (2007).[23] Scott also provides much useful Solomons and Pacific colonial history but particularly useful are Judith Bennett's magisterial *The Wealth of the Solomons* (1987) and *Pacific Forest* (2000).[24] After 1970, Mamaloni appears in the parliamentary records and newspapers, as well as the memories of political colleagues, friends and the public.[25] There are also 10 printed biographies and autobiographies of Solomon Islanders, a number of them contemporaries of Mamaloni, plus three memoirs of former colonial administrators that provide excellent detail and insights into the colonial mentality.[26] Kenilorea's *Tell It As It Is* is particularly relevant because he and Mamaloni were in school, public service and politics together until 1991 when Kenilorea left politics.

I now have great appreciation for archives and archivists. The National Library of Australia and the Pacific Manuscripts Bureau at The Australian National University are treasure troves, with facilities for digital copying. The National Archives in Honiara is sadly neglected but rewarded diligence and provided moments of elation, such as finding Mamaloni's confidential files and reports by the first District Officer, F.M. Campbell, which I copied for his family in Makira.

---

21 Church of Melanesia journals such as *Southern Cross Log* and *Melanesian Messenger*, sourced through Rev. Terry Brown, former Bishop of Malaita, and the Solomon Islands National Archives. SSEM history from C. Moore, *Florence Young and the Queensland Kanaka Mission 1886–1906: Beginnings of an Indigenous Pacific Church* (Honiara 2009).
22 S. Sayes, *An Ethnohistory of Arosi, San Cristoval*, MA thesis (Auckland 1976). Sayes' thesis is an excellent source of written materials on Arosi; Sayes was assisting Dr Charles Fox in his final years.
23 Two essential sources on the anthropology of Makira are C. Fox, *The Threshold of the Pacific: an Account of the Social Organization, Magic and Religion of the People of San Cristoval in the Solomon Islands* (New York 1924); and, more recently, M. Scott, *The Severed Snake*, Chapter 3.
24 Two magisterial works are J. Bennett, Wealth of the Solomons: *A History of a Pacific Archipelago, 1800–1978*, Pacific Islands Monograph Series, no. 3 (Honolulu 1987); and J. Bennett, Pacific Forest: *a History of Resource Control and Contest in the Solomon Islands, c.1800–1997* (Cambridge 2000).
25 Parliamentary sources – Proceedings of Governing Council (1970–74), Legislative Assembly (1974–78), National Parliament (1978 to present), available at the Solomon Islands Parliamentary Library, Honiara.
26 Three very informative memoirs by colonial administrators are T. Russell, *I Have the Honour To Be: a Memoir of a Career Covering Fifty-two Years of Service for British Overseas Territories* (Spennymoor 2003); J. Tedder, Solomon Island *Years: a District Administrator in the Islands 1952–1974* (Stuarts Point 2010); J. Smith, *An Island in the Autumn* (2010).

Perhaps the archival coup was finding the records of Suharahu, Mamaloni's great grandfather, who was executed without trial by a Royal Navy Australian Station firing squad at Rumahui in 1892.[27]

I conducted six months of very enjoyable fieldwork between 2009 and 2011 in Honiara and Makira, Mamaloni's home island, interspersed with internet, library, and archival research in Solomon Islands, Australia, New Zealand and the United Kingdom. I interviewed nearly 160 people. Supporters, opponents, family and friends have been primary sources of original material, including former Governor-Generals and Prime Ministers, who were excellent and gracious informants, as indeed was almost everyone I interviewed. One former Prime Minister and another Opposition Leader refused to be interviewed, still furious about what Mamaloni had done to the country. There were many anecdotes and stories about Mamaloni, some apocryphal, others embellished, with many examples of his famous wit and informality.

Table 3: Summary of interviews conducted by Christopher Chevalier (to March 2013)

Family members	34
Fellow Makirans	24
Friends and school mates	13
Political peers	9
Colleagues and supporters	19
Critics and opponents	23
Neutrals	10
Academics	15
Former administrators	8
Total	**155**

Source: Author's compilation.

Navigating the hidden tracts

> How a biographer finds his or her own way through the deliberately hidden tracts of a private life becomes a challenge that will be recognised by many.[28]

Many informants were happy to provide details about 'Solo' as a private and family man. Mamaloni was always fond of women and related easily to them, especially pretty ones. He had four partners who each bore him three children.

---

27 RNAS and WPHC references (see fn 2).
28 N. Gunson, 'Telling Pacific Lives', xi.

In a highly Christianised country, he attracted much criticism for his messy personal life and revolving-door marriages. There is anecdotal evidence of infidelity and domestic violence, not unusual in marriages throughout the Pacific, particularly among powerful men. But the biography will not intrude too closely on this area of his life, heeding the advice that 'good biographers should go up to the bedroom door but do not go beyond'.[29]

Interviews provided original and fascinating insights not available from the public record. Not all details could be corroborated or justify publication, including reports of domestic violence and infidelity. This is particularly relevant in a Melanesian compensation culture and one reason that I have given draft chapters to other researchers and key family members for correction of facts and advice. Respondents are often unreliable about dates and events, which is where newspapers and magazines have proved essential, as well as providing detail, commentary, and quotes. Although, as Clive Moore points out, they are unreliable as single historical sources, I have used print media to assemble the factual narrative, a form of bricolage.[30] I have then sequenced the chapters by decades rather than by broad themes, which would have been another possible approach.

Table 4: Newspapers and magazines relating to the Solomon Islands

BSIP Newssheet (Government Information Service) – weekly government newspaper (to 1975)
Solomon News Drum (Government Information Service), renamed the *Solomon Star* in 1982
Kakamora Reporter 1970–75 (private radical paper)
Solomons Toktok 1977, first tabloid (mildly sensationalist paper)
Solomon Star 1982–2000
Island Business 1980–2000
Pacific Islands Monthly 1946–2000

Source: Author's compilation.

Learning from biography

> '[H]istory … should always be tempered by sensitive appreciation of context, contingency and circumstance.'[31]

29　A. Sebba, *That Woman: The Life of Wallis Simpson, Duchess of Windsor* (St Martin's Griffin 2012).
30　On the unreliability of newspapers, see C. Moore, 'Biography of a Nation: Compiling a Historical Dictionary of the Solomon Islands', in B. Lal and V. Luker (eds), *Telling Pacific Lives*, 279–80.
31　N. Gunson, 'Telling Pacific Lives', xvii.

Writing the biography has been a journey of learning and understanding about Mamaloni, the Solomons, and also myself. If his life story is a prism on the Solomon Islands, it is inevitably filtered through the lenses of my own experience and attitudes. My research has taught me a more nuanced understanding of colonialism, Christianisation, and commerce. I particularly admire Mamaloni for fighting against racism and colonialism throughout his career. Britain was always a reluctant colonial master in the Pacific, overseeing such a vast area with little commercial value and a great distance from Whitehall. Compared to the French, Germans, and Australians, the British were more subtle and experienced colonialists. Their different impacts and political heritages resulted in the various political systems in Melanesia today.

Solomon Islands politics is highly personalised and individuals appear to be responsible for success and failure when in fact they are only part of larger forces beyond their control. The road to independence is a case in point, with Mamaloni and Kenilorea credited with struggling to bring the country to self-government and independence. But independence was a well-travelled route and, in the words of the last Governor of the Solomon Islands, Sir Colin Allen: 'It is not true that there was a struggle for independence. If there was any struggle, it was on the part of Her Majesty's Government to get them to independence.'[32]

The reverse is also true, that is, that politicians appear to be more responsible for failures than they deserve. For example, the government of Kenilorea and Alebua from 1984 to 1989 had to manage an economy experiencing declining terms of trade, as did most other Pacific countries. This allowed Mamaloni to claim superior economic credentials during his stewardship between 1981 and 1984. Given the performance of his 1989 to 1993 and 1994 to 1997 governments, this is ironic – even laughable. But it also raises the larger question of how much leaders of small countries in a global economic context can be held responsible for the economic fortunes of the country. Mamaloni was only one player in a world where much larger historical and economic forces were operating. Where he can be held personally responsible was in being so erratic, careless and reckless with his own resources and those of the nation. *'Tout comprendre, c'est tout pardonner'* (to understand all is to forgive all) is a useful caution when making judgments.

Opinions and judgments can be upturned or moderated by a new fact or piece of the puzzle. One example is Mamloni's exam failures at King George VI and Te Aute, which I attributed to laziness or inattention to detail, and certainly not

---

32 B. Standish, 'The Struggle for Independence', *Melanesian Neighbours: the Politics of PNG, the Solomon Islands and the Republic of Vanuatu*, Basic Paper No. 9, Legislative Research, Department of the Parliamentary Library, Parliament of the Commonwealth of Australia, (Canberra 1984), 104.

due to lack of intelligence. However, my visit to New Zealand and interviews with informants who had been to Te Aute College revealed that Maori and Islander students often failed matriculation; they did not sit exams well and were disadvantaged in written English.[33] Details from his exam results and probation reports in the administration reveal that his English was 'only fair'. Moreover, exam results mattered less than they do today with many more graduates and greater competition. What mattered more was that Mamaloni left a prestigious overseas school as an avid reader with a lifelong interest in history and strong confidence in indigenous culture and ownership.

Psychological interpretations are irresistible when trying to understand one's subject. According to Niel Gunson:

> Clinical study of the biographical subject enables the historian to understand the workings of the subject's mind and prompts him or her to ask particular questions and look for particular signs. The historian becomes a profiler.[34]

Beneath his benign exterior, Mamaloni was a complex character affected by a number of psychological factors and events. The severe yaws he suffered as a child left him in the care of gentle women and unable to play robustly for several years. He had a difficult relationship with his mother, who did not look after him, and he had an ambivalent attitude to women – relaxed and charming to some but callous and cruel to others. He was very short and displayed aspects of 'short man syndrome'.[35] Like many politicians he suffered from hubris. David Owen has described hubris syndrome as an occupational hazard of leaders. Even before when he was elected to Parliament, he made great play of being synonymous with the wisdom of Solomon and the country itself.[36] In each of his administrations, he overestimated his powers and was damaged by scandal. Ill health also affected his behaviour; he became increasingly fractious, tetchy, and difficult as his medical problems grew.[37]

---

33 Noel Vickridge, former headmaster of Te Aute College, interview, 8 March 2013.
34 N. Gunson, 'Telling Pacific Lives', 6.
35 Short men have been found to be most jealous in the presence of powerful, tall, strong and rich potential rivals. Mamaloni displayed traits of short men, such as being prone to bouts of aggression, showing off and keeping a close eye on their wives or girlfriends.
36 David Owen and Jonathan Davidson define hubris syndrome as a personality disorder acquired in high office. It is characterised by excessive confidence, becoming 'impossible' and not listening to others. D. Owen and J. Davidson, 'Hubris Syndrome: an Acquired Personality Disorder? A study of US Presidents and UK Prime Ministers over the last 100 years', *Brain*, Oxford Journals (2009) brain.awp008.full.pdf.
37 David Owen's analysis of leadership in American presidents and British prime ministers also shows how health and decision making are related. D. Owen, *Sickness and Health: Illness in Government and Leadership in the Last 100 Years* (London 2011).

As human beings, we live our lives without knowing how events will actually turn out. But to the biographer, trends and traits become evident in retrospect. As Neil Ascherson writes:

> A biographer's classic problem is an acute case of hindsight. It is easy to judge in retrospect and to link events over time. Knowing the end means that many previous episodes can seem to converge towards events ... the omens are easy to pick out.[38]

For example, Mamaloni's disregard for convention led to repeated scandals that seriously undermined his credibility and the integrity of his governments. It is notable that he was never re-elected immediately after each of his terms. His superiors in the colonial administration had noted that he did not do what he was asked to do and did not do his job properly; this neatly and prophetically describes his performance as Prime Minister.

Hopefully, *Understanding Mamaloni* will be well enough researched, have few factual errors, and have interpretations that are well supported. I hope that I will do justice to the life of a man who was the most interesting and significant leader that Solomon Islands has so far produced. Ultimately, the 'best one can do is to be sincere, to gather all the information that is humanly possible and, while enthusiasm lasts, set it down.'[39]

---

38 N. Ascherson, 'An Acute Case of Hindsight, a Classic Biographer's Problem', *London Review of Books* (2010), 102.
39 T. Pocock, *Alan Moorhead* (2011), 207.

4. The 'Pawa Meri' Project

Producing film biographies about women in Papua New Guinea

Ceridwen Spark

Introduction

Who should tell a life story? For whom should they write? These questions confront most life writers. Such questions are crucial for outsiders writing about Pacific lives but they are also important for insiders. In late 2011 I was in the process of planning a research project which involved producing six films about leading Papua New Guinean women. The project, to be funded by the gender division of AusAID, was to be conducted in collaboration with the Centre for Social and Creative Media at the University of Goroka. In the spirit of 'rewriting history from the bottom up', the project entitled 'Pawa Meri' (powerful or strong women) aimed to celebrate 'ordinary' women achieving extraordinary things.[1] Having written about some of the challenges facing educated women in Papua New Guinea (PNG), I considered it important to balance this account with stories about women in PNG who inspired. In particular, I wanted to do this in a way that would be accessible to Papua New Guineans. Because of low literacy levels, films seemed an appropriate way to communicate the life stories of Papua New Guinean women.

During this period I ran into a colleague with strong connections to PNG and a history of working there. Mentioning that I was compiling a list of possible subjects, I asked whether there were any women she would recommend to be included. Her response was swift and discouraging; she could not see the point of making *bik hets* (show offs) of a few individual women by focusing on their achievements. In her view, no one in PNG got anywhere without the support of *wontoks* (friends and family) and, consequently, using film to tell the stories of six individual women was fundamentally problematic. These biographical films would only cause division and jealousy. Moreover, the project represented a misguided attempt to 'help' and would contribute little of use to Papua New Guineans.

---

1 R. Smyth, 'Reel Pacific History: The Pacific Islands on Film, Video and Television', in B. Lal (ed.), *Pacific Islands History: Journeys and Transformations* (Canberra 1992), 206.

Her criticisms were provocative. Apologising for being negative, she said, 'I just spend so much time trying to stop people from "helping"'. Her assumption appears to have been that in making these films and putting particular women forward as role models, I was motivated by a desire to show Papua New Guineans what to aspire to and how to 'do development'.

Was my desire to make these films motivated by misguided benevolence? Did celebrating particular kinds of women reflect problematic assumptions about the kinds of women who were worth honouring? And to what extent would my perceptions about the great women of PNG be different from local perspectives? Peter Hempenstall has discussed Marilyn Strathern's argument that in Melanesia, '"persons" cannot be abstracted, or conceptualised, distinct from the relations that bring them together'.[2] Whether or not one agrees with the particulars of Strathern's argument, Melanesian society does tend to be characterised by a greater emphasis on a person's place within a social group than is the case in most western settings.[3] As such, it seems reasonable to query the appropriateness of biography – which tends to focus on the achievements of individual, 'bounded' subjects – for telling stories in PNG.

In what follows, I reflect on these points and the ways in which they have helped me to think through the aims, processes and intended outcomes of the Pawa Meri project. At the time of writing, the project is halfway through its 18-month life. I make no claim to have resolved these matters, nor to pretend they will be resolved when the project is completed. Rather, the essay discusses some thoughts and experiences so far in order to highlight some of the challenges, practical and ethical, that are involved in the production of cross-cultural life stories.

Film-making in PNG

The question of who is telling the story is especially pertinent in a medium as powerful as film. In her essay, 'Reel Pacific History: The Pacific Islands on Film, Video and Television', Rosaleen Smyth recalls Lenin's description of cinema as 'the most persuasive of all the arts'. She writes:

> The makers of film history, like the conventional historians of the print media, are all motivated by some idea about the purpose of history – to show how it really was; to rewrite history from the bottom up; to put

---

2 P. Hempenstall, 'Sniffing the Person: Writing Lives in Pacific History', in B. Lal and P. Hempenstall (eds), *Pacific Lives, Pacific Places: Bursting Boundaries in Pacific History* (Canberra 2006), 43.
3 Martha Macintyre discusses and disagrees with Strathern in M. Macintyre, 'Violent Bodies and Vicious Exchanges: Objectification and Personification in the Massim', *Social Analysis*, 37 (1995), 29–43.

a minority viewpoint or a woman's eye view; to decolonise colonial history by viewing it through an ethno- as opposed to Euro-centric lens; or to promote national consciousness.[4]

Film-makers have different agendas, so it is important to consider how films reflect the values and beliefs of those making them and the eras in which they are produced. The following 'potted history' of film-making in PNG helps to outline the politics of representation that has preceded and informed the making of the Pawa Meri film biographies.

Film-making in PNG is usually thought to have begun with the making of *Pearls and Savages* (1921), Frank Hurley's now famous depiction of his journey through the Torres Strait and into two villages in the Gulf of Papua. As Liz McNiven, Senior Curator of Indigenous Collections at the National Film and Sound Archive, writes:

> This film may appear ethnographic but Frank Hurley was primarily a photographer. His interest lay in the commercial image rather than the production of an ethnographic record: he used the camera to create art rather than to document actuality.[5]

Bearing in mind the fluid boundary between ethnography and art, film-making in PNG can be said to have been primarily ethnographic until at least the 1950s. In these films, the 'natives' and their ways are the objects of curiosity and explanation. Hank Nelson reflects: '[t]he anthropologists, particularly Gregory Bateson and Margaret Mead, had made good use of moving film by the 1950s. But all this was taking images from Papua New Guinea and displaying them to astonish and inform distant audiences'.[6]

While ethnographic films are still made in PNG, something of a shift occurred in the 1950s when the Australian Commonwealth Film Unit (CFU) became the main producer of films about PNG. As Jane Landman notes, the CFU 'made a series of documentaries on Papua and New Guinea for ABC [Australian Broadcasting Corporation] Television', the primary purpose of which was to inform Australians watching 'at home' about the 'progress' being made by their northern neighbours. These films were 'friendly and ... not detached, salacious or sensationalising'.[7] However, like the anthropological films before them, they were not made with indigenous audiences in mind. 'Neither the ABC nor the CFU in the early 1960s, in Australia or in the territories, encompassed

---

4   Smyth, 'Reel Pacific History', 205–6.
5   Curator's notes, available online at aso.gov.au/titles/documentaries/pearls-and-savages/notes.
6   H. Nelson, 'Write History, Reel History', in B. Lal (ed.), *Pacific Islands History: Journeys and Transformations* (Canberra 1992), 190.
7   J. Landman, 'At Home With Our Colonial Work: ABC TV's New Look at New Guinea', *Continuum: Journal of Media & Cultural Studies*, 24: 3 (2010), 357.

Indigenous peoples in their civic address. Papua New Guineans were "the problem" or "curiosities"'.⁸ Maslyn Williams, the senior producer appointed to the CFU series, estimates that 40 films about PNG were made during the ten years between 1956 and 1966.⁹ Even though the unit 'aimed to film in all districts, and at times … encouraged Papua New Guineans to direct the camera at what they thought was important', the primary purpose of the films was to tell Australians about Papua New Guinea rather than to explore Papua New Guinean perspectives.¹⁰

Following the period in which the CFU was the leading producer of films about PNG, politics and art took a postcolonial turn. Reflecting this, some of the expatriate film-makers working in the country began to challenge the idea that Papua New Guinean traditions needed to be abandoned in favour of modernisation. Leading up to and after independence in 1975, film-making in PNG was dominated by outsiders, including some who have come to be synonymous with films about PNG. These include British-Australian film-maker, Chris Owen, who later became the Director of the National Film Institute; and famously, Bob Connolly and Robin Anderson. Nelson comments of this group:

> Robin Anderson, Bob Connolly, Gary Kildea, Les McLaren, Dennis O'Rourke and Chris Owen … were in Papua New Guinea for long periods, learnt Tok Pisin, and were prepared to spend months in the field to get the raw footage, and months in the editing room to shape the content accurately and elegantly.¹¹

Considering this dominance by outsiders in *Taking Pictures*, the self-reflective documentary he co-directed with Annie Stiven, Les McLaren states, '… the cameras have been mostly in our hands'.¹²

Despite the proliferation of expatriate film-makers operating in PNG in the decade or so after independence, the period also spawned some examples of Papua New Guinean film-making. These were largely contingent on the willingness of individual expatriates to support local film-makers. Two key films to note in this early period of collaboration are *Tukana: Husat i Asua* and *Stolen Moments*.¹³ In the case of *Tukana*, a feature film, Albert Toro, the now well-known Bougainvillean actor and star of the film, wrote the semi-autobiographical script and co-directed the film with Chris Owen, who was

---

8   Ibid., 367.
9   J. Landman, 'Visualising the Subject of Development: 1950s Government Film-making in the Territories of Papua New Guinea', *Journal of Pacific History*, 45: 1 (2010), 72.
10 Nelson, 'Write History, Reel History', 192.
11 Ibid., 197.
12 L. McLaren and A. Stiven, directors, *Taking Pictures*, Australia (1996).
13 A. Toro and C. Owen, directors, *Tukana: Husat i Asua* (1982); M. Wilson and N. Sullivan, directors, *Stolen Moments* (1989).

also the producer. The lesser known *Stolen Moments* represents a collaboration between Mount Hagen film-maker, Maggie Wilson, and North American academic, Nancy Sullivan. Wilson wrote, co-directed and shot the film with the support of Sullivan who was 'producer and co-director'. Sullivan notes:

> The importance of this production is that, notwithstanding my presence, it was local to Mt Hagen on all levels: from the themes and attitudes of the story, to the financing, the production goals, and the organization of the project itself. Here, as in other productions, it was more the manner in which the story was made than the presence/absence of a European that rendered the project "indigenous".[14]

The effort to support indigenous film-makers was consolidated somewhat in the early 1980s with the establishment of the *Skul Bilong Wokim Piksa* in Goroka, the capital of the Eastern Highlands Province. Sullivan has discussed the history and role of the *Skul* more fully than I can here.[15] Suffice it to say that the *Skul* was set up by Goroka architect, Australian Paul Frame, and that it was instrumental in training several of the country's now more established film-makers, including Martin Maden, the director of cinematography for *Tinpis Run*, the maker of *Crater Mountain Story* and, more recently, *Return to High Valley*.[16] Elsewhere I have discussed *The Last Real Men*, a film made by another graduate of the *Skul*, Ruth Ketau, who currently works for the National Film Institute (NFI).[17]

The recent films by Maden and Ketau provide evidence of indigenous film-making in PNG. Notwithstanding such examples, it is fair to say that there was minimal activity during the 1990s and in the early years of this millennium. Reflecting this lack of activity, Kingston Namun, a blogger from Divine Word University, wrote in 2003:

> From Demolition Man to Spiderman to Star Wars, Papua New Guineans have watched these Western films so many times that they have become household names. Whether they be on DVD, video cassettes or on HBO, we have become so accustomed to American movies that we never give a second thought to the possibility that we could make our own.[18]

---

14 N. Sullivan, 'Film and Television Production in Papua New Guinea: How Media Become the Message', *Public Culture*, 5 (1993), 544.
15 Ibid.
16 P. Nengo, director, *Tinpis Run* (1990); M. Maden, director, *Crater Mountain Story*, Papua New Guinea, 52min (2006); M. Maden, director, *Return to High Valley* (2012).
17 R. Ketau, director, *The Last Real Men: The Neheya Initiation* (2011). This is discussed in Ceridwen Spark, 'Sisters Doing it for Themselves', (forthcoming).
18 K. Namun, 'Film Making in PNG', available online at malumnalu.blogspot.com.au/2008/09/why-film-making-is-not-taking-off-in.html.

Happily, over the last decade, the increasing accessibility of film-making equipment has resulted in the production of more films by Papua New Guineans. At least a dozen PNG-made films were shown at the 2012 Human Rights Film Festival in Port Moresby, a festival which explicitly highlights development issues via a focus on 'the current situation in Papua New Guinea and what can be done to further implement human rights in those key areas'.[19] At the inaugural Human Rights Film Festival in 2010, only two of the films on the whole program were about PNG and both were funded by externally based aid agencies. As such, the number shown in 2012 represents a significant increase. Supporting this, film-makers I have interviewed tell stories of people they know, including village-dwelling and older people, documenting everything from their own life stories to environmental change in their local areas. For instance, at home in Melbourne, I recently watched a music video about police destroying homes at the Paga Hill settlement in Port Moresby in May 2012.[20] This demonstrates that, via the internet, home-made stories are being communicated 'unadulterated to audiences around the world', thereby adding to the public record of PNG by its peoples.[21]

In addition to representing themselves, Papua New Guineans also want to watch themselves. Historically, they have had limited opportunities to see people on screen whose lives, concerns and humour resemble their own. As Llane Munau, a Bougainvillean woman who works at the NFI says, 'a lot of Papua New Guineas want to watch themselves but they don't have any opportunities'.[22] Film-makers have noted the 'visceral power and connection' viewers feel when they see people who look like them and with whom they can identify on screen.[23] Such comments reveal the intricate link between the ethnicities and identifications of the film-makers, the ways in which this impacts on the films they make, and the capacity of these films to engage local audiences.

The above analysis reveals a gradual, but encouraging, increase in the number of films made by Papua New Guineans. The question of who Papua New Guineans are addressing when they make films is, however, little discussed. In the next section, I consider the 'imagined audience' in films made in and about PNG, in order to reflect more deeply on the importance of addressing Papua New Guinean audiences.

---

19 Human Rights Film Network, available online at www.humanrightsfilmnetwork.org/festivals/papua-new-guinea-human-rights-film-festival.
20 PNGexposed, available online at pngexposed.wordpress.com/2012/12/18/human-cost-of-paga-hill-demolition-captured-in-new-music-video/.
21 N. Sullivan, 'How Media Become the Message in Papua New Guinea: A Coda', available online at www.nancysullivan.net/articles.htm.
22 L. Munau, interview, April 14, Goroka, PNG (2012).
23 S. Frilot, in K. Hankin, 'And Introducing ... The Female Director: Documentaries about Women Film-makers as Feminist Activism', *NWSA Journal*, 19: 1 (2007), 68.

The question of audience: who is watching the films?

With the exception of some popular local films, including *Tukana*, *Tin Pis Run* and, more recently, *The Road to Wabag* and *Return to High Valley*, the overwhelming majority of films made in and about PNG have been directed to an international audience. This causes consternation among Papua New Guineans of all backgrounds, whether educated middle class, student or village dweller. As Les McLaren shows in *Taking Pictures*, there is resistance to filming in public places because of the widespread belief that these images are used to portray Papua New Guineans in a negative light overseas.[24] Moreover, the national ire about this is not confined to criticism of expatriate film-makers. For instance, Kymberley Kepore, the Engan woman who made *Tanim*, has been criticised for making a film for international audiences that depicts the people of Enga in a poor light.[25] Shot during the 2002 election in Enga, *Tanim* reveals the violence, vote rigging and corruption involved in local efforts to secure power. The repercussions of making this powerful film have been more difficult and lasting for Kepore than for the outsiders with whom she collaborated on the project.

To make matters worse, the few films that have addressed local audiences in PNG have done so in explicitly pedagogical and patronising ways. While, as noted above, the imagined audience of the CFU films was Australians watching at home, in the early 1960s the unit did produce some films for local audiences. These were designed to teach PNG people the behaviour that the Australian government and its representatives saw as desirable and appropriate. Reflecting the broader attempt to smooth their transition into a modern democracy, these productions tended to construct the newly constituted group of ethnically diverse peoples known as 'Papuans' and 'New Guineans' as inferior beings in need of instruction.

One such film, *A Woman Called Gima*, explicitly addresses women.[26] Encouraging local women to participate in women's groups and through these to learn about good hygiene and health, the 21-minute film models the modern, efficient and, by implication, superior way for women to get together. The 'star' of the film is Gima, a neatly dressed and apparently educated Papua New Guinean woman who stands out from the other women in the village. Gima's distinction

---

24 *Taking Pictures*, Australia (1996).
25 J. Frankham, director, *Tanim* (2002).
26 M. Williams, director, *A Woman Called Gima* (1963).

is enacted physically; she is shown standing apart from the other women, shaking her head disapprovingly at those who talk and make *bilums* during meetings. The script is as follows:

> This is Gima. She is the wife of the new school teacher. She shakes her head sadly when she sees what a bad meeting this is … Gima … knows that the Secretary, Mary, should keep a book with the names of the women who come to each meeting and should write down what happens. Gima also knows that Dora, the treasurer, has to keep a book and know how much money the club has saved. Gima knows all these things and thinks she can help them.[27]

Gima then proceeds to show the apparently incapable and too relaxed village women a 'better' way, including how to hold an orderly meeting, mark attendance and manage a budget. By the end of the film, the women of the village are doing as the film (via Gima) instructs. The clear message is that they will reap the benefits in the form of healthier and more productive lives. Through these behaviours, previously unfocused and unknowing village women can themselves become women like Gima.

Given this history, it becomes crucial to consider how to make films for a local audience in a way that does not replicate the pedagogical imperialism of the past. While the involvement of Papua New Guineans does not guarantee either that power inequities will be flattened out or that the films produced will be well-received by local audiences, it is an important first step. In particular, the challenge is to work across cultural differences to try to achieve co-authorship.

Collaboration and control: co-authoring the Pawa Meri films

> Film is different from the loneliness of writing: it is cooperative, different skills are required and the technology forces compromises… But undoubtedly the most satisfying involvement is at the level of producer/director – keeping close to all activities and always having the right to influence, if not command.[28]

So wrote Hank Nelson, reflecting on his involvement in the production of the film *Angels of War* which explores the story of Papua New Guinean involvement in World War II.[29] Nelson's description suggests that the role of 'producer/director'

---

27   Ibid.
28   Nelson, 'Write History, Reel History', 199.
29   G. Daws and A. Pike, directors, *Angels of War* (1982).

is akin to that of 'author' in that it involves 'influence, if not command'. If the Pawa Meri films are to reflect collaboration and mutual control, the power to command (to author) must also be shared. It is not enough to have Papua New Guineans involved as technical crew. But co-authorship is challenging at the best of times. Nelson co-directed and co-produced with two other Australian men, Gavan Daws and Andrew Pike, to make *Angels of War*. In the case of the Pawa Meri films, the process of 'authorship' involves ongoing cross-cultural interaction, including between me, an Australian born and raised in PNG; the German producer, Verena Thomas; and the women who are the subjects and directors of the films, as well as their families and friends. This situation is variously stimulating and difficult.

Each of the six Pawa Meri films will be directed by a Papua New Guinean woman. It is hoped this will help the stories to be seen through PNG eyes. But this is not a matter of 'handing over the means of production' in the naïve belief that when 'outsiders' relinquish control authentic PNG films will emerge.[30] For a start, the funding, provided by the gender division of AusAID, entails unstated obligations on the part of those involved. We could not, for example, make a film celebrating a woman's decision to remain subservient to a husband who beats her. The sceptical colleague I mentioned at the outset of this essay might perceive our need to convey certain messages and not others as imperialism masquerading as development. However, the alternative – that is, that the films do not get made at all – would seem a pity given the power of the cinematic medium to shift perceptions and institute change. 'Handing over' control might be acceptable and effective if one perceives all to be well in the world of gender relations in PNG. The alternative view is that cross-cultural interaction around gender issues offers an opportunity for people of different backgrounds and mindsets to respectfully listen to and acknowledge other points of view and, in doing so, reach a new position together. The best way to illustrate this is by example.

Choosing the subjects

I lived in Goroka for some months in 2012. During this time, I had discussions with many people to try to identify six women about whom we might make these biographical films. In the course of these discussions, various Papua New Guineans made clear that they valued leaders who remained connected with the 'grass roots', as opposed to those who direct their energies to shoring up their own privilege and power. Given PNG's much-discussed diversity, it was

---

30 Sullivan discusses the matter of '"handing over" the means of production' in 'How Media Become the Message', 2003.

important to try to achieve a balance across the series in terms of the province of origin, area of contribution and expertise of the six women, and as far as possible in relation to other factors, such as age range. It would not be appropriate, for example, to make six films about educated, employed women living in urban centres such as Port Moresby and Goroka. Doing so would risk alienating the majority of PNG's population, many of whom live in rural areas, may never be employed in the formal economy and are unlikely to have completed secondary, let alone tertiary, education. In PNG, educated women are often portrayed as 'inauthentic and non-representative'.[31] This construction can be used to dismiss their claims and exclude them from power. As such, and while aware that it would be wrong to make six films about formally educated, urban women, I would be reluctant to pretend that this is not an important group to represent in the context of six films about leading women in PNG.

These issues are pertinent when deciding whether or not the educated daughter of an Australian teacher and a well-known politician ought to be one of the subjects for the films. Some expressed doubts, including the educated young women involved in the project, who thought this potential subject would be considered privileged and thus hard to relate to. I was of the view that educated, socio-economically advantaged people of mixed heritage were part of contemporary PNG and thus no more or less authentic than anyone else. Moreover, in order to avoid excluding the category of young women, we needed a subject who was less advanced in years than most of the women we were identifying.

Arguably, my desire to include a younger, educated woman with Australian parentage among the six 'Pawa Meris' simply reflects my own cultural biases, including a tendency to value youth and a sense of comfort with the 'middle-class'. Nevertheless, this does not mean the outcome – exploring and celebrating the life of someone whose experience is atypical in PNG – is wrong. Indeed, the exploration of exceptional lives can reveal a privileged person's very ordinariness and humanity.

I am told by the director working on the film about this subject, and who has already conducted most of the filming, that the team involved with her is now excited and happy to tell her story, precisely because the person in question values her connection to PNG and its people above a potentially easier and more comfortable life in Australia. For the team, such choices reveal the subject's strength of character and commitment.

---

31 M. Macintyre, '"Hear Us, Women of Papua New Guinea": Melanesian Women and Human Rights', in A. Hilsdon, M. Macintyre, V. Mackie and M. Stivens (eds), *Human Rights and Gender Politics: Perspectives on the Asia-Pacific Region,* (London 2000), 153.

Now it is my turn to be challenged. Just as the Papua New Guineans working on the Pawa Meri films have been forced to confront their prejudices so too must I, for in telling this particular life story, as in a number of the Pawa Meri films, the subject's strong Christian beliefs are a key part of how she narrates her resilience and success. As a secular Australian, I perceive the widespread religious devotion of Papua New Guineans to be an explicable but sometimes alienating facet of life. But I cannot dismiss or 'write out' the enormous significance of Christianity in this context. As such, co-authoring this life story with a devout director and subject will require a genuine sharing of control, while endeavouring to ensure the film does not become a vehicle for proselytising.

Conclusion: transforming the genre from within the Pacific?

Producing jointly told stories across cultural and religious differences is no easy task and we have a long way to go. Nevertheless, at this point in the Pawa Meri project, I do not consider the collaboration irredeemably problematic in the ways my sceptical colleague implied. Although there are challenges involved, co-authoring these life stories seems a worthwhile endeavour because in the process those of us involved are required to confront and question the beliefs we hold dear, and which differentiate us, while at the same time delineate new ground through a growing sense of the values and beliefs we share. I also think it is unlikely the films will make *bik hets* of a few individual women. Rather, what seems to be emerging are films in which six strong and courageous women reveal, in true Papua New Guinean style, the extent to which they are made, sustained and enabled by those around them. As such, I hope that the Pawa Meri films will come to represent an exciting and unique contribution to the genre of life stories, requiring those of us involved in their production to think differently about our sometimes too 'de-socialised' accounts of the lives of individual subjects. This being so, rather than reflecting the imposition of a western genre on Pacific peoples, the films may come to represent an instance in which the genre itself was transformed by being practised collaboratively in a new location.

5. 'End of a Phase of History'
Writing the life of a reluctant Fiji politician

Brij V. Lal

> The author who speaks about his own books is almost as bad as the mother who talks about her own children.

Fiji is an ethnically divided society where public memory has long been racially archived. This raises particular questions about what to write and from whose perspective; it turns 'insider' into the 'outsider', and vice versa. In this chapter, I reflect on writing the life of one figure, Jai Ram Reddy. He was the dominant leader of the Indo-Fijians from the mid-1970s to the late 1990s when his political life ended in a massive defeat and he departed the political scene for good. The post-independence years were deeply fraught for Fiji in general and for Indo-Fijians in particular. Independence had been achieved peacefully in 1970, but the colonial-era race-based constitutional architecture adopted then, and the values and assumptions which underpinned it, effectively consigned Indo-Fijians to a life of prolonged political opposition from which escape seemed well-nigh impossible. Fijians would control the levers of power if they remained united, and Indo-Fijians would be invited to the table of national decision-making on terms and conditions determined by the ruling elite. Tokenism was the order of the day. When Indo-Fijians finally managed, in partnership with a small number of indigenous Fijians, to win power at the ballot box in 1987, they were rudely removed from office after only a month by a military coup in the name of protecting indigenous interests. There then followed a dark period of political persecution, rampant racism and religious bigotry against Indo-Fijians on a scale never seen before. Mercifully, common sense returned a decade later in the form of an amicably negotiated multiracial constitution in 1997, but its life was cut short by yet another military coup a decade later. But that is a different story.

As the leader of his people, Jai Ram Reddy witnessed this tumultuous series of events at close quarters. His life might therefore afford close and intimate glimpses into the processes of politics in this period as well as insight into the personalities who drove them. I had watched Reddy intermittently from a distance from the 1970s to the early 1990s, and cannot recall more than a couple of very brief conversations with him during that time. My first meeting with him had begun on an inauspicious note. I met Reddy at a farewell party hosted by a friend in Lautoka on the eve of my departure for Hawaii in July 1983. Reddy was aloof, but later in the evening he bore into me. I had written an assessment of the 1982 general elections in which I had suggested that if the National Federation Party (NFP) had not widely distributed a controversial *Four Corners* video alleging misuse of Australian aid money by the ruling Alliance Party, implicating Prime Minister Ratu Mara in the sordid affair, it might have won the election.[1] In other words, associating the party with the video too closely was a bad strategic move. Reddy was livid: 'Who the hell are you to write such rubbish? I have had it with you academics, sitting on the sidelines and making carping comments. I am not going to waste my breath talking to you.' I was sufficiently perplexed by the encounter to note it down in my diary. But it was not anger and disappointment that remained with me over the incident, rather a vague sense of respect; respect for a man who stood by his words and deeds. He was in possession of certain facts which he felt duty bound, as Opposition Leader, to make available to the public irrespective of political consequences for himself or his party.[2] He did the right thing, was I so obtuse not to see that? I have had disagreements with Reddy on subsequent occasions but learnt not to take these personally. Most people who have had any close association with Reddy will tell a similar story of sudden eruptions of anger at some perceived slight or difference of opinion, but the disappointment evaporates quickly.

For several years, living in different countries and pursuing separate careers, we lost all contact until the 1987 coups. I became a vocal critic of the coups (as I have remained ever since) and wrote a book about them as well as a general history of Fiji.[3] I was to discover much later that Reddy had read some of my writings, not always with complete approval it has to be said, though he spoke approvingly of my account of Fiji's first military takeover. But there was no correspondence, no talk – political relationships in Fiji are like that, people are bad at writing. In 1993 I was asked to address the annual convention of Reddy's NFP in Nadi. This was unexpected. Political conventions were, and still are, partisan political affairs to re-energise the party faithful with stirring rhetoric about possibilities and potentials, not a place for sober political discourse. I gave a carefully prepared talk on the flaws of the 1990 Constitution and the need to create an inclusive, non-racial political culture in Fiji. The speech was widely publicised. I spoke both in English as well as Hindi, to the surprise of some in the audience and the appreciation of others that, for the first time, a practising academic had addressed a gathering of what some saw as a communal party, that is, an Indo-Fijian party. From then on, our acquaintance deepened. Reddy would occasionally ask for notes for a speech he had in mind or a talk he had to

---

1   See my article 'The Fiji General Elections of 1982: The Tidal Wave That Never Came,' *Journal of Pacific History*, 18: 2 (1983), 134–57.
2   As he told the Sir John White Commission enquiring into the allegations made during the 1982 general elections.
3   B. Lal, *Power and Prejudice: The Making of the Fiji Crisis* (Wellington 1988); B. Lal, *Broken Waves: A History of the Fiji Islands in the 20th Century* (Honolulu 1992).

give, and I would oblige with that and other relevant material. By the time he nominated me to the Fiji Constitution Review Commission in March 1995 he was very well briefed on my scholarly work and about my stance on crucial issues — the 1987 coups, for example.[4] Nonetheless, putting me on the commission was still a big gamble for him politically.

I continued to write about political developments in Fiji in the 1990s, along with the biography of the founding NFP leader, A.D. Patel, for whom Reddy had worked as a young lawyer from 1961 to 1966.[5] Reddy was pleased with this work,[6] but a study of his own life was never mentioned, nor did it occur to me to ask. After the completion of the constitution review work, I resumed my academic life in Canberra, returning to Fiji in 1999 to speak about the review work at some NFP rallies at Reddy's request, to the utter disappointment of his opponents in the Fiji Labour Party. The election was a rout for Reddy and his party. They failed to win a single seat in parliament. To everyone's surprise, Reddy fell to a novice. NFP stands for 'Not Fit for Parliament', opponents shouted. The results raised more questions than I could find answers for. Why such a massive defeat for a party which had played a crucial role in the review of the constitution? What caused the rejection by the Indo-Fijian electorate of a man widely seen as the dominant figure in the Indo-Fijian community and who was respected across the nation? It was then that I seriously contemplated writing Reddy's life as a prism into the history of post-independence Fiji. There was a certain logic to the project. In the Patel book I had taken the story of the Indo-Fijian political experience from the 1920s to the late 1960s; with this book the experience of the twentieth century would be complete.

******

Reddy was interested in the project in a detached kind of way, in the manner of an ever cautious lawyer. That is also in the nature of the man. Unlike most politicians, Reddy was reluctant to talk about himself; he was firmly focused on the present and on the future, and on trying to avoid the debilitating pitfalls of the past. But he promised to give me access to his and his party's papers, which were kept in massive cardboard boxes at his country house in Lautoka. The papers covered his life from the 1990s onwards; most of the papers dealing with the earlier period Reddy had burnt when he left parliament in December 1983, convinced that his political career in Fiji was over for good. I told Reddy

---

4 The 1988 book is titled *Power and Prejudice*. I deal with the work of the Commission in my 1998 *Another Way: The Politics of Constitutional Reform in Post-coup Fiji*, Asia Pacific Press, Canberra.
5 B. Lal, *A Vision for Change: AD Patel and the Politics of Fiji* (Canberra 1997); re-issued in 2011 by ANU E Press along with a collection of his speeches and writings.
6 As he said launching the book at the Sri Vivekananda College in Nadi: 'This exhaustively researched and well documented book is long overdue. We all owe a debt of gratitude to Dr Lal for his industry and perseverance in producing this excellent book.'

to his face that what he had done was a criminal act. He said nothing; there was nothing he could say. He had, though, kept some sensitive correspondence in a separate file which he gave me later. The papers, which are preserved for future researchers at the Pacific Research Archives at ANU, were a vital source for my research, containing correspondence with party people and other leaders, drafts of speeches, newspaper coverage of important events, policy documents, manifestos, campaign literature and other marginalia.[7]

These were supplemented with haphazardly organised material from the head office of the NFP in Tamavua, Suva. The building which housed the office was also the home of Kamal Iyer, a man with a phenomenal (and unforgiving) memory of recent political events. He had once worked in the Office of the Leader of the Opposition. He was effectively the custodian of the papers and gave me complete, unrestricted access to them. I do not know where these papers are now – probably lost to posterity. Mary Chapman, Secretary-General of the Fijian Parliament, was extremely helpful with insights about meetings which Reddy attended and the rapport between him and Rabuka; and generous in sharing, under supervision, closed records of committee meetings and other parliamentary proceedings not yet in the public domain.[8] The staff at the Fiji Parliamentary Library let me have free rein with their mostly published records and a full set of the daily newspapers. These were also consulted, with less cooperation, at the Pacific Collection of the University of the South Pacific Library.

The lesson I learnt from my archival searches was, unsurprisingly, that the records about the contemporary period are sketchy and, furthermore, prey to the ravages of humidity and cockroaches. The National Archives of Fiji, chronically under-funded and under-staffed, is of very little help about the contemporary period. They simply cannot afford a systematic program of information gathering routinely undertaken in many other countries such as Australia. Private individuals often have fading or fractured memories of events of long ago, but no papers, and memories coloured in many cases by events of the intervening years. Newspapers help trace the contours of the past political landscape, but there is very little beyond the headline and the skimpy paragraph that follows. There are few people around to verify or amplify the accuracy of the reports, the situation aggravated by the migration of many past actors and party strategists. The past is now a foreign country to them and they are often reluctant to revisit it for fear of opening old wounds. Recordings of past campaign speeches by the Fiji Broadcasting Commission (now the Fiji Broadcasting Corporation) have all but vanished. All that any assiduous

---
7   The Pacific Manuscripts Bureau in Canberra has a microfilm of the papers.
8   They are at the National Archives of Fiji, accessible under the 30-year rule, I assume.

researcher can do is to assemble as much documentary material as he can, from whatever source he can access, and construct his narrative accordingly. He knows that his research is partial, but that is in the nature of the enterprise.[9]

The written, archival material would have to be supplemented by interviews I quickly realised. I began with colleagues I knew, who were willing to talk, who were sympathetic to my project, or were political allies of Jai Ram Reddy. Long-forgotten anecdotes were recalled around the *tanoa* bowl long into the night, along with quotable quotes from past fiery speeches, the machinations undermining an opponent, the trimming of truth (always by the other side, never your own), the internal jockeying for power. The essentially partial recollections were interesting, but they were partial; often they added much colour and variety but little substance. There were no great revelations. I asked for names of people on the other side of the political divide who might be willing to talk, not names of prominent leaders but others hidden in the shadows. This was easily given and I followed up the leads.

The picture I got from talking to them was often diametrically opposed to what I have heard before. For every event, there is an alternative explanation, casting Reddy in the role of a villain, a divider, a second-fiddle player. Some say that he was the right man in the wrong party. In many cases, the speakers preferred to remain anonymous; Fiji is a very small place and word gets around quickly. Their preference was respected. The interviews, if that is not too strong a word, were always informal, interspersed with frequent forays into irrelevance and trivia, but all this was part of the process, and things cannot be rushed. I did not carry a tape recorder with me, that stifles free-flowing conversation. A small notebook was all I had for recording dates and other precise information. Immediately afterwards, I wrote down the full text of our exchanges. I didn't have university ethical clearance routinely required for oral interviews these days; I was not unduly troubled. I belong to an earlier generation of researchers who did not need to be told to exercise prudence, judgement and fairness in their treatment of words spoken to them, to always place texts in context. I do not need to be told how to go about the business for which I was trained. Nevertheless, as a standard procedure, I checked back with my interviewees whenever I could about the accuracy of the quotes I attributed to them.

Reddy was aware that I was talking to people, but never once, on the rare occasion when we did meet, did we talk about my research. He was characteristically meticulous in the observance of the protocol of the law. That is his nature; but the arm's-length approach is also, I realised, a good thing to have. He can, in good conscience, disclaim any connection to the project if he does not like

---

9   The use of 'he' is not indicative of any gender bias on my part, but the constant use of 'he or she, his and hers' is tedious. My apologies.

what I have written. After all, it is my book, not his. By now, he knows me well enough to know that I would be fair-minded in my assessment of his life and work, which obviates the need for any discreet enquiry. If he could trust me to be his nominee on the Reeves Commission at one of the most critical moments in his political career, surely he could trust me with the biography project.

Having assembled the bulk of documentary material, I needed to have an informed conversation with Reddy about what I had read, about the gaps in what I had uncovered, and about what others had said. I was anxious. This was new territory for me. With the Patel book, I worked primarily with archival material, personal correspondence and a limited number of oral interviews. The man himself was long dead (in 1969) when I began research for the book (in the 1980s).

In 2004, I invited Reddy to Canberra (as part of the Distinguished Pacific Visitors Scheme) to talk at length about his life in politics. We sat in an empty office next to mine and talked over several days about the major political events in which he was a participant, his take on things, and his assessment of people. The conversation was recorded (now in digitised form for future researchers). Reddy speaks with clarity, candour and precision, in the manner of a persuasive barrister, never evading a hard question, always to the point. We talked about the major crises of the mid-1970s; about the NFP's failure to form government in April 1977; his statement over the radio about why the NFP could not govern on its own; and why Siddiq Koya was unable to become prime minister. We also talked about the enactment of the Agricultural Landlord and Tenant Act, which subsequently divided the party irreparably; we talked about the *Four Corners* programme and its role in the 1982 elections; we talked about the 1987 coups, its causes and consequences; and we traversed the tumultuous events of the 1990s, including the process that led to the formulation of the 1997 Constitution. This list was by no means exhaustive. I was grateful for the candour with which Reddy spoke. It certainly helped put hitherto misunderstood or misrepresented events into perspective.

I had enough new material from the interview to know that interpretations which have become part of the Fijian historical orthodoxy would no longer be viewed in the same way after the publication of my book. In popular mythology, Koya and Reddy are portrayed as sworn enemies, daggers drawn to the end. Reddy said he could never really dislike Koya, and Koya said that there was 'compassion' between the two men. Fijian nationalists targeted Reddy as a virulent anti-Fijian politician. Reddy, however, talked of warm relations with Ratu Sir Penaia Ganilau ('an honourable adversary'), though not with Ratu Mara, between the two of whom there was mutual antagonism. He could 'talk for hours' with Fijian nationalist lawyers Kelemedi Bulewa and Etuate Tavai, and Apisai Tora, the founder of the fire-breathing Taukei Movement, would give Reddy 'respect' — 'he would not shun me.' There was a revelation in the interviews on Reddy's relations with Sitiveni Rabuka. There was no bitterness or anger but a forgiving, understanding tone; a warm appreciation of Rabuka's openness and willingness to listen, and of his 'masterful' leadership of the constitutional review process. Perhaps the fact that Rabuka was a commoner, with no aristocratic pretensions and proclivities, made it easier for Reddy to deal with him, Reddy speculates with some justification.

Equally revealing for me was the discovery of how much of the reconciliation process of the 1990s — which led to the successful promulgation of the 1997 Constitution — was led by men outside the formal process, who facilitated dialogue and discussion away from the public eye, in informal get-togethers and dinners. Reddy especially mentioned the contributions of American Ambassador Don Givertz, House of Representatives Speaker Dr Apenisa Kurusiqila, and President of the Methodist Church Ilaita Tuwere. All this was new information, available nowhere else. The book is the richer for it. Reddy set the record straight about various allegations made against him by his opponents in the Fiji Labour Party: about his role in the enactment of the Agricultural Landlord and Tenant Act; about contentious issues in the sugar industry; about his role in the constitutional review process; and that he escaped Fiji at 'the height' of the 1987 coups. These clearly false allegations still hurt Reddy.

There was a certain sadness in the way Reddy recalled his political life to me; this most outstanding criminal lawyer of his generation who could have gone places in his beloved profession, his great love, but who reluctantly got drafted into politics at great personal cost. In one of my early conversations with him, I had asked how he would sum up his life. 'It is a wasted thirty years,' he said. 'I gave up thirty years of my life for nothing. All that sacrifice, for what?' It was an admission that had 'an arresting effect on me', says the biographer Doug Munro. 'It was such a sad thing to read: it really hit you in the face.'[10] It evidently had a similar effect on another scholar, Jack Corbett, who made it the centrepiece of his review of the book,[11] and also on Professor Yash Ghai whose words conclude this chapter. Sometimes, in my darker moments, I have similar thoughts about having spent or rather misspent my entire professional life working on Fiji, its past and its present, only to bear witness to more pain and avoidable, unnecessary tragedy.

******

---

10 Correspondence from Doug Munro, 21 March 2013.
11 See J. Corbett, 'In the Eye of the Storm: Jai Ram Reddy and the Politics of Postcolonial Fiji', *Journal of Imperial and Commonwealth History*, 39: 2 (2011), 344–46.

I realised as I began writing that Reddy and I had not agreed to any precise condition about the use to which I would put the material, written and oral, he had provided me. At some point, whether I volunteered or Reddy requested (I cannot now say), he would read the final manuscript to point out any egregious errors of fact or interpretation, but that would be the extent of his intervention. The final say would be mine about what would go into the book and what would not. It was my account after all. Reddy was not concerned about the essential truth of what he told me; he was vaguely concerned about the impact of his comments about his adversaries on their families. Children should not pay for the sins of their fathers was his view. This very humane and entirely legitimate concern, I said, should be weighed against the concern for historical truth. Many wrong turns had been taken in the past, including by Reddy himself, but all this had to be confronted and, if possible, lessons drawn from them. We agreed to be mutually accommodating of each other's point of view. But there is nothing beyond that vague understanding. Reddy remarked several times, not entirely in jest I think, that I should publish the book after he was dead. Each time, I deflected his wish with a playful request for precise information about the date of his departure from this world!

By early 2007, the research was complete but the writing refused to get done. I got easily distracted, although, to be fair, there were many things happening in Fiji to distract one's attention, such as a military coup and the subsequent deluge from the media, both local and international, for commentary and assessment. That engagement still continues, much to my distress; I would like nothing more than for a return of more stable times in Fiji. But the claims of the past on my time and learning cannot be avoided. Constant movement between Suva (where my wife then lived and worked) and Canberra (my principal residence) did not help. Each day, the enormity of the writing task ahead drained me. I was probably suffering 'writer's block' and I began to entertain serious doubts as to whether I would ever be able to finish the project. I had a surreal sense of impending mortality, much to my wife's alarm, especially when I mentioned to her the person I would like to complete the book if I was gone. Nothing was going right for me until the day I was invited by an old student of mine to address his history class at a high school in Nasinu. His students, who had seen me on television, were keen to meet a 'real live' historian, he said. Could I say something about the value of reading and writing history to convince the non-believers that history was not necessarily for no-hopers. I spoke about what I was doing and asked the class of about 20 whether they knew who Jai Ram Reddy was. Not a single student knew, including the Indo-Fijians in the class, though they had heard of Sitiveni Rabuka and George Speight. This historical amnesia among Fiji's best and brightest horrified me.

Around the same time as my Nasinu talk, I came across an old issue of the *Fiji Times* lying about our Suva Point home. It contained a story about some Miss Hibiscus contestants visiting the Naboro Prison where they met its most infamous inmate, George Speight. One of them was quoted as saying: 'Meeting Mr Speight was like meeting Mr Mandela.' She gushed: 'He was really friendly and meeting him would be one of the biggest highlights of my life. This is a trip I would remember in years to come.' Another said that meeting Speight was 'like meeting one of the Hollywood celebrities', a memory she would 'cherish for the rest of my life'. Another contestant was reported to be 'in a world of her own when she visited Mr Speight and through all the trips they have taken, she described the prison visit as the most memorable'. I was speechless – what future for Fiji with role models like these? It was then that all my dithering and diversions disappeared and I began to write furiously, often six to eight hours a day. I had renewed determination that I would finish the book before it finished me. By May 2009, a year later, a good draft of a 230,000-word manuscript was completed.

People wondered politely about how the writing was going, but I quickly changed the subject. I don't like 'pissing in the wind', as Gavan Daws once said. Research and writing are for me solitary exercises, and I am wary of sharing my thoughts with others before they are fully formed. This, I imagine, is how most historians approach their task, unlike social scientists who are comfortable about working in teams and sharing ideas as they go along. As I was writing, I sometimes wondered about the reception the book would have in Fiji. It was a depressing thought. I was under no illusion that my book was going to be read in Fiji. People in Fiji just don't read, even, or especially, those who make their living from teaching in tertiary institutions. There would be no review forums, no university seminars beyond comments about my industry and perseverance – not even criticism that I was interfering from afar in matters that no longer concerned me.

My worst fears turned out to be well founded. Nearly five years after its publication, not a single review has appeared in Fiji. No one has written to me even privately to express their views, critical or otherwise, about the book. It is as if the book did not exist. So why do I write? I certainly do not write for a non-existent Fiji readership. In a sense, they do not matter anymore. I write because I have to, to bear witness to the time in which I have lived. I see writing as an act of revenge against a culture of indifference and forgetfulness, an act of revenge against historical amnesia. Words, as Winston Churchill once said, are the only things that last forever. And historians, if they are to be true to their vocation as guardians of public memory, must find a place at the table of posterity for both victors as well as the vanquished.

Writing history – writing anything – does not come easily to me. Writing the history of the present is especially fraught. Contemporary history, some would say, is an oxymoron, like family vacation or friendly fire. You write as the gun is still smoking. You have no sense of how things will turn out in the future. Other accounts will come to light, fresh evidence unearthed that might throw a different light on the period or contradict your account.[12] I am not unduly troubled by this. There can be no question of finality in historical discourse. History, as someone has said, is a long conversation without an end. We all live within our own histories, not outside or beyond them. Timeless historical texts, – for example, by Gibbon or Macaulay or Trevelyan, or Thomas Carlyle on the French Revoultion – are as rare as the clichéd hen's teeth; and they are enjoyed today more for their style and craftsmanship than for their historical content.[13] Then there is the forbidding thought that the person you are writing about is alive and will read what you have written. And not just him alone, but his numerous colleagues and friends (as well as foes) who were part of the action you describe and who will each have their own personal recollections, their own take on events, which they will not hesitate to communicate to you in no uncertain terms. I can't say – what writer can – that I have got everything absolutely right, but if the broad picture I have painted is seen as credible and authentic, I should be pleased.

As promised, I sent the completed manuscript to Reddy for his perusal. Several weeks passed and I didn't hear from him. I was worried enough to ring him. He was complimentary about the depth of my research – he had forgotten about half the events and episodes narrated in the book – but there was a hint of hesitation in his voice. 'I am not sure this should he published,' he said in a tone that I found deeply worrying. 'There are too many things here that will unnecessarily upset too many people. I have finished my career and I want to be left alone in peace.' He continued:

> This book will bring back memories of old controversies better left buried. What is done is done. Why unnecessarily hurt children of my former political opponents? I am not sure I want my grandchildren to read all this one day.

I was disappointed, to say the least, to be told that after all the years of research, the book should not be published. In response, I raised the historian's traditional defence. 'The past cannot be erased, no matter how much we may wish it to go away,' I told him. 'If I don't write, someone else will; you are a figure of history

---

12   See D. Munro, *The Ivory Tower and Beyond* (Newcastle upon Tyne 2009), 273–80.
13   See J. Clive, 'Why Read the Great Nineteenth Century Historians,' in J. Clive, *Not By Fact Alone* (Boston 1989) 34–47.

and will be judged accordingly; you have an obligation to allow your story to be told.' I went on like this for a while, but I was not sure Reddy was listening. I was not sure I had convinced him to see my point of view.

In a curious kind of way, I understand Reddy's reaction. He has firmly shut the door on his political past and has moved on to retirement after several years as a Permanent Judge on the International Criminal Tribunal for Rwanda. But I was not about to give up. 'You have encountered some of the biographer's worse nightmares,' a colleague sympathises. There are several, he says:

> They include serious disapproval from Guardians of the Great Spirit, who don't want you going anywhere near their esteemed and departed friend. There is denial of access to sources. Then there is a previously cooperative 'living' subject spitting the dummy. What started as a cuddly relationship turns sour when they see what you've said.

As a make-or-break initiative, I invited Reddy to Canberra for a face-to-face conversation so that I could get a better understanding of his objections. If the manuscript had to be junked … the thought remains unfinished. Over several days, we went through the whole manuscript, page by page, chapter by chapter. We agreed in advance that Reddy would have no say over my use of material gathered independently from other sources (such as newspaper reports), but only over that which came directly from him orally. That is the only veto power he would have. It is a fair compromise; it is always possible to get things wrong or distorted when dealing with oral evidence. Things said in the heat of the moment can be reconsidered. Perhaps things were said in confidence and not intended for public dissemination. I approached the encounter with much trepidation. But I was relieved that contrary to my deepest apprehension, Reddy did not find any egregious fault with my overall interpretation. A face-to-face meeting made all the difference, with the opportunity for a prolonged conversation, digressions, breaks over cups of coffee and lunches. There was give and take. I accepted that I might have misunderstood Reddy's intentions, which might have caused me to react too strongly.

The meeting went well. There was no difference over substance, or very little, but difference only over style. Reddy did not deny the quotes I attributed to him. He was concerned primarily about how they might come across, or how they might give inadvertent offence. As a scrupulous lawyer, he was especially concerned about protecting the privacy of confidential information. Why revisit the darkest period of his party's and his community's life with a blow-by-blow account? What purpose would that serve except to give comfort to his detractors? He suggested a way out. Could I say the same thing indirectly, allusively, without altering the substance of the text? I had no problems with that at all; in a way, I found Reddy's concern about the discomfort his words might cause to his erstwhile foes admirable. That speaks volumes for the kind of man Reddy is and why he is so widely admired by those who remember him.

I respected Reddy's concerns and readily amended words and phrases and direct attribution that might have given offence. I am now glad that he had an opportunity to read the final manuscript with great care. After all, I had written a book about him. But as readers will see when they compare the final published version with the penultimate draft of the manuscript (preserved for future researchers), there is not an iota of difference, none, in interpretation between the two versions. It is easy to be wise after the fact. In the book, I quote Theodore Roosevelt in support of the principle of authorial humility: 'It is not the critic who counts, not the man who points out how the strong man stumbles or where the doer of deeds could have done them better.'[14] The credit, he continues,

> belongs to the man who is actually in the arena, whose face is marred by dust and sweat and blood, who strives valiantly, who errs and comes up short again and again, who spends himself in a worthy cause; who, at best, knows, in the end, the triumph of high achievement, and who at the worst, if he fails, at least he fails while daring greatly.

There should be room for criticism and evaluation, as good scholarship demands, but 'it should always be tempered by a sensitive appreciation of context, contingency and circumstance'.

To that end, I appended at the end of each chapter one or two of Reddy's speeches on topics covered in it. This, I hoped, would enable readers to weigh Reddy's words and judgements against my interpretation of them. Their inclusion made the book bulkier, but several readers wrote to express their thanks for the archival value the speeches added to the book, especially as most of the speeches were not in the public domain, and some were lost forever. I will give an example. One of the most controversial topics in post-independence Fiji was a proposal floated by Ratu Sir Kamisese Mara for a government of national unity. He later claimed that Reddy had rejected the proposal, and that claim has become a part of the myth about Reddy's recalcitrance. I assessed this and other contentions in the book, but included two papers on the subject. One is the original paper written by Alliance politician Ahmed Ali outlining the problem and proposing solutions. Reddy subjected the paper to a clinical analysis at the NFP's Ba Convention in 1980; the paper is reprinted in the book. Reading the two papers together gives the reader a good sense of the complexity of the

---

14 B. Lal, *In the Eye of the Storm: Jai Ram Reddy and the Politics of Postcolonial Fiji* (Canberra 2010), xviii.

5. 'End of a Phase of History'

subject and the political calculations which sounded it. No serious discussion of the government of national unity proposal would ever be complete without reference to Reddy's reply.

******

I acknowledge the danger of forming conclusions about the past through the eyes of one individual.

> It is far too tempting, in this approach, to impute too much importance and impact to the actions and thoughts of one person when, as is often the case, the person actually represents the consensus of a larger group of which he was merely a spokesman.

The approach, I continued, 'could also potentially frustrate an understanding of the deeper forces of change over time that transcends the range of personal experience.' All that conceded, I agreed,

> but it is still true that some men and women do achieve a level of eminence and practical authority in the affairs of their societies and are able, by force of personality and personal intervention, charisma and cunning, to mould events to suit their purposes and thus affect the course of history.[15]

Jai Ram Reddy was such an Indo-Fijian leader, just as A.D. Patel had been the charismatic leader in pre-independence Fiji. But seeing the past through Reddy's eyes and experience also alerted me to patterns and changes which would otherwise have eluded me. I saw, for example, how and why in the 1980s and 1990s the NFP moved away from its demand for common roll to consociationalism. I saw close range the deep fractures and fissures in the Indo-Fijian community which acquired a political dimension in the 1990s, the North Indian–South Indian divide, for example. I saw how false it was to see the political process in Fiji solely through the prism of race, just as it was false to see the Indo-Fijian community as homogenous in its intentions and motives.

Most readers will likely see *In the Eye of the Storm* as an exercise in biographical writing. It is that, to be sure, but it is also something different. Reddy is the centrepiece of the book, and there is a long treatment of his childhood, his cultural and social background, and his early education and upbringing. But there is no deep probing of his interior life, no psychological analysis. I am candid with the readers. The book is not a biography in the conventional sense of the word. Rather, it is more in the nature of a political history of the subject.[16]

---

15   Ibid., xv.
16   Ibid., xiv.

> The focus is not on Reddy the man and his interior life or his private emotional world. Such an approach would require an intimacy with the subject I do not possess. Moreover, that kind of project is beyond my competence or even inclination to pursue. The Oedipus complex and all that are not for me. I accept for the purpose of this project that the public self is the 'real' self. Hence the focus on Jai Ram Reddy's public life and his engagement with the dominant political issues and concerns of his time shaped by the master narratives of colonialism and postcolonialism.[17]

Every writer of the life of a major contemporary figure, especially of his own community and country, will invariably face the question of how objective he is in his assessment of the subject. It is a fair question, but my firm view is that the writer must have a sympathetic understanding of the subject: the choices the writer made, the context in which he operated, and the constraints he experienced. It is very easy to shoot fish in a fish bowl. I am upfront with my readers:

> I am in broad sympathy with Jai Ram Reddy's political philosophy and approach to politics in Fiji and the fundamental transformation he sought to bring about in its political culture and orientation. The essential course that Reddy attempted to chart for his people and his vision for their place in the larger scheme of things were intrinsically right.[18]

And there was a personal dimension too. I was in my early university years when Reddy entered politics in the early 1970s. I witnessed at first hand the unfolding drama in which Reddy had a leading part. I was an interested bystander for most of the time, a student of it too and, for a brief period, a minor participant in the story I was narrating. In a very real sense, Reddy's story was my story too. 'Reddy's story is inevitably refracted through the lens of my own personal experience and political perspective.' At least some readers have appreciated this candid declaration of reflexivity on my part.

All scholarship is paradoxically both a solitary and a collective endeavour. You have got to face the tyranny of the blank screen all on your own, but you realise that you have reached that stage through the sacrifice and support of many people. I have had the good fortune of having friends and colleagues who have put aside their own work to read mine, to correct my prose and my stylistic blemishes, to seek clarification of points blindingly obvious to me but obscure to others. On the basis of friendship and regard we ask others to comment on our work, knowing that they will be honest and frank, to the point of asking

---

17 Ibid.
18 Ibid., xvi.

hard questions and coming out with hard criticisms. Things can be said in this context that go down very badly if coming from others. Having close and caring readers of your work in its formative stages is an invaluable asset; it lightens the burden and alerts you to new, unseen possibilities. But it is an asset in diminishing supply as the pressures and perils of academic life increase in these days of bureaucratic accounting.

In the Eye of the Storm has been well received, even in quarters where I expected hostility. But, as noted above, in Fiji there has been deafening silence. There is no reading culture there anymore. It is intellectually and morally an arid place, empty, the creative spirit and quest for fearless investigation corroded by two decades of coup-inspired turbulence. A conforming intellectual culture subservient to the regime in power, looking the other way as human rights violations proliferate, is rapidly becoming the order of the day. People who might have once been looked up to for leadership – intellectual and moral (vice chancellors, scholars, religious leaders) – have, many of them, offered their services to the military regime in return for minor rewards and recognition in their twilight years, but all the while camouflaging their personal pecuniary and business interests with the rhetoric of altruistic service and sacrifice. 'Menopausal males,' someone has called the do-gooders from overseas, former Fiji citizens, returning to offer their services for hefty fees and other forms of recognition. I have lost all hope of scholarship informing public discourse in Fiji any time soon, of effecting a change in attitude, of underpinning public policy. Colonels and commodores, not artists, scholars and thinkers, are paraded as role models for the younger generation.

So why do I write? In addition to what I have said before, because writing matters, because preserving memories from the ravages of time and human vanity matters, and because I want to leave my imprint upon my time and place. At my age and stage, and in contrast to younger scholars, I can ignore university demands to publish in highly ranked journals and the like; the 'brownie points system' of today simply washes over me.

All that and more; writing *In the Eye of the Storm* was also a cathartic experience for me. I relived the tumultuous events of the post-independence years that I had witnessed as a bystander: the pettiness of political leaders, corrupt and self-serving; the rampant racism; the arrogance of power; the coups and chaos; the fractured hopes and betrayal of promises; and the struggle of one man, not perfect by any means, hobbled by bitter divisions among his own people and facing the wrath of men convinced of their God-given right to rule irrespective of the verdict of the ballot box; the struggle by one man to find an honourable middle course for his people and for his country. All that sacrifice, all that anguish and heartache, came to nought in the end. To relive all this was a deeply painful experience for Reddy, as it was for me. I know in my heart that

I would not be able to write this book now; the grief is simply overwhelming at how we ended up where we are: in a cul-de-sac where the prospects of genuine democracy look exceedingly bleak, where guns, not good arguments, rule the day. I am reminded of the words of William Butler Yeats: 'Time drops in decay/ Like a candle burnt out'.

I conclude with the words of Professor Yash Ghai, the distinguished constitutional lawyer who has himself played a part in Fiji's recent history:

> The book ends, at least as it strikes me, both on the note of the achievement of a great man and sadness. There is sadness at Reddy's own assessment of his life in politics, living in 'exile' and caring at a distance for the welfare of Fiji. And sadness about the Indo-Fijian community (despite its resilience): rejection in its land of adoption despite humiliation and exploitation it suffered there: the inhumanity of the indenture system, 'denial of the humanity of the individual man and woman, the wilful negation of their cultural identity by those in authority.' Now dispersed again, a second migration, bonds of family weakened, foreshadowing the disappearance of the Indo-Fijian, the end of a chapter, end of a phase of history.[19]

---

19 Y. Ghai, 'In the Eye of the Storm: Jai Ram Reddy and the Politics of Postcolonial Fiji. By Brij V. Lal', in *The Journal of Pacific History*, 46: 3 (2011), 400.

6. Random Thoughts of an Occasional Practitioner

Deryck Scarr

Like many other contributors to this volume, I came to life writing quite by chance and I hesitate to add reflections that touch upon theory in any shape or form, unless in argument against paying overmuch attention to psychological analysis even of the living let alone of the dead. The authorities who deal in psychology were once likened to 'Romans consulting Sibylline books', but admittedly by a novelist in wartime.[1] And while I have always greatly admired works like Carola Oman's *Life of Nelson*, I had never particularly seen myself as setting up as a biographer in any major way, and had not much more idea of it than that the subject should be central and have left a sufficient direct record to be able to speak up for him or herself to a considerable degree.

If I had gone ahead with a history of sixteenth-century Plymouth at the Institute of Historical Research in London, as envisaged during my final months as an undergraduate in England, instead of venturing, via the Research School of Pacific Studies, into the South Seas when I graduated and becoming entrapped by tropical islands, Francis Drake and John Hawkins would presumably have made appearances as sea dogs ashore but perhaps not much more.

The first thing of any size that I ever did – a study of the Western Pacific High Commission (WPHC) based on archives admirably housed at that time in seductive Fiji – was actually rather criticised by an examiner for lacking biographies.

As a considerably expanded doctoral thesis, it was probably a big enough book as it stood and, by way of exemplifying the perversity of these things, a senior scholar then of these ANU halls found it seriously improper for me to have said of Sir John Gorrie, then the Chief Judicial Commissioner to the WPHC, that '[i]n his desire to see the law amended to what he considered it should be, he was invariably confused as to what it actually was'.[2] In further contrast, the Deputy British Resident Commissioner of the New Hebrides in those days found this comment very much to his taste when he read the original thesis, perhaps because administrators are often at loggerheads with lawyers, and, to the benefit

---

1 M. Davie (ed.), *The Diaries of Evelyn Waugh* (London 1995), 544.
2 D. Scarr, *Fragments of Empire: a History of the Western Pacific High Commission 1877–1914* (Canberra 1967), 43.

of the ensuing book, he opened up the Condominium Joint Court archives in Vila. Later, as Governor of Seychelles, Sir Colin Allan suggested I write a history of Seychelles. As it eventuated, this was not at all to the joy of the revolutionary government coming far from bloodlessly into power between my two long visits in 1976–7; but the book does in fact have a few outline portraits of its own: named slaves from the late eighteenth century onward; estate- and slave-owners documented from the notaries' extensive archives for generations since the 1770s; and a post-World War II Chief Justice from Britain who presided in court in Port Victoria wearing nothing but wig and gown on the bench because, after all, it can be so warm in Seychelles.[3]

******

Major figures leaving substantial records may very well impose themselves upon even an initially reluctant biographer. While I was working in the WPHC archives with Fiji all around, this happened in the case of the European whose portrait – which was signed with his Fijian nickname *K'oi Au, Na Kena Vai*, meaning 'I, the Very Bayonet', according to exceptionally sound Fijian opinion – was, to my knowledge, the only one hanging in the office of the Secretary for Fijian Affairs in Suva when that post was held by a Fijian.

The WPHC was, after all, set up to avoid the necessity of further direct responsibilities being assumed by Britain in the Pacific after the Cession of Fiji in 1874–5. And his major appearances in WPHC record quite apart, this unusual *Vavalagi* had already turned up in Foreign Office correspondence when, as Acting British Consul at Levuka in the mid to late 1860s, he was, among much else, doing his utmost to prevent speculators on the scale of the Polynesia Company of Melbourne from acquiring doubtful title to vast areas of land in Fiji. He came very much to the fore again in the records of the Cakobau Government as its inspirational Chief Secretary in the early 1870s. And you can hardly fail to recognise his style in the Fiji press of those very fraught years when editorials in the rival newspaper to the settlers' much-preferred *Fiji Times* declared:

> What is wanted by a certain class of men is an Utopia of rampant Anglo-Saxons, with a subject population of Fijians (among them, in proportion as 70 to 1) – among whom to live, and among whom to find, or make, hewers of wood and drawers of water – to be regarded as the ancient Phoenician regarded the Iberian, – or the modern Spaniard

---

3   D. Scarr, *Seychelles since 1770: History of a Slave and Post-Slavery Society* (London 1999).

the aborigines of Hayti; and, in due time, as these countries, and more modern and neighbouring ones have done – to furnish forth its perfect Iliad of woes.[4]

For settlers, after all, had been announcing that his government's

> line of policy has been a systematic attempt to demonstrate the possibility of placing the superior race in a utter subserviency to the inferior one; but we being men of Anglo Saxon descent are unwilling and determined not to be a medium for the solution of such a problem.[5]

As he put it, their desire was

> [t]o reduce the Kingdom of Fiji to the position of a British Colony, and to subject its Sovereign, Chiefs, and people to some such status as that of the aboriginal races of other countries which have been thus 'annexed' and subjected.[6]

And then from 1875 until his death in 1897 at 61 he is never out of the enormously rich record of colonial Fiji.

This was J.B. Thurston – Sir John, eventually – London-born, Jersey-residing as a young boy, a merchant seaman from the age of 13, castaway on Rotuma during a plant-hunting trip at 25, planter and labour-recruiter. He was the right arm of King Cakobau's Government before he became Colonial Secretary after the conditional cession of the islands, and then Governor of Fiji as well as High Commissioner and Consul-General for the Western Pacific – a founder of the Fijian Administration and the Native Tax System which put money into Fijian hands through the refunds paid after the tax assessments were met; unchanging in his belief in a serious degree of Fijian autonomy; unlikely to have allowed the indentured Indian population to rise beyond the 18,000 it had reached by 1897 when he died; a demolisher of the argument that Fijians were inevitably doomed to die out; and an inveterate prolific private as well as official correspondent about pretty well everything in the Southwest Pacific. Robert Louis Stevenson was put rather sharply in his place when his interference in Samoan politics came under the High Commissioner's eye, but the eventual olive branch from the Apia-residing novelist was well received.

---

4 *Fiji Gazette*, 5 November 1873; and quoted D. Scarr, *The Majesty of Colour: a Life of Sir John Bates Thurston: Volume One: I, the Very Bayonet* (Canberra 1973), 206.
5 Encl. Stirling to Admiralty 18 April 1873, British National Archives: Adm. 1/6261 and quoted Scarr, *Bayonet*, 223.
6 *Fiji Gazette*, 30 August 1873; Scarr, *Bayonet*, 206.

Yet very little was known of J.B. Thurston's background, nor a great deal in detailed context either, and it was great fun to track all this down in the Fiji archives, the Public Record Office in London, and in widely spread private letters and occasional journals around the world. Commonly, his tone was sardonic and his arguments well founded. As he asked a fellow Commissioner to Samoa, the American G.H. Bates, to tell Mrs Bates in 1889,

> not only does the American Government senselessly block my way in putting down robbery – murder & all abominations though it practically has no trading interests in the Western Pacific – but contrary to the Statute at Large, *English built* vessels cruise about here under American colours nominally owned by Americans –or soi-disant Americans, in order to evade the jurisdiction of the British High Cmmr. Just now when the Sovereign people are warm upon the subject of their 'Duties in Samoa' they might take up the wider question of their Duty in the Western Pacific.[7]

Thurston kept no private press-copy letter-book and for this jibe you have to search the George Hardy Bates Papers at the University of New Delaware.

For much else there are the archives at Kew Gardens and the Aborigines Protection Society, among other places, because the amateur botanist commented on politics and the Aborigines Protection Society needed protection from successors to supposed philanthropists like the merchant William MacArthur, who had possessed its ear in pressing for Fiji's annexation in settlers' interests during the 1870s. But the official record itself is vast, of course, and the manner there is very often unofficial too. Again, you place these private communications and the letters Thurston wrote to his sisters alongside the official dispatches and minutes and you check to see whether they add up. Are they consistent?

They always are – and when the established yet still controversial head of a colonial administration declares in a minute for his juniors that 'one half of the young *maramas* who are sometimes supposed to be guilty of indiscretions with young fellows in the evening, simply get into obscure corners in order to enjoy the luxury of a smoke', because the Methodist Church banned tobacco, you may continue to be intrigued.[8]

Thurston possessed genuine personal ties in Fiji and when, among much else, I asked his eldest daughter and last surviving child – then in her early 80s but aged 12 when he died – whether she remembered Ratu Josefa Lalabalavu, son of the Tui Cakau of the 1860s and 1870s and holder of this title himself, she immediately replied: 'Of course – my father's adopted son.'

---

7   D. Scarr, *Viceroy of the Pacific: the Majesty of Colour: a Life of Sir John Bates Thurston* (Canberra 1980), 263.
8   National Archives of Fiji: Colonial Secretary's Office: CSO93/2765; Scarr, *Viceroy of the Pacific*, 209.

So this biography really rather imposed itself with the Pacific background as well as the central subject leaping from the written record, but nothing on similar lines was planned. There were other things to work on, the study of Seychelles from human settlement around 1770 onward at the Governor's invitation among them; and I was away in or in search of Seychelles when, having read the Thurston biography's first volume, with its culminating point at Cession in 1874–5, a committee in Fiji asked if I would do its long-considered biography of Ratu Sir Lala Sukuna.

******

That could have been a pretty startling prospect as it would be the more-or-less official life of a high chief born in 1888, a decorated and wounded World War I French Foreign Legionnaire, an Oxford graduate, a barrister of the Inns of Court in London, a major recruiter of Fijian servicemen in the World War II, the first Fijian Secretary for Fijian Affairs, principal spokesman for the Fijian people for about 30 years until his death in 1958, and a man closely related to the chairman of the biography committee, Ratu Sir Kamisese Mara, at that time the Prime Minister. Ratu Sir Lala Sukuna was Ratu Mara's great-uncle and, it was generally thought or assumed, had been very much his mentor in youth and early manhood.

A prospect to baulk at, perhaps, although, after months in Seychelles, I was accustomed to free access to records and people. In fact, the revolutionary post-coup government actually rather congratulated me by taking exception to my simple narration of inconvenient fact and managed to frighten off publishers for two decades.

But of Ratu Mara's sophistication I had not the least doubt. Obviously he had been the up-and-coming man since I was first in Fiji on a series of long visits from 1962, initially not working primarily on Fiji at all but surrounded by it. And, while naturally keeping very quiet, having absolutely nothing to contribute anyway, I had a reasonable number of contacts as well as at least one very good friend who knew him well. Whatever reservations I had gathered there about Ratu Mara's thin skin and uncertain temper, I had never heard that if he asked you to do a job he did not leave you alone to do it with all the help he could give.

In fact, I found him entirely supportive and non-interfering. Nor as a whole was the committee other than unobtrusive and helpful. The word went out that I was to be well received wherever I turned up around the country, with or without an accompanying *matanivanua*, although usually with someone from the region in question – and stories such as Ratu Sukuna's miraculous ability to be in two or more places at the same time flowed.

Mere conceit, perhaps, had prevented me from supposing that anyone in the world would imagine they could make me or indeed would want a tool for such a project anyway, and an ardently Ratu Sukuna-admiring committee member eager to take on the biography himself had been suppressed. Other members rather enjoyed making sure of this, I thought. The committee's secretary, Dr Isireli Lasaqa, then Secretary to Prime Minister and Cabinet, was an ANU PhD graduate in geography and we knew each other well; and I not only noticed Ratu Mara observing a mild exchange or two between me and the aspiring committee member with amusement, but I also found him frank and open in private conversation about how he and Ratu Sukuna had related during Ratu Mara's rebellious days as an undergraduate and District Officer. Medicine, not administration-cum-politics, had been Ratu Mara's strongly preferred career; he had resented Ratu Sir Lala's insistence on his giving up medical studies in Dunedin for Modern History at Oxford, and he sometimes regretted having given in.

A great power's ambassador was once kept waiting for half an hour while we talked – and nothing Ratu Mara said was declared to be private, even though, in light of the general public perceptions about his relationship with Ratu Sukuna, some clearly could have been.

In other contexts, Mahatma Gandhi's emissary to Fiji of the late 1920s, S.B. Patel, lawyer and long-time quiet political eminence in Fiji, provided illuminating comments as a non-attending committee member. In the past he had rather mocked Ratu Sukuna's pronounced Britishness – the voice, the attachment to the Crown, the implicit determination that Fiji should not pass into the hands of people whose forebears had been in the islands for so short a time and whose betters, as Ratu Sukuna once put it in an uncommon moment of open exasperation, were not making a particularly good job of governing the subcontinent of India itself. As he had said, both echoing and speaking for his own people, the British Government was primarily there to look after the interests of Fijians anyway – but others' interests were also to be protected.

Ratu Sukuna invariably passed for a conservative leader and so in fact he was. As a District Commissioner in the 1930s, he was obliged to keep a detailed official diary, and I could only bless the central government's insistence on it. According to him, the semi-autonomous Fijian Administration, which had effectively died with Sir John Thurston, still provided the model. And individual Fijian families on farms of their own might be all very well in theory, but the relative isolation was very hard on wives. Village-based production under provincial control always struck him as the better plan anyway. Quite often it worked, but not invariably. Men of hereditary rank were reckoned the 'natural leaders of society' and may often still remain so in the people's eyes – but rank, he himself had always told his peers, was not an ornament. In fact, the man he appointed over Tailevu, long regarded as the leading province of Fiji, was Joeli Ravai – a conspicuous member of Viti Cauravou or the Young Fiji Society, a man with no rank but of powerful personality, the schoolmaster of whom Ratu Mara said in his memoirs that 'I attribute to my time under him much of my ability to face hardship and difficulty'.[9] And as Ratu Sir Lala told the Legislative Council in 1947, while regretting that, for instance, there was so little real eagerness for multiracial education: 'Frankly, Fijians fear Indianisation and for this reason: Indians possess an ancient culture of which they are justly proud and from which they have no intention of departing.'[10]

Often he was accused of confining higher education in his own society to men of rank, but in a conspicuous case his reluctance may have been based more on perception of character. In another instance, this certainly appeared in a letter to his great-nephew at Oxford in 1946, saying that, whatever Ratu Mara might think about his own role and current or future importance, people outside his own islands in Lau would not give two hoots for him until he had done something useful for them.[11]

As a matter of course, and with the quiet comment to me from Ratu Mara years later that he had sent Ratu Sir Lala an explanatory telegram from Oxford on the spot, this went into the volume of Ratu Sir Lala's writings that, on the heels of the biography subtitled *Soldier, Statesman, Man of Two Worlds*, came out with his letters from World War I battlefields, official diary extracts, minutes, annual reports on Fijian affairs, and such private correspondence as I could find. I particularly enjoyed his spoof but evidently heartfelt draft Annual Report on Fijian Affairs for 1948. It began: '1948 cannot lay claim to any spectacular achievement of policy; in fact, it can hardly lay claim to any achievement at all.'[12]

******

Compliments for this volume, *Fiji: The Three Legged Stool*, came to the biographer-editor and were duly passed on to the shade of Ratu Sir Lala Sukuna to whom they belonged; but about a dozen years after the biography's appearance in 1980 there were quiet indications that a life of Ratu Mara was rather expected of me. By then he was the President. A biography had actually been proposed by a leading National Federation Party parliamentarian in the late 1970s, but the offer had not been taken up by Ratu Sir Kamasese, as he then was, although still more usually just Ratu Mara.

---

9   R.S.K. Mara, *The Pacific Way: A Memoir* (Honolulu 1997), 15.
10 J.L.V. Sukuna, in D. Scarr (eds), *Fiji: the Three Legged Stool: Selected Writings of Ratu Sir Lala Sukuna* (Suva 1983), 422.
11 Ibid., 451.
12 Ibid., 427.

I was not at all sure how I felt about the proposition, although I had been watching him since he gave the Cession Day speech for 1962 at Levuka with, as it seemed to me, an air of disquiet about him. This I had put down to the fact that, as Commissioner Eastern and as the Tui Lau recently installed by Tongan kingmakers at Lomaloma into the bargain, he was introduced to a crowd largely of his own people by a non-Fijian, the editor of the *Fiji Times*. However, when the Colonial Office's archival record became available much later, it was clear that, during a year in London spent largely at the London School of Economics and Politics, but with forays into officialdom, Ratu Mara had become very well aware that the British Cabinet intended to leave Fiji as soon as a multiracial regime could be put together to inherit the independent state.

His own people's general reaction to this proposition he could easily foresee and, frankly speaking, so could any reasonably alert observer who was prepared to pay attention in the 1960s when young Fijians were quietly saying that they did not intend to end up like the Hawaiians and Maori.

Some 30 years later, when the idea of a biography came up, it was possible to make oneself very well acquainted with Britain's policy in detail. The archival resources, along with many more conversations with people at large, made a biography perfectly feasible. And, to my knowledge, Ratu Mara had not jibbed a bit about my book on the 1987 coups, not all of which I imagine he could have relished since, following the first coup, I had spent time with rebellious Taukei Movement members in the streets who did not love his concern for other people besides Fijians or, as they saw it, for his own international reputation either. When I called to see him at Government House, he was as open as ever, and again I remembered a confidential colonial assessment of about 1965 saying that he had the manner of an Oxbridge Don. An uncommonly good one, I feel obliged to say. And had he mentioned the idea, I should have agreed on all the usual generally unspoken conditions.

At the very least, it would have been interesting to be considering the career of a man who could have answered back, and perfectly feasible to have run a well-informed late draft past him. By contrast, Ratu Sukuna was famously reserved in private as well as in public; and Thurston had been reticent with the author who produced a work that appeared after his death.[13] The first Governor of Fiji, Sir Arthur Gordon, by then Lord Stanmore, had considered writing one soon after Thurston died, and it would have been fascinating; perhaps finding Lady Thurston unappreciative, he had not gone ahead with it.[14]

---

13 C. Stuart Ross, *Fiji and the Western Pacific* (Geelong 1909).
14 Stanmore to Arundel, 9 December 1987, J.T. Arundel Papers, National Library of Australia; Scarr, *Bayonet*, xxx.

But while Ratu Sir Kamisese Mara remained very conspicuously in harness as President of Fiji, with very delicate affairs of state still before him, the better option by far, as I thought at the time, was a volume such as the memoirs that he published in 1997. Following this, the circumstances of his leaving office in 2000 – to the glee of the Speight Gang in the captured parliament buildings but effectively at the behest of the army, which could have enabled George Speight's coup to be suppressed by negotiation if officers had acted immediately on Ratu Mara's orders as Commander-in-Chief to close off parliament so that marchers could not flow in as a human shield – did not seem to me to invite intrusion during the years before he died in 2004, when, I gathered, he was mentally as alert as ever. And I had preoccupations of my own. Actually, I regret not having made the approach, but there was a very rich archival record as well as lively memories since 1962 and some conversations from the late 1970s to help produce the biography that came out in 2008 under the title *Tuimacilai*.

As well as relating to a particularly boisterous stretch of sea in Lau, the province of his birth and always his place of retreat from a difficult world, this was also, after all, one of his given names; but if I had used his own or his speechwriter's image, the book could equally well have been called *Man on a Tightrope*, for this was what he had to be in a balancing act between rival ethnic forces for the whole of his political life.

Again, and rather more than with Ratu Sir Lala Sukuna, although not in Sir John Thurston's case where not much knowledge at all could be assumed in the majority of readers foreign to the Western Pacific, it was necessary to do a good deal more than sketch the background in order to illustrate the nature and scale of the drop lying below a political leader who was aspiring to win support from every community in the country, controversial and often misunderstood if not actually misrepresented as Ratu Mara's circumstances have sometimes been. More analysis was needed, as it was when Carola Oman wrote about Admiral Nelson, as I've lately reminded myself by reading a new edition, for she had to make and keep twentieth-century readers aware of the politics of Naples as well as the inner workings of the Royal Navy more than 200 years ago.

For Ratu Maru, one has to analyse perceptions as well as politics for decades before his birth, and it needed to be established that his perceptions were often unusual. For one thing, he did not love the *mataqali* as a unit of land tenure. For another, he told Ratu Sir Lala Sukuna from Oxford that 'there will be no peace of mind if we keep on underlining the differences between Indians and Fijians. Neither race seeing anything in common. One thinking the other privileged.' As a District Officer in the 1950s, he fought hard to get the colonial government's idea of multiracial local government across to all the rural communities but, as his official diary shows, he found Indian leaders quite as opposed to this obvious and intended nursery for future politicians at the national level as the Fijians and Europeans were.[15]

Later in the pre- and post-general elections, his own Alliance Party governments always had a good many more Indian votes than the opposition National Federation Party or Fiji Labour Party ever secured from Fijians, and when the voting system was rendered so opaque under the 1997 constitution it was his active support for Mahendra Chaudhry's Labour Government in 1999–2000 that put him at such risk from sections of his own people. For as he had pointed out in the pre-independence negotiations of 1969–70, with the National Federation Party pressing hard for the common electoral roll in expectation of taking government itself as a result, the cultural gulf was not an imaginary one, not least because Federation politicians confessedly had no idea how a great many indigenous Fijians thought and felt, and nor was inter-ethnic rivalry imaginary either.

'I am almost going to persuade my electors, "Let us have common roll"', Ratu Maru had said, believing in it himself in principle, 'and let us see what will happen in this country; *and don't blame me because I won't be alive.*'[16]

Thirty years later, the Army deserted him, as did some of his powerful relations, and he went home to Lakeba very much wishing at times again that he had told his great-uncle to go to the devil in 1945 and stuck to medicine after all. Very bad for the country if he had done so, though, and I think that the evidence for this comes out in the biography. They might call him Pharoah, or the Towering Inferno, but it might have been difficult to get very far with the word 'dictator' before well-informed people without ending up speaking into a deep silence if not being openly challenged or laughed at.

******

So my ideas of a biography go not much further than the idea that the subject of it should probably open the work. Without prejudice to background and contemporaries, the subject should maintain a certain precedence throughout; and the subject again should have left a considerable personal record.

Since the lives of painters or even of novelists I admire, like Graham Greene, so far tend largely to leave me underwhelmed, biography seems, for my part, to mean becoming involved on the page with well-recorded authoritative individuals of whom all three left a significant record and one, in particular,

---

15   D. Scarr, *Tuimacilai: a Life of Ratu Sir Kamisese Mara* (Adelaide 2008), 75.
16   Ibid., 184.

the most inaccessible in time, an amazingly extensive but scattered collection of minutes, dispatches, journals and private letters that would amusingly fill several thick volumes of their own.

Thurston received two volumes of biography in what might seem an authorial indulgence except that my condensation of the first volume in typescript, while what would then have become the second half of a single volume was being written, struck several people as being not so worthwhile when compared with the larger work from which it had been distilled. In a supporting instance, Elizabeth Longford's *Wellington* is likely to strike readers as exceptional unless they have read her *Wellington: the Years of the Sword* and *Wellington: Pillar of the State* of which the single volume is her expert abridgement.

My major subjects have rather chosen themselves, then, or have been suggested, and they come from the Southwestern Pacific. Yet I can imagine taking on a literate Mascareignean slave, or slave-owner, or slaving sea captain, or French privateersman of the eighteen- or nineteenth-century Indian Ocean. Harking back to school and undergraduate days, I would certainly consider Drake or Hawkins or anyone sailing with them, if more trunks of unread or half-digested documents in the subjects' own hands or from their well-attested dictation ever came to light. On the same terms, the Lord Protector Oliver Cromwell would appeal too. Yet by stretching the imagination a great deal further, and with archival understanding as well as direct knowledge of Indian Ocean islands, one might find it rewarding to take the unlettered slave Robert Sans Chagrin at his illegal arrival in Seychelles from Mozambique, where he had very different names, and to imagine if not actually trace his experiences on Silhouette and Mahé where he was known, and on any other island where he can be supposed to have lived.

Such at any rate are the passing random thoughts of an occasional practitioner.

7. Walking the Line between *Anga Fakatonga* and *Anga Fakapalangi*[1]

My experience researching the life of a Tongan king

Areti Metuamate

In this chapter I discuss the challenges of writing the biography of a fellow Pacific Islander and elaborate on the approach I adopt. The issues I confront are not unique but are variously shared by other contributors. During a visit to Tonga in early 2012 I was told by a Tongan friend that as a person of Pasifika heritage[2] I did not quite fit the mould of being a *palangi* in Tonga because I share a common connection as a native of Polynesia. At the same time, however, because I was not Tongan I was also not considered an 'insider'.[3] My friend explained that from a Tongan perspective only a Tongan could be an insider and a *palangi* was, by definition, an outsider. However, she suggested that my position was unique because I was neither; I was walking the line between the two. 'You can do what a Tongan and a *palangi* cannot do,' she said, 'but you have to walk that line carefully so people know you are not pretending to be either.'[4] She was referring to my research on the life of King George Tupou V, the previous king of Tonga.

Reflecting on what my friend said to me and what it means to be neither an insider nor an outsider in Tonga, I concluded that I would adopt the analogy she used. 'But what', I asked her, 'does that actually make me?' 'You're just in the middle,'[5] she replied. This was a particularly interesting conversation as my friend has no academic background studying the insider/outsider dynamics of societies and was simply explaining what she saw as my position in a language we both understood, English. However, in the context, I felt it was much better coming from someone who simply saw things from the perspective of a local and who says it how she sees it. Whether her view would be widely held by other Tongans is something I am uncertain of, but I warmed to the idea that I was walking the line between being a Tongan insider and a *palangi* outsider. I was, in a sense, an in-betweener.

---

1   *Anga fakatonga*, simply defined, is the Tongan way or Tongan custom, while *anga fakapalangi* is the way of the *palangi* (non-Tongan, usually of European descent).
2   Maori, Cook Island and Tahitian.
3   Conversation with the author, 15 July 2012.
4   Ibid.
5   Ibid.

An important question arises when considering my friend's comment and that is whether it is appropriate for a non-Tongan to write a biography of a Tongan king, a question I have pondered deeply and sought advice on. My considered position is that it is appropriate for a non-Tongan to do this. Even though, as I will discuss later in this chapter, I have no expertise in Tongan language or history and no first-hand experience of living in Tonga, in many ways it is easier for me to undertake this research than it is for a Tongan, especially a commoner.[6] In her book on Queen Salote, Wood-Ellem points out that 'it would be difficult for a Tongan to write about such a chief, a chief who achieved the sacred mana'[7] because a Tongan would be restricted in so many ways with cultural barriers and protocols that a non-Tongan would not be subject to or expected to adhere to. Most Tongan commoners, for example, would find it difficult to interview a member of the royal family and almost impossible to interview the king because of the many restrictions on questions that could be asked, ways of engaging, what can be recorded, et cetera.

In addition, there are a myriad of sensitive relationships that a Tongan would need to bear in mind when writing a biography of their king, in terms of historical relationships (between the author's family and the royal family), perceptions of these relationships, and the general view of the Tongan public as to whether the author is of the right rank or status to be writing about Tonga's most sacred and revered person. While these may also be considerations for me, they are not barriers in the way they could be for a Tongan. My friend acknowledged this point when she said that I 'can do what a Tongan and a *palangi* cannot do'. She was referring to my distance from Tonga and yet at the same time my closeness as a fellow Pacific Islander/Polynesian which would facilitate a unique access and perspective in my research journey, as the line I walked might be more permeable as neither outsider nor insider. At the same time, her words 'but you have to walk that line carefully so people know you are not pretending to be either' held particular resonance with me. I realised that I would need to be sensitive to the similarities and differences between Tongan and Maōri or Cook Islands culture and at the same time have confidence that our close Pacific relationships and shared values would help guide my steps in my research of Tupou V's life.

This chapter will discuss my research journey and the main considerations I have grappled with while, as my friend put it, 'walking the line'. Before doing so, I will provide a brief background of my subject, King George Tupou V.

---

6   Commoner, while a word I do not personally favour, is the word Tongans have used to me in interviews to describe a person who is not of royal or noble birth, noble being between royal and commoner status.
7   E. Wood-Ellem, *Queen Salote of Tonga: The Story of an Era* (Auckland 1999).

The fifth Tongan monarch

According to Tongan history, Tupou V is a direct descendant of the god Tangaloa and a Tongan woman. Tupou V's birth name was Siaosi (George) Tāufaʻāhau Manumataongo Tukuʻaho; he was the fifth monarch of the Kingdom of Tonga, the only Polynesian monarchy that still exists today.[8] Since 1875 there have been five kings and one queen, but before that there was a long line of traditional Tongan chiefs known as the Tuʻi Kanokupolu. Tupou V was the 23rd Tuʻi Kanokupolu.[9] Aged 63 when he died in March 2012, after less than six years as king, Tupou V was not very old compared with his immediate predecessors. His father, King Tāufaʻāhau Tupou IV, lived until his late 80s and served 40 years as Tonga's monarch, seven years less than his own mother, Queen Salote Tupou III, who ruled for almost half a century.[10]

While the official record, the Tongan Line of Succession,[11] shows that Tupou V had no children, it is acknowledged by many in Tonga that he had an illegitimate daughter in 1974. Her recognition, including by some members of Tupou V's own family, has no legal force and, even if Tupou V had himself publicly acknowledged her as his daughter (which he did not), the law, based on the Tongan constitution of 1875, is very clear that only a child of a legal marriage can succeed to the throne of his or her parent.[12] There are also complex Tongan social dynamics and traditions that would make it very difficult for Tupou V's daughter to be recognised as the daughter of the king; for example, the tradition that only men can inherit land and that a child's rank is determined by the rank of one's mother.[13] (Tupou V's daughter was not born of two royal/noble families and she lives her life as a commoner.)

Although referred to by western news media as 'eccentric' and out of touch,[14] the misunderstood Tupou V was considered by Tongans to be highly educated and sophisticated, speaking several languages and regularly travelling abroad for both public engagements and personal interest.[15] He attended schools in New Zealand and Switzerland, studied at Oxford University and trained at the Royal Military College Sandhurst in England. He was in many senses a 'man of the world',[16] one who read a great deal and enjoyed debating matters related to

---

8 M. Daly, *Tonga: A New Bibliography* (Honolulu 2009).
9 E. Wood-Ellem, *Queen Salote of Tonga*.
10 Ibid.
11 Tongan Ministry of Information and Communications website, available online at www.mic.gov.to.
12 Tongan Constitution, Part 2, Sec. 32.
13 Conversation with the Hon. Lupepauʻu Tuita, 14 December 2012.
14 J. Phare, 'The Madness of King George of Tonga', *The New Zealand Herald*, 17 June 2008, available online at www.nzherald.co.nz/world/news/article.cfm?c_id=2&objectid=10401690.
15 Conversation with H.M. King Tupou VI, 16 July 2012.
16 Conversation with the author, 15 July 2012.

history, religion and international politics of the day.[17] Tupou V's commercial involvements over many years, which included owning one of the main telecommunications companies, being the Chair of the electricity and water boards and owning, or part-owning, other smaller businesses, show a flair for business and entrepreneurship. He had many and varied interests, including producing films, horse riding, cooking, and designing military uniforms, both for himself and the Tongan military.[18]

At Tupou V's funeral I could not help but be struck by the massive contradictions in the perceptions of his person. Here was a man who was born and raised to be the king of Tonga but who also spent many years living like a playboy bachelor travelling abroad, seemingly without a care in the world. Yet at the moment of his funeral such individual pursuits and styles seemed irrelevant. The focus was exclusively on the king as king, as the occupant of a divine role and descendant of a long royal lineage.

My research on Tupou V's life is primarily to inform my PhD thesis at The Australian National University. It will be presented as a narrative of the life of the late king. I am choosing to write a narrative of his life because I am interested in the genre of biography and because the life of one person, particularly a monarch, is a lens through which we might view the broader subject of Tonga, its culture and history.

There is a scarcity of literature available on Tupou V's life apart from references to him in works written on his father and grandmother, and in some Tongan songs and poems, such as the *Upe o Tāufa'āhau* composed by his grandmother, Queen Salote.[19] There is a significant body of information available from the news media, particularly in New Zealand and Australia, but it is rarely factual or correct. As a non-Tongan researcher, the richest sources of information have been people with professional, personal, and familial relationships with the king, or with Tonga. Therefore a large part of my research involves interviewing people ranging from current and former Tongan government officials, academics specialising in Tonga, friends and family of Tupou V, members of the wider Tongan community (both in Tonga and the Tongan diaspora), and pro-democracy activists. I have found that Tongans are very willing to talk about their king and their views on him are always respectful, even if they disagree with behaviours he displayed or decisions he made. Essentially, it is the views, opinions and insights of the Tongan people, along with friends and colleagues of Tupou V that inform my research.

---

17   Conversation with Angus and Jenny Rogers, 20 February 2013.
18   Ibid.
19   E. Wood-Ellem, *Songs and Poems of Queen Salote* (Tonga 2004), 207.

Tonga culture and history

Undertaking research on a foreign country or people entails empathy and immersion in the intricacies of another culture. It is important to reiterate that Tonga and Tongans are not my area of expertise. My own upbringing was in a trilingual, multicultural family where we walked in the worlds of Pakeha, Maori and the Cook Islands. But even with my own Oceanic experience, it was challenging to consider Tongan matters from the cultural lens of a Tongan. At first I made a number of assumptions about similarities between the Cook Islands and Tonga, and Maori culture and Tongan culture. This was partly due to cultural similarities and shared traditional values and practices. Further to this, our languages come from the same Austronesian family of languages; I noticed as a young child that many words in *lea fakatonga* (the Tongan language) have the same or similar meanings to words we use in *te Reo Maori* (the Maori language) and *Maori Kuki Airani* (Cook Islands Maori). Tongans have not expected me to be fluent in their language, and are very forgiving of my lack of knowledge on some matters, but I remain conscious of the need to respectfully demonstrate my ignorance and maintain a culturally sensitive approach to my engagement. For example, when I informally asked a Tongan noble and his wife, 'What was your relationship with the king?', the immediate response was, 'Oh, we cannot answer that. It is impolite for one to talk of how they are related to the king.'[20] That was an interesting response as my question did not necessarily imply an answer as to how they were related genealogically to the king, but more about their broader social relation to the king (and the king to them). Nevertheless, a careful rephrasing of the question: 'What was the nature of your interaction and relations with the King?' has been more compatible with Tongan courtesies and protocols. This is despite the fact that it would be fair to assume that most Tongans would know in detail how their family is related to the king because of the importance Tongans place on knowing one's genealogy and one's place in relation to other people in society.

Tupou V compared with other kings/queens and leaders

Tupou V's father and grandmother appear to be the two people who most influenced his life, especially as a child and young man. Two excellent works have been written about his grandmother Queen Salote's life. The first is by Margaret Hixon titled *Salote, Queen of Paradise* and the second by Elizabeth

---

20   Conversation with the author, 17 June 2012.

Wood-Ellem titled *Queen Salote of Tonga: The Story of an Era*. Both accounts are foundational to understanding Tupou V, and the authors spent a great deal of time learning about Tonga directly from Tongans and in Tonga.

Fanny Wong Veys' article on King Tāufa'āhau Tupou IV's funeral also brings to light an interesting perspective regarding the different elements that make the Tongan king who he is. Her reference to Tupou IV as a 'descendant of a mythical ruler, the fourth king in a modern Christian dynasty and as a contemporary ruler who reformed both education and economy'[21] reinforces the argument made by Wood-Ellem in her work on Queen Salote, that the Tongan monarch is a complex and multifaceted personality, not like any other person in Tonga.[22]

The very question of how Tupou V styled himself is one that I will examine, especially in relation to his dress and the way he spoke. His British/Oxford manner does raise questions around how Tupou V viewed himself; however, it has also been noted that his father and great grandfather, Tupou II, both wore British-looking military uniforms. Hixon suggests that Tupou I, perhaps best demonstrated by the constitution he developed in 1875 that had many adaptations from Britain, was very keen on modelling the Tongan royal tradition on that of Britain.[23] More recently, I have learnt that Tupou V was himself one-sixteenth English,[24] a fact that is not widely known, or at least not widely discussed in Tonga or by Tongans.[25]

Tonga's constitutional and political reform

Tonga has been through some major constitutional and civic reforms in the past few years. A recently published report by Guy Powles[26] has given an excellent analysis of where the reforms are at, and a book by Ian Campbell, *Tonga's Way to Democracy,* provides a comprehensive discussion about the history and journey Tonga has taken towards democracy.[27] The underlying purpose of the recent reforms[28] was to move Tonga towards democracy and, as Powles implies in the title of his report, *Political Reform Opens the Door,* to make government more accessible and transparent to the people.

---

21 F.W. Veys, 'Materialising the King: the Royal Funeral of King Taufa'ahau Tupou IV of Tonga'. *The Australian Journal of Anthropology*, 20 (2009), 131–49.
22 E. Wood-Ellem, *Queen Salote of Tonga: The Story of an Era*.
23 M. Hixon, *Salote, Queen of Paradise* (Dunedin 2000).
24 Tupou V's mother, Queen Halaevalu Mata'aho, was the daughter of 'Ahome'e, the son of 'Amelia, who was the daughter of Ma'ata Ane Blake, who was the daughter of Alexander George Blake and Matelita Fusilangoia. Blake was a British subject who travelled and settled in Tonga.
25 Conversation with Semisi Taumoepeau, 18 February 2013.
26 G. Powles, *Political Reform Opens the Door: the Kingdom of Tonga's Path to Democracy* (Wellington 2012).
27 C. Campbell, *Tonga's Way to Democracy* (Christchurch 2011).
28 From 2006 onwards.

Both Powles and Campbell show that Tupou V, in his short time as king, was largely the power behind the reforms, although it is important to note that there were clear demonstrations by the people that they also wanted change. From a position of having near absolute power over the affairs of government, Tupou V ceded most of the monarch's executive powers to the Cabinet of Ministers[29] and this came to fruition when, on 25 November 2010, the people of Tonga had a government elected by them instead of appointed by the king.[30] The number of elected members of parliament representing the people increased from nine to 17 while the number of elected nobles stayed at nine.[31] It would be the first time the general public had more seats in parliament than nobles since it was established in 1875.[32] Even the new prime minister was elected among his peers in parliament rather than appointed by the monarch; the king had made it clear the day before the election that 'in the future the Sovereign shall act only on the advice of His Prime Minister'.[33] With this new elected government, Tonga's political system would change forever and, to Tupou V, 25 November 2010 would be 'the greatest and most historic day for our Kingdom'.[34] Certainly for him, it would be a day he would never forget. That was the day he relinquished much of his power to the Tongan people. In his address to the nation, he said:

> At sunrise on Election Day you will feel the warmth of the sun as well as the gaze of your ancestors from the past and those of countless unborn generations in the future turn towards you. For a few brief moments in our meagre lives we shall occupy the attention of history itself and we will be judged on how we have kept its trust. It will be at this moment that our true character as a nation will show.[35]

Tupou V clearly saw the reforms as a positive move in the history of his kingdom and they will surely be his main legacy.

It would be fair to say that the story of democratisation is one I am still in the early stages of researching, but I intend to gather further insights into Tupou V's motives behind supporting, or leading, the reform and in understanding what the reforms now mean for the role of the king in Tonga. What are his powers now? And what impact does the king have on the day-to-day life of the ordinary citizen? These, and other questions, continue to be on my research agenda.

---

29 Powles, *Political Reform Opens the Door*.
30 Ibid.
31 Ibid.
32 Ibid.
33 V. Tupou, Address to the Nation on 24 November 2010, Office of the Prime Minister of Tonga, available online at www.pmo.gov.to.
34 Ibid.
35 V. Tupou, Address to the Nation on 24 November 2010.

Biography

My preliminary research on biography, and particularly on biography in the Pacific, has precipitated important questions in framing my approach to researching the life of a Tongan king. Neil Gunson in *Telling Pacific Lives* argues that 'the biographer from outside is often tempted to ignore or dismiss facets of a subject's life that appear alien or irrelevant to him or her'.[36] As mentioned above, my own assumptions around the similarities between my cultural lens and that of Tongans were challenged very early and I realised it would take a great deal of work to acquire even a basic understanding of *anga fakatonga*.

In Gunson's paper he also observes that 'kinship provides the basic framework for identifying the individual life'[37] and Brij Lal and Vicki Luker argue further, in the preface of the same book, that in the Pacific:

> … personhood is defined largely by relations with kin, alive and dead – Western concepts of the individual, together with the consciousness of the self on which 'biography' and 'autobiography' in important Western senses depend, are alien and, some would argue, inconceivable.[38]

This has become more and more apparent in my research so far. Not only is the king seen by Tongans as a descendant of so-and-so, and from such-and-such clan, he is also very rarely seen as an individual person but rather through his role and relations. His kinship ties are what people, usually privileged, valued. In the case of Tupou V, I was told people would often see traits of his father and his grandmother in him and that gave them a different perspective of him than if they were to look at him simply as an individual, as a western biographer might presume.[39]

One of the long-standing debates in the literature on biography comes from the Victorian era and concerns the ethics of biography. I have found reference to two especially useful articles in Ray Monk's work, both titled 'The Ethics of Biography' which, ironically, take opposite views on the matter.[40] Margaret Oliphant argues that a biographer 'has a greater obligation to [preserve] the good reputation of his or her subject than to the truth',[41] whereas Edmund Gosse argues that the responsibility of the biographer is 'to be as indiscreet as possible.'[42] This tension

---

36 N. Gunson, 'Telling Pacific Lives: From Archetype to Icon' in B. Lal and V. Luker (eds), *Telling Pacific Lives*, (Canberra 2004).
37 Ibid.
38 B. Lal and V. Luker, 'Preface' in *Telling Pacific Lives*, (Canberra 2004).
39 Conversation with 'Akanesi Palu-Tatafu.
40 R. Monk, 'Life without Theory: Biography as an Exemplar of Philosophical Understanding', *Poetics Today*, 83: 3 (2007).
41 Ibid.
42 Ibid.

is one I have reflected on a great deal in my work so far, and a recent debate at the ANU-hosted symposium on political life writing in the Pacific helped me to define my own position. During the course of discussion on Chris Chevalier's paper (see this volume), one of the scholars in the audience commented that he believed 'that a good biographer goes up to the bedroom door [of their subject] and not beyond'. I found myself disagreeing with this point and, when it came time for me to present my own paper, I made the following comments:

> For public figures in positions who make decisions that impact on the private lives of others (such as politicians, judges, monarchs et cetera), there has to be a level of acceptance that their own private lives will come under scrutiny or review from others as par for the course when in such a position. If it is right for you to make decisions that affect an aspect of another person's life, then that aspect of your own life should be transparent, even if it is something usually confined to the bedroom.[43]

Although I disagree with the idea that a good biographer goes no further than the bedroom door of their subject, I can see that such an approach may have merit in certain cases. In the case of my subject, Tupou V, the fact that he had an illegitimate daughter is highly relevant in the context of Tonga's hereditary positions, land titles and the questions around power and influence over other people. If Tupou V were a private citizen simply going about his business, having an illegitimate daughter would be much less relevant. His position as king, a fundamentally public role and, at least before the democratic reforms were implemented, an immensely influential one in the day-to-day lives of other Tongans, lessens any claim to the right of privacy on his part. This does not make the job of his biographer any easier, however, because there will always be questions around what is relevant in his private life and his public life, and discerning what information to share and what not requires careful judgment and consideration.

It would be fair to say that my approach to biography would lie somewhere between the two extremes outlined in the twin 'Ethics of Biography' works of Oliphant and Gosse.[44] Because of personal friendships I have with some of my subject's relatives and the people of Tonga, I could not aim to be, as Gosse would argue, as 'indiscreet as possible'[45] without damaging these relationships and, potentially, causing more harm than good from the results of my research (both for myself and my university). I believe that being as indiscreet as possible is a dangerous way of approaching the writing of another person's life. On the other hand, I consider it unethical to do as Oliphant suggests and write a thesis

---

43 Notes for presentation to ANU Symposium on Political Life Writing in the Pacific, 18 October 2012.
44 Monk, 'Life without Theory'.
45 Ibid.

that paints my subject in a positive light at the expense of confiding information crucial to understanding the truth of his life, or at least one view of that truth. To hide or sugar-coat the truth to ensure one's biographical subject has a 'good reputation'[46] is an approach that undermines academic inquiry and weakens the integrity of the words written.

People – the heart of my research

I am in a fortunate position, as I touched on earlier in this chapter, of having personal friendships with members of Tupou V's family, specifically a number of his nieces and nephews. These friendships hold personal significance but they also bring about both advantages and challenges for my research. Clearly, being able to interview my friends and through them other members of Tupou V's family, such as the current king, is an extremely valuable and privileged opportunity for my research. I am hugely grateful to them for their help. On the other hand, when people in Tonga become aware of my personal relationships with members of the royal family, there is a risk of distrust regarding my motives and objectivity. They may assume I might not take what they have to say too seriously because they were not as close to Tupou V as the people I already know,[47] or that I will simply write a biography that will please my friends.[48] The challenge is for me to reassure every interviewee that their perspective has value and that anything they share with me enriches my research. I also make an active effort to outline that even though my friendships are important to me, I would never compromise the integrity of my academic work (I often point out the Gosse/Oliphant debate and position myself in the middle) and neither would my PhD supervisors allow me to. This is possibly the biggest challenge I have faced in my research so far.

Another challenge I have faced stems from the fact that few people get to meet a king personally and even fewer get to know one. In the case of Tupou V, his family and close friends knew him well and, although he was well-known internationally, few people actually knew him. As is the nature of the position of a king, uninformed opinions abound; however, this can be useful because it means no shortage of information available from those who have opinions on the king. The challenge here is to balance these with information from people who actually knew him and who have credible material about his life – and that is not always easy. Even though I have friendships with Tupou V's family members, he had numerous friends across the world and many of them

---

46   Ibid.
47   As relayed to me by one of my earlier interlocutors in Tonga, who would prefer to remain unnamed.
48   A perception that has been discussed with my PhD supervisors and others in Tonga.

were not known to his family. Discovering these people and attaining access to them can be difficult, especially when you consider who friends of a king are likely to be. They range from other royals, presidents, governors-general, major businesspeople, celebrities and top lawyers. This is proving to be one of the more interesting elements of my research at the current time – trying to get in touch with people like Sir Michael Hill the jeweller, Lord Glenarthur of Britain and the King of Bhutan! Surprisingly, the social media website Facebook has been very useful for contacting friends of Tupou V. I was shown Tupou V's Facebook page by some of his close friends (he used an alias) and was told that he was a regular Facebook user just before he died. From that I have been able to go to his Facebook page and see who his personal Facebook 'friends' were and make contact accordingly. The responses have been very positive as people are very willing to talk about their friend.

Each of my interlocutors is supporting my research and I have a deep sense of gratitude to them all. Meeting family and friends of Tupou V is both fascinating and valuable, but speaking with the local dairy owner on Tonga's main strip, or having a chat with a waitress from the restaurant I eat at, unearths equally interesting insights and colourful stories. My research is greatly enriched by the sharing of their perspectives, and it is very apparent to me that without the support of these people I would not be able to undertake research on this doctoral topic. I believe that it simply would not be possible for a non-Tongan to write the life history of the king without having some connection to the people and their culture.

Conclusion

In Tonga the king sits at the pinnacle of society. He is the head of state, the highest traditional chief, the most prominent celebrity and a person of divine descent. Writing the life history of such a person, one whom every single member of Tongan society knows of and has a view on, requires the researcher to have a depth and breadth of interviews with people from all sections of society. For any researcher, Tongan or not, that is a huge task.

I started this chapter quoting a comment made to me by a Tongan friend while on a recent visit to Tonga. Her words helped me to position myself as a young scholar thinking about what perspective I bring to academia in the Pacific and how I relate to people I engage with. People, and the relationships I build along the journey, are at the core of my research. It is only through the perspectives of other people that I will get to know my subject. Throughout my research so far I have proudly seen myself as someone walking the line between being an insider and an outsider. An in-betweener may not be a term that catches on in the academic community but an in-betweener I am. This is the position I see myself in on this journey, researching the life of King George Tupou V.

8. Writing Influential Lives

Nicole Haley

This chapter is written to honour the life and memory of Sane Noma, a ritual leader, land mediator and visionary, who died in 2006. It is not just Sane's story though; it is also my story and that of my daughter Aliria, who was born some two years after Sane's death. It is a deeply personal account of lives irrevocably entangled through dreams, prophesies and shared experiences past, present and future.

> Mummy I got into a fight with a boy at school today. I told the class that when I get bigger I am going to be able to turn into a dragonfly. He didn't believe me. He said I was lying. But I wasn't lying. Sane could turn into a dragonfly and when I get bigger I know I will too.[1]

Sane Noma was born at Huguni in the mid-Tumbudu Valley area in what is now Lake Kopiago District, Hela Province, Papua New Guinea. He was born in the early 1900s and lived through the twentieth century, witnessing epidemics, first contact, the colonial period, and Papua New Guinea's Independence, not to mention a radical transformation in the ideals of masculinity.[2] He lived a truly remarkable life and one worthy of biography, although it was not a political life in the conventional sense. Sane was a ritual leader and custodian of the *Haroli Palena* bachelor cult through which young Duna boys were raised into men. He was the last in a long line of such leaders, following in the footsteps of his father, Noma, grandfather Yalepa, and great-grandfather Ariako. Somewhat remarkably, Sane lived to be over 100. He attributed his longevity to his extended involvement with the bachelor cult.

Almost without exception, every piece of academic writing throughout my career has been informed or inspired in some way or another by Sane and, in particular, by the insights imparted to me over the last 12 years of his life. My first scholarly publication introduced Sane and his spirit familiar, Tsiri Harola, and detailed Sane's renown for reading signs, revisioning the past and prophesying future events.[3] Much of my writing since then has continued Sane's story, albeit in a piecemeal fashion. What I have not acknowledged is

---

[1] Aliria Haley-Kenny, February, 2013.
[2] See N. Haley, 'Sung Adornment: Changing Masculinities at Lake Kopiago, Papua New Guinea', in J. Taylor (ed.), *Changing Pacific Masculinities*, The Australian Journal of Anthropology, Special Issue 19: 2 (2008), 213–29.
[3] N. Haley, *Altered Texts and Contexts: Narratives, History and Identity among the Duna*, BA(Hons) Thesis (Sydney 1993), 282.

that much of my adult life has played out as the fulfilment of Sane's various prophesies, something I found extremely disconcerting at first but something I now embrace.

For the best part of two decades I have wanted to tell Sane's broader story, but have struggled with the task. Where do I start? What form should such a story take? Who would it be written for? Would anyone be interested in the life history of a ritual leader who served his community by presiding over a now defunct cult? For the most part these questions remained unresolved; however, since the birth of my daughter I feel compelled to tell Sane's story. Not least because his story is now her story and it is part of the legacy I leave her, for better or worse. I tell it now with much trepidation and at the risk of exposing myself to ridicule, in particular to the charge of 'having gone native'.

I first met Sane in April 1994, during a six-week preliminary field trip, undertaken two months into my PhD candidature. After arriving at Lake Kopiago in the early hours of the morning after an exhausting two-day trek from Koroba, I was woken at daybreak by Sane knocking on the door of the Lake Kopiago Council Guest House. As I opened the door I was confronted by an elderly, somewhat unkempt old man who reached out and shook my hand, saying:

> Siragura. Yu kam pinis ya? Gutpela. Planti wok istap. No ken slip, sixty go, was na redi. Mi bai kam back na stori. Karu pe?

> Morning. You're here. Good. There is plenty of work to be done. No time for sleep. As fast as you can have a shower and get ready. I will be back and we will talk. Ok?

As was often the case, Sane spoke in mixed *Tok Pisin* and *Tok Ples*. He didn't bother to introduce himself. Perhaps he thought I would know who he was. Certainly he knew much about me, as I would soon learn.

That first conversation set the tone for our working relationship, or more particularly my instruction over the next decade or so. Central to our work was Sane's sense of duty to record the past and his attempts to preserve Duna culture for future generations.

I had not intended to undertake my PhD fieldwork at Lake Kopiago, but intended instead to work in the Auwi-Pori area among bilingual Duna and Huli speakers. A great deal of ethnographic research had already been undertaken in the Huli-speaking area by Robert Glasse, Laurence Goldman, Stephen Fraenkel and Chris Ballard, and in Kopiago District by Nick Charles Modjeska, Thomas Maracek, Andrew Strathern and Gabriele Stürzenhofecker. No one had worked in the area in-between. More importantly, one of my supervisors had received an email from Strathern, warning me off undertaking fieldwork in Kopiago

District. Before establishing myself in the Auwi-Pori area, I had intended to survey the Duna-speaking area to familiarise myself with the broader landscape. I had walked down the Tumbudu Valley, planned to visit the Aluni Valley and then return to Tari via the Auwi-Pori-Logaiyu Valley, having identified a field site for my PhD fieldwork. Sane had an altogether different plan.

When he returned he did so with key members of the District Management Team who informed me that the local council had resolved just weeks before to invite an anthropologist to work at Lake Kopiago to document their culture and history before the current generation of leaders passed away. Being situated between the Ok Tedi gold and copper mine and the Porgera Gold mine, they were also keen to encourage further mineral exploration with a view to seeing a mine established in their area. They desired development and explained that anthropologists had worked in all the other areas where mining was now underway, and my work would be a necessary precursor to the future they envisioned. They had agreed to provide accommodation and offered me a large house on the government station. They also offered to schedule meetings and interviews, and certainly kept me busy from dawn to dusk during my preliminary visit. Needless to say I abandoned my plans and resolved to return to Lake Kopiago for my fieldwork proper.

During our first month together, Sane introduced me to Tsiri Harola – his spirit familiar – a water spirit, that had been associated with his father, grandfather and great-grandfather; the key originary narratives of the Duna area, including his apical ancestor who could transform into a dragonfly (an ability Sane likewise claimed to possess); a series of prophesies concerning gold, copper, oil and gas; flying lakes; spirit women and some absolutely mind-blowing spells. At first much of what he told me seemed entirely fanciful, but as I got to know Sane and heard his stories, memories and prophesies recounted and given voice to by other men and women, I came to realise that I was working with someone altogether different from the other Big Men and leaders at Lake Kopiago.

Working with Sane, I saw things and witnessed things that challenged my sense of reality. For example, within weeks of our first meeting Sane cut his foot with an axe while working in the garden. The cut extended from his big toe and encompassed a third of his foot. He arrived at my doorstep with the foot wrapped in an old shirt and bound with cane, and asked for some pain medicine. I gave him some paracetamol and offered to stitch the wound. Sane declined, pointing out that he had a spell for mending broken bones and one for healing wounds. He sat down on the guesthouse floor, unwrapped the foot and proceeded to remove bone chips from the open wound. When he was done, he took some stinging nettles from his bag and started rubbing them on the wound reciting the spell for mending broken bones. Within 10 minutes or so the wound had completely healed leaving a large keloid scar.

Had I not witnessed such miraculous healing with my own eyes, I would have considered it completely implausible; so too the notion of flying lakes and spell-induced earthquakes. And yet in May 1994, Ipa Noma, a sacred lake named after Sane's father, was relocated from Arou at Huguni to Waneke to be closer to Sane and to Noma's skull and Tsiri Harola's *auwi* (ancestral stone relic) which were being kept in ossuaries nearby.[4] In October 2003 Sane caused a series of earth tremors while teaching me the earthquake spell.

Looking back, I struggled in the early days to know what to make of my sessions with Sane. They often seemed disconnected. What I know now is that I initially lacked the scaffolding to make sense of his stories. Working with Sane was like putting together the pieces of a three-dimensional jigsaw puzzle. Everything important was conveyed or revealed in piecemeal fashion: myths, spells, stories about his own past, accounts of the colonial period, not to mention his prophesies. Much energy went into connecting the dots, so to speak. It is this which makes writing Sane's life history particularly difficult.

My relationship with Sane was somewhat unconventional and attracted much attention locally. Many considered it improper that we spent so much time together and that his knowledge was being conveyed to a woman. But this was very much Sane's choice. Some anthropologists describe being adopted into communities, as having sponsors and fictive kin. And while this was also true in my case, Sane was neither my sponsor nor family. He was my mentor and I was his student. For a ritual leader like Sane, the relationship was a familiar one as I would come to learn.

For the most part, our conversations and interviews which were tape-recorded took place in a mix of Tok Pisin and in the vernacular, Duna. Sane did not speak English and could neither read nor write. He had no formal schooling, being close to 60 when the government patrol post and airstrip at Lake Kopiago were established in 1961. In the early years our sessions took place with the assistance of a translator, notably at Sane's insistence a female translator to whom he was distantly related. On numerous occasions, Sane made it clear that he would not have conveyed his knowledge to a male anthropologist or a male translator for fear they may have sought to use his spells. In the hands of women such spells were held to have little efficacy.

******

---

4 N. Haley, *Ipakana Yakaiya: Mapping Landscapes, Mapping Lives – Contemporary Land Politics among the Duna*, PhD Thesis (Canberra 2002), 48–9.

Sane was born soon after the turn of the last century. At birth his mother named him Pele. One of his earliest memories concerned the 1918 flu pandemic. For Sane the event was truly life changing, and his account of it harrowing. He lost his mother, Lupame, and his younger brother, Rale, in the space of a few days during one of his father's extended absences. In the wake of the event, relatives renamed him after a small creek nearby the place where his mother and brother died.

> This is the story of the big sick, *kenekenekene* (death death). It is also my story. One time when I was like Jona [approximately 15 years old] my mother told me to stay in the house and look after my small brother while she went to the garden. My father was no longer with us. He was living on the Huli side with his second wife.[5] He and the other ritual specialists had gathered at Gelogili to determine the cause of the sick.
>
> My brother was sleeping when my mother left. He woke briefly but seemed distressed and disorientated. I tried to wake him properly but he went back to sleep. When my mother came she checked on Rale and found he was already dead. My mother started screaming and crying inconsolably. 'My son is dead. Who killed my son? I left my two boys in the house. Pele is here, but Rale is dead. Who killed Rale? Who is responsible?'
>
> While my mother was crying it got dark and then turned to morning again. She spent three days holding my brother and crying. I didn't know what to do. My father was far away on the Huli side. He was busy trying to end the sick. My mother said, 'You are still but a boy. We don't have a man to bury him and we don't have an axe to build a burial platform, so I will just sit here like this and rest your brother on my legs until his body rots away and his bones are exposed.' My mother sat there holding my brother. His body swelled up and blood came out his nose. After some days my mother became sick too. I worried that she too would die and wondered who would look after me and bring me food. I thought for sure I would die too. I had not eaten in many days and was really hungry.
>
> I ventured outside and found some fruit that had fallen from a fig tree. I ate that fruit. First I ate fruit that had fallen on the ground, and when I had finished those I climbed the tree. While I was sitting in the tree I heard a noise coming from inside the house. It was a big pig, one my father had given to my mother. I went down to check and found that the

---

5   Sane's father Noma had two wives. Lupame, Sane's mother, was the first wife. The second wife, Londome, was a Huli woman from Gelogili. She had one son, Kandale.

pig had got hold of my brother's leg and was eating it. I was shocked and frightened. The pig was eating my brother. When I entered the house the pig ran off, taking my small brother with it.

My mother was so weak she could not stand. She was crying, 'My son, my son is gone, please go outside and find him and bring him to me. Pele, Pele, please try and find Rale and bring him back to me I want to hold him one last time before I die.' I went outside and looked for the body. I tracked the pig. The pig was dragging my brother's body. I eventually caught up with them after my brother's head got caught between two banana trees. I tried to chase the pig away and retrieve my brother's body, but the pig was big and strong. It pulled the leg side while I pulled the head side. I wrestled the body away from the pig but it came after me and attacked me.[6] I was bleeding and in a huge amount of pain, but managed to fight off the pig. As I did I thought to myself, 'My mother must truly want me to die too.' I grabbed my brother's body and ran back to the house. All that was left was the head and the torso. I ran to the house, opened the door and threw my brother's body to my mother. I said, 'Mother here is Rale, you can hold him now.' I fastened the door behind me. My mother did not move. She didn't reach out to touch him as she too was dead.

I could hear the pig outside. It was trying force its way into the house. I grabbed a piece of firewood and prepared to hit the pig. It forced its way inside and went straight for my brother and mother, who by then were really smelly. I escaped outside and took refuge in a nearby tree. I stayed there for several days not knowing what to do. I could hear wailing across the valley and knew many many people had died. While I was there some men came along. They checked the house. They buried my mother and brother and set fire to the house. They set fire to many houses in the same manner. I didn't know what to do or where to go.

I fled to the bush and stayed there by myself for several months. I survived on bush foods like a wild man. After some months my father came in search of me. He came with ten men. I hid from them. I was angry at my father. A man named Kakayale eventually found me. He had been sent by my father. Kakayale was strikingly handsome and was nicely dressed. He was custodian of the *Haroli Palena* bachelor cult. He said, 'You are going to come and live with me at the Palena place'. I was happy to go with him.

---

6   Sane was left with scarring on his face and several large prominent scars on his left forearm from this attack.

During pre-colonial times, most young men spent at least their adolescent years in seclusion within one of the local bachelor cults situated in the high bush.[7] There, they were 'grown' into strong, attractive and desirable men, ready to embrace the challenges of adult life. While in the cult, young men learnt how to protect themselves from the polluting effects of women, were taught spells (*ngao*) to promote growth and healing, were introduced to spirit beings and learnt the secret names for places, plants, and animals – the keys to unlocking the more esoteric aspects of parish histories and ritual performance. Bachelor cult boys spent their days either in the bush or within the bachelor cult compound under instruction from the cult leaders and senior bachelors. Indeed, all aspects of their lives were regulated and closely monitored by the cult leaders, with formal testing an integral part of the cult experience.

While in the cult the Palena boys observed strict behavioural and dietary regimes – they couldn't go out in the sun, sleep close to a fire, smoke, or eat warm foods of any sort. They ate only bush foods, unblemished sugar cane and pandanus nuts, and cold sweet potato that had been harvested and cooked by the cult leaders. During the day they cleansed their bodies, received instruction on how to adorn and convey themselves properly, tended their ritual plants (*palena*), practised and sought to memorise the various spells (*palena ngao*) associated with the cult, and committed to memory the specialised vocabulary of praise name (*kei yaka*) and hidden talk (*paraya haka*) upon which these were based.[8] At night they received instruction in dream interpretation and sought to commune with the female spirits (*paiyame ima*) looking over them.

As far as I was best able to ascertain, Sane spent close to 50 years in or presiding over the bachelor cult. He eventually assumed the role of cult leader – something that set him apart from other adult men. During his time in the cult he simultaneously trained as a ritual specialist.

> Kakayale was my teacher. I stayed with him at the Palena place. He taught me many things – hidden talk and spells of all kinds. I then taught the younger boys. When Kakayale married I became custodian of the bachelor cult. My father trained Kakayale and entrusted the

---

7 Bachelor cults have also been reported among the Enga, for example, see M.J. Meggitt, 'Male-female Relationships in the Highlands of Australian New Guinea', *American Anthropologist*, 66: 4 (1964), 204–224; M.J. Meggitt, 'The Mae Enga of the Western Highlands', in P. Lawrence and M.J. Meggitt (eds), *Gods, Ghosts and Men in Melanesia: Some Religions of Australian New Guinea and the New Hebrides* (Melbourne 1965); R. Bulmer, 'The Kyaka of the Western Highlands', in Lawrence and Meggitt, *Gods Ghosts and Men in Melanesia* (Melbourne 1965); P. Wiessner and A. Tumu, *Historical Vines: Enga Networks of Exchange* (District of Columbia 1998); Ipili (P. Gibbs, *Ipili Religion Past and Present*, Diploma of Anthropology, Thesis (Sydney 1975)); Paiela (A. Biersack, 'Ginger Gardens for the Gender Woman: Rites of Passage in a Melanesian Society', *Man*, 17: 2 (1982), 239–258); and Huli (R.M. Glasse, 'The Huli of the Southern Highlands', in Lawrence and Meggitt, *Gods, Ghosts and Men in Melanesia* (Melbourne 1965); L. Goldman, *Talk Never Dies: The Language of Huli Disputes* (London 1983); S. Frankel, *The Huli Response to Illness* (Cambridge 1986)); and were present among the Hewa and Bogaia as well.
8 P. Weissner and A. Temu, *Historical Vines*, 218.

> *HaroliPalena* to him when he married my mother and moved to Gelogili. Kakayale then trained me and when he was ready to marry he passed the cult to me.
>
> Nowadays young boys go to school. Before the white man came we didn't go to school. Instead the boys went to the *Haroli Palena*. All of the leaders around here went inside. I looked after them and raised them. I took them through each stage. I looked after them as they grew their hair and escorted them to courting parties.[9] When they were ready to graduate, I would play my *hiliyula* (jew's harp) to determine who they should marry. I married all of those men — some before the white men came and some after. They all have adult children now. Their children are like my own. I did not marry quickly as I was looking after those boys. Had I married as a young man, my own children would have been like the men I raised. Instead my children are like their children.

The bachelor cult served the important purpose of regulating relations between different generations of men. In the Duna case, the long seclusion period coupled with the late age of marriage meant that men emerging from the cult were not only free to but were expected to forthrightly embrace adult life as their own fathers were often dead. Certainly Sane's own father died while he was in the cult. And although Sane felt a strong sense of abandonment by his father, due to his father's extended absences during his childhood, Sane sought to recover his father's skull and continue his father's work. 'When I heard he had died I went with my bush knife and cut off my father's head. I told his wife to bury his body and legs. I brought his head and buried it near my house. I later exhumed it and put it there in the cave.'

For Duna men, like Sane, the colonial period was one of massive upheaval. It changed relations between successive generations of men, giving rise to new forms of leadership and wondrous expectations. In the Duna case, it also generated a project of forgetting and self-deprecating portrayals of Duna culture.[10]

In the decade from 1955, as the Duna-speaking area progressively came under colonial control, practically all indigenous ritual activity ceased and the bachelor cult, which had until then dominated young men's lives, was abandoned. The Bisamu-Yalia bachelor cult, over which Sane presided, persisted the longest, and was still operating when the colonial administration established a presence

---

9   In the fifth and final stages of the cult, the senior bachelors were permitted to attend the *yekia*, the formal institution through which courting took place. They attended these courting parties in the company of, and under the watchful eye of, the cult leaders. The *yekia* provided the bachelors with an opportunity to present themselves to potential marriage partners and to allure and attract the girls of their choice.
10 Haley, *Altered Texts and Contexts*; Haley, *Ipakana Yakaiya*.

at Lake Kopiago. For instance, Sane was in the bush at Bisamu with a group of bachelor cult boys when a light plane dropping supplies to James Sinclair's 1957 Strickland patrol crashed at Lake Kopiago.

> I saw that plane crash at Rilaparu. At that time we did not know what a plane was although I had seen them flying in formation some years before. Later another plane came, a sea plane. It landed on the lake and went back, leaving some men and a small boat. Those men sat on the small boat and rescued the survivors. At the behest of the patrol officers we took that plane apart piece by piece and carried it back to Koroba. Only the engine was left. It was too heavy to carry. During that period I worked with the Patrol Officers from Koroba. I carried for them and sought to understand their ways. I was there when the people at Aiyuguli died. I saw the cargo fall on them. They were really dead, like squashed tomatoes. After the cargo killed those people we wondered whether the white men were really trying to drop cargo or kill people. Many of the carriers ran away. I stayed and went all the way to Tari. I saw they were building the Tari airstrip. I didn't stay. I came back with the patrol. When we got back the patrol officer gave me some soap and a jumper. I washed and put the jumper on. When I got to the men's house one of the leaders said, 'You smell, get out of my house!' I left and slept outside. I didn't go back to Koroba.

Sane stayed on at Kopiago and worked on the airstrip briefly before returning to the bush with a group of young bachelors. He was still in the bush when the missions came.

> I married after the missions came. Before doing so I married off all the boys I had trained. One time soon after, the patrol officers cut a very big long pole. It was so big it needed 10 to 20 men to carry it. They planted it down on the main playing field. They wrapped cloth, cowrie shells, tin duck and kina shells in a *laplap* and hung it at the top of the pole. They then put mud and dripping on the pole and invited the men to try and get the parcel tied to the top. Plenty of men tried. They found it impossible to climb up. Their legs were slippery and they fell down. I tried and successfully managed to get to the top. I sat there right on the very top and ate the tin duck. I then threw down the *laplap* and it landed on an old man's head. He took the *laplap* and handed it to his daughter, and she said, 'If the man who owns the *laplap* asks me, I will go to his house and marry him.' That is how I came to marry my wife, Londa. I didn't make any payment for her because she had already joined the SDA church and the SDA missionaries had told people not to eat pig or to pay for young girls.

******

Unlike Noma and Kakayale, Sane did not train an immediate successor. Had he done so, it would most likely have been Kakayale's son because in the Duna case ritual knowledge was vested in paired clans. Typically it passed between clans from fathers to sons via key knowledge intermediaries.

When I met Sane, his elder son Tsalas was in his early 20s and his younger son Drai was approximately eight years old. Tsalas was already married with two small children and he and Sane were somewhat estranged. Sane hoped Drai would one day inherit his knowledge and continue his work. During one of our final sessions together, Sane prophesied his own death at the hands of his elder son and revealed to me his expectation that I would one day share the knowledge I had gained from him with his younger son Drai. This is something I intend to do when the time is right. He also revealed and entrusted to me the history his own father had revealed on his deathbed some 70 years before.

> Tsalas came to see me and said he wants to take you to court. He is angry that I chose you. He wanted money so I gave him the K500 you gave me. I dreamed that he is going to kill me so now I am coming to tell you this. When you come back next I won't be here. I will have died but you will come and see my grave.

> When my father died he called me and told me the history I am about to tell you. I am close to death now … You are my heir and I am entrusting to you the things my father entrusted to me. What I am about to tell you will anger many people. Everyone up to the National Member and the Prime Minister will want me dead for entrusting these things to you. It was my decision to allow you, a woman, to come inside. It is not our way, but our history has shown us that true power rests with women and that men just spoil their hard work. Had I been able to find a Papua New Guinean woman who could speak and who shared your strong mind and strength of character that would have been good. I could have entrusted these things to her.

> Instead I chose you. Your skin might be different. But remember you are not alone. Drai is there. You and he are bound together. This is your origin place. We are of the same place. Everything I have told you over the years belongs to you now. It is your history. The trees and stones belong to both of us. That PNG woman will come behind. She is at the back of you.

In a subsequent session, Sane indicated that he would send me a sign when Drai was mature enough to be entrusted with his legacy. He expressed a confidence that his work would continue and that the positive Duna future he had long envisioned would be realised after his death. He stressed repeatedly that my replacement would be his replacement. At the time I assumed he was talking about my son Nelson. Certainly he talked extensively about the need to raise Nelson, whom he referred to using the honorific *Ikiko Ilurali*, properly so that he might embrace his destiny.

Had it not been for past experience, I may have found these conversations somewhat disconcerting. Yet, as noted at the outset, much of my adult life has played out as the fulfilment of Sane's prophesies. Indeed, a decade or so before, Sane came to me and told me that my long-term partner of ten years would soon leave and return to Australia. Within five months our relationship had ended. He talked at that time of a subsequent relationship which would bear fruit and, after the birth of my son Nelson in 1999, made many predictions about his future, including a broken bone in his kindergarten year.

When I returned to Kopiago in 2004, soon after having experienced a miscarriage, Sane approached me on the airstrip and immediately sought to console me, saying, 'In time there will be another'. Several more miscarriages and the breakdown of my marriage followed, leading me to question his assertion that there would be another. By the time of Sane's death in 2006, I had all but given up hope of a younger sibling for Nelson.

I was not present when Sane died. However, I am told that his last talk took the form of a series of prophesies, several of which concerned me. Key among these was the prediction that I, *IkikoIlurali's* mother, would within a year or two give birth to a child whose father's name was Kenny. He named the child as the true heir to his knowledge. Sane's prophesy gave rise to much speculation, especially as I was still married to Nelson's father at the time. True to Sane's word, however, I did give birth – to a daughter Aliria Haley-Kenny – some two years after Sane's death. She will soon turn five. Aliria talks of Sane regularly, claims that he appears to her in her dreams and that he visits us in the form of a dragonfly. There is no doubt we are connected though time and space and that Sane's history is now Aliria's history. Fathers and sons, mothers and daughters, irrevocably entwined through interfluent histories. How this story ends remains unclear to me but if Sane's prophesies are correct, it has something to do with a big plane, a flying fox, a waterfall and a power place – but that's Aliria's life history, which is still to be written.

9. Celebrating My Journey

The Value of Autobiography in Recording History

Sethy Regenvanu

Why do public figures in the Pacific need to record their lives? What are the benefits, pitfalls, opportunities and challenges of this enterprise? I cannot speak for others but in my case I can safely say that I did not always intend to write about my life. Indeed, I was about 55 years old when I started to collect the materials that make up my autobiography: *Laef Blong Mi: From Village to Nation: An Autobiography*.[1] If you haven't read my book, here is a very brief background of my life. I grew up in a village in rural Vanuatu on the island of Malakula and began formal education at age 11. After eight years of schooling, I trained to be a church pastor and worked as Christian Education Director of the Presbyterian Church of Vanuatu for six years. During this time I was heavily involved in the struggle for independence, and was elected to the first Parliament of independent Vanuatu. I served as minister in various portfolios for 16 years. But in the election of 1995, I failed to regain my seat.

Personal reasons for writing my autobiography

I had felt that I still had the support from my electorate which I used to enjoy until that point. However, the results of the election showed otherwise, because my support base had been split between my former Vanua'aku Pati and the new National United Party which I had joined. My defeat hit me somewhat hard and it took me a while to fully recover from the hurt this inflicted on me. As I reflected on what might have contributed to my downfall, one factor that appeared to be the major cause was the infighting within the leadership of the Vanua'aku Pati which resulted in the split of that party and, another, the ensuing false accusations thrown at those of us who stood up for our principles. The anger that I felt stirred me up to do something about it, and especially to expose the truth behind the political turmoil and intrigue which had preceded the election.

---

1 S.J. Regenvanu, *Laef Blong Mi: From Village to Nation: An Autobiography* (Port Vila 2004).

Meanwhile, many of my friends who had stood by me and had worked together with me expressed their support and encouraged me to return to the field the next time around and re-contest. I didn't want to do that, but some encouraged me to write a book about my life and my experience as a statesman. The idea of writing down my experience as a leader had also been mooted by one of my own children. When he listened to me trying to tell him and his brothers about the experiences I had in the period leading up to the independence of Vanuatu, and my work in the government of Vanuatu, he suggested that I should write all that down. I think he could see that I had a great deal that would be of value to them and to other young people who had not actually witnessed these things themselves, and that trying to relate this verbally would not do justice to it.

So the combination of the hurt I felt over my downfall and the encouragement I received to record my experiences gave me the impetus to want to write. And at that stage I had time on my hands that I did not know what to do with. Indeed I had not anticipated a situation in my life when I would have nothing to do, as I had always been busy doing something and, might I add, I loved to be busy. I therefore had not prepared myself for when I would be without a job and have the associated free time.

I felt I owed it to those people who, like me, loved Vanuatu and had made their own contribution to its wellbeing, to share with them the part I myself had played in the service of the country. They had made their own contributions too, in one form or another, in making me who I was, both as an individual and as a leader and statesman. Without them, I would not have been able to accomplish what I had up to that point, both in the church and in national politics and government. This feeling of indebtedness was another reason why I wanted to write, to give something back to all those who had influenced and shaped my life. Furthermore, I was sure that there were people out there who would be interested to know a little bit more about me and that they would be interested to read a book about my life. And now I had no excuse not to do something about that, as I had time on my side to do it.

The need to record important history

Another reason for writing was to place on record an account of the colonial situation that existed in our country, and the engagement of our people in the process of achieving political emancipation, popularly referred to as 'our political struggle' to free our country from colonial rule. Indeed, my lifetime up to that point had been part of the political struggle waged by the people of Vanuatu to regain their right to human dignity, human rights and justice, national identity and international recognition.

9. Celebrating My Journey

Our colonial situation was quite unique in the Pacific, and perhaps in the world, and in a way quite absurd. Our country was ruled under three regimes – the British National Service, the French National Service and the Joint administration, popularly known as the Condominium. None of these existed for the benefit of the indigenous people of the New Hebrides (the name of our islands before independence). In fact we were legally stateless: 'no people' under the law in our own country. The Anglo-French Condominium was totally unjust and openly discriminatory in that it existed to serve foreign interests and to promote their establishment in the country with no formal recognition of the indigenous people of the land. The people were left to fend for themselves for their survival and existence in so far as formal governance was concerned. For their subsistence and community life our people relied on their land and their culture and traditional wisdom and experience, which had sustained them for thousands of years.

However, the things that were important to us as a people – our language and culture, our land and our unity – were disappearing before our eyes and we had no means to address this as we had no voice in the governing of our country. The only option available to us was to unify ourselves into a strong political force with unity of purpose.

Fortunately, the churches were on our side. They were the sole providers of any level of education and health for the people of New Hebrides during most of the colonial period. This explains why it was that the first leaders in the fight for political independence and justice for the land were all church people, many of whom were ordained clergy and lay leaders of the church. My own church's involvement, the Presbyterian Church, in the struggle was significant.

Our independence and the building of our new nation, Vanuatu, was not a ready-made package prepared by our colonial masters to be handed over for our adoption. As is covered in some detail in my book, we had to fight every inch of the way for justice and our rights, and even the right to formulate our own constitution. In the process we became unpopular in the eyes of the establishment. We risked our lives in the struggle but the goals and objectives of what that fight was all about were worth the sacrifice.

While this period in our history was abhorrent, and something one would want to forget rather than trying to remember or glorify it, I hold the view that it is an important part of Vanuatu's history which should not be overlooked. It must be made known and not forgotten. In a way, I consider myself somewhat fortunate to have experienced living under that colonial situation. I therefore felt duty bound to tell future generations of Vanuatu what I could about our colonial condition. And I have seen the proof of the rightness of this decision as I watch the reaction of people today whenever I talk about the colonial condition that Vanuatu was once under. They react with intense interest, disbelief and dismay.

The other side of the coin is that it is important for people to know how our country became emancipated from the colonial stranglehold. This was the political struggle of all our people. It took certain important strategic approaches to take the country out of its chaotic, colonial system. These included the development of a new level of national consciousness, unity of purpose, awareness of our land rights, political consciousness and willingness and commitment to make sacrifices to achieve the ultimate goal of winning back freedom, justice and our political independence. It is important that all of this not be lost sight of. People who take these things for granted make a weak, confused and corrupt nation; but knowledge, appreciation and memory of this struggle make a strong nation as Vanuatu should be.

An opportunity to bring some issues out into the open

In addition, I saw the writing of the book not just as an opportunity to record our struggle for independence but also as an opportunity to expose what I knew about the period that came after, especially after 1987 when, in a sense, all we had worked for began to fall apart. I wanted to bring out into the open what I considered to be the root causes of many of the political and national problems that Vanuatu has experienced for a long time until today. I wanted to give my side of what I considered to be the rottenness and corruption within the leadership of the Vanua'aku Pati and the national government at that time. I saw that selfish interests and greed for power and money had taken a strong grip on some leaders, who were intent on resorting to any course of action to achieve their desires, and which manifested itself in the demonstration and riot of 1988 in Port Vila, the split within the Vanua'aku Pati, and the dishonesty and lies fed to the people of Vanuatu to cover up the wrongs of the leaders.

It had never occurred to me before that people in leadership positions in political parties or government could behave like this, and so I wanted to record and expose such behaviour to set the record straight, and as a warning for future leaders.

To encourage others to write

My final reason for writing the book was to encourage other people to also write their stories and to give their own account of what happened at that time and the part they played in these events.

We Ni-Vanuatu, like other Pacific Island people, come from cultures in which the traditional means of communication is oral. We pass information from one person to another or from one generation to another by word of mouth, whether through conversation or by means of stories, myths, legends, and songs, or in art forms such as painting, drawing or dances. Information about the past is kept in the memory of individuals and is often shared only with certain people under tight customary rules.

The point should also be made here that people of Vanuatu, like their fellow Islanders throughout the Pacific, have a wealth of information and knowledge which they do not necessarily want to share with others, unless they are encouraged to do so for a particular reason. It may be that they think the information and knowledge may be of no interest to anyone else, or they are reluctant to share tribal 'secrets' with outsiders. Also, when young people move out of the village to go to school or to live in town, the older generation may not have any traditionally approved channel through which to pass on their knowledge or the stories of their lives. When the information held by one custodian, or even a whole generation of people, is not recorded, it can be lost forever, thereby depriving the incoming generation of the heritage that should be theirs by right. I recall a remark once made at a memorial occasion for a dead member of a community: 'Our dead are buried with a wealth of information and knowledge accumulated over many years of their life time and we are left poorer as a result.'

There has to be a new way for our people to pass on to others the wealth of information and knowledge associated with their life experience. They have to *write*, especially for the younger and future generations of their own community who were not part of a particular period in the life of their country but who are now literate, and often computer literate as well, and are used to accessing written information. The knowledge of that history can have an important bearing on the country and its people from one generation to another, as discussed earlier in this paper. And the onus is on those people, the leaders who had the vision and who directed the course of action towards the realisation of their vision, to pass their experiences on to the coming generations of younger people in a written form.

I was keen that those of us who were the leaders at the time of independence should tell the story of our experience. While we all were involved in the development of Vanuatu in more or less the same period towards one overall national goal, the accounts given by each would convey different aspects. The diverse accounts would reflect the varying circumstances of the contributors. And all this taken together would make a very rich and valuable account of what happened during that period.

So my last reason for writing was to encourage my compatriots to come out and write their own versions of our history. I believe that those of us who were leaders at that time have the ability to write, given the level of education each has achieved and the free time we have. I dedicated my book as a challenge to other Ni-Vanuatu to write.

Why write an autobiography?

The four reasons above represent the main thrust and aim of my book. But why write it as an autobiography? And why do I want others to write their autobiographies?

Firstly, I wanted our people to hear their history from us, the first-hand actors, and not through someone else telling our story. No one is better qualified to communicate an experience than the people who themselves have been part of that experience, whether as actors themselves or as recipients. I want our people to write their own life stories in the way they want to tell them and in their own words, and not have someone else writing about them. I believe our people will feel prouder to hear from their own leaders directly. What they hear from us will make a greater impact on their lives than if non-nationals or non-indigenous try to relate it, as has often been the case in the past. Another advantage of having Pacific Islanders themselves write about their experiences is that the language used will be simpler and easier for Pacific people to understand. Pacific writers telling the stories of their own lives will use less complicated English, the language of storytelling, rather than the jargon and academic language of university researchers and non-indigenous writers.

Secondly, as I was writing my book I felt it would be helpful to persons reading it to have not only the historical facts about our struggle for independence but also some idea about the prevailing conditions and circumstances at the time, and the environment surrounding my life at different stages. It was for this reason that I included such details as my childhood, my life at school and my family life, as well as references to my personal conduct, hobbies and beliefs. Such anecdotal details help readers to see and understand the conditions of life at that time and the background to the historical events, seen through the eyes of someone who actually experienced them. In addition, the village life and the school conditions I experienced are now a thing of the past, but still of great interest to today's children and young people, as well as an essential background for understanding the context of the historical events that took place.

Such anecdotes also help the reader to understand a person better with all his or her character, sentiments and personality, even if they have not seen that person. In addition, personal stories about a writer's life help to lighten the writing and make reading easier and more interesting, as the readers see the human side of politics and national life reflected in the values and failings of the main characters. Many people who have read the book have commented favourably on it and said they were especially interested and intrigued by the personal details and stories. For example, a recent review I found on the internet commented:

> The narrative brims with cultural insights, particularly in the early sections. From learning the lost art of fishing with black sea slugs to discovering the rituals of a Vanuatuan circumcision ceremony, the reader encounters a whole host of information about traditional life on the islands. Despite having a total population of fewer than 250,000 people, the archipelago is divided into a series of communities that differ enormously from one another – so much so that when Regenvanu went away to school on mainland Efate he was the only pupil there who spoke his language.
>
> However, perhaps most striking of all is the revelation that Regenvanu, having no official birth date and finding himself obliged to 'pinpoint when [he] had begun' by the Franco-British colonial administration, plumped for the date 1 April 1945, both from a sense of lightheartedness – because this is the Western April Fools' Day – and because this is the day the UN was founded.[2]

Even strangers come up to me in the supermarket or on the road and say that they recognise me from the photos in the book, and that they feel they know me. To me this is a result of the 'personal touch' that comes with autobiography.

Another point I'd like to add here is that I was writing at a time when my level of interest in national politics was very high. I cared about the welfare of the country, and about the work and development we had made. I believe political writing, especially in the form of autobiography, is best done at an active age and at a time when one is still politically focused. Also, at that stage my mental capacity to remember and evaluate my life experience was still at a high level. I could still

---

2   Available online at ayearofreadingtheworld.com/2012/08/06/vanuatu-a-global-village.

remember vividly those experiences I had had, which were so important to me. They became my passion, the driving force within me to make me want to share my life experience with others. Accounts of historical events given subjectively in autobiography can have this quality of genuineness, passion, and a sense of purpose and urgency that is often missing from other forms of writing. This is why I think that autobiography is an ideal form for historical writing.

The challenges of writing in the Pacific

I would like to finish this paper with a short discussion of the technical side of writing and especially of the challenges that we Pacific writers face to get our work published.

My personal experience

Once I decided what to write about I got down to it. I simply wrote down as much as I could remember, as if I was telling it. When I had exhausted what I could remember about one topic, I would start on another topic. Often I would get up in the middle of the night or in the early hours of the morning and write what I had recalled, and insert it in the appropriate section.

I wrote the entire book in my own handwriting. I did not have a typewriter to work with, let alone a computer. As I pointed out in the book, I was fortunate at the time that there was someone with the time and knowledge in using computers who offered to type my written manuscripts for me. Initially it was not easy for that person, as my writing is not easy for other people to read. Even I find it difficult to read my own writing at times.

Also, I had been collecting photos of interest over the years, resulting in a large collection of photo albums now sitting in my house. I had been doing this simply as a hobby I enjoyed, but when the need to use photos and pictures to go with the stories that I had written came up, I had a huge collection to choose from to publish with different parts of the book. I believe the photos have helped to make the book more enjoyable to read, and I have watched many people flipping over the pages just looking at the photos.

However, my written manuscript would have remained just that had it not been for the active interest of other people with the skills and knowledge I did not have. Without these people, the book would never have been published. I have mentioned the assistance in the typing of the book. But the greatest assistance came from a long-time friend, Dr Howard Van Trease, who, as an historian, took a keen and active interest in my project. His close connection with the University of the South Pacific (USP), and especially the Institute of Pacific Studies (IPS), helped to facilitate the final process in getting my book published as we have it today. And I am forever grateful to Howard for that.

Difficulties for writers today

Having said that, however, I know for a fact that there are people today in my own country, and also in Fiji where I have worked, and I am sure in other Pacific countries generally who, like me, appreciate the value and importance of telling their own stories but have great difficulty in getting those stories published. I know of many who have actually written down the story of their lives, what they have done for their people and their countries, and what that means to them. Many have lived through exciting times and experiences and want to share their experiences with the incoming generations through writing. But often they are frustrated because they arrive at a point where they can make no further progress. They lack the finance and the technical assistance in the form of editing and organising their material, so it just sits somewhere in their house, unfinished and inaccessible to others.

Some have managed to have their life stories written by other people and published by them, but this is not the same as an autobiographical account. Many people today with experiences to tell are getting older and are losing their memories; and some have already died, thus missing out on the opportunity to pass on their stories.

This situation should become a challenge to us as individuals and as institutions. What role can we play to get people who have something worth sharing in written form to do so while their interest and passion is still high?

I believe that IPS, which was founded by Professor Ron Crocombe and had as its primary goal to encourage research and writing by Pacific people and facilitate publication of their works, has been replaced at USP by a more conventional publishing operation. IPS subsidised its publications and did not pay royalties to the authors, but was able to publish books by Pacific Island writers as a result. This might not have been accepted by publishing houses operating for profit. The loss of IPS means that opportunities of financial and editorial support for Pacific writers are fewer nowadays. I am not aware of any other publishing options in the Pacific similar to that provided in the past by IPS.

I hope that this book might be an important first step in understanding the difficulties Pacific authors face and may result in a plan to assist them in their efforts. I would suggest, for example, that programs be run by universities in the region to teach the art of book writing and publication. In this respect I would hope that one outcome of this book would be to encourage regular opportunities for discovering and assisting potential authors in the Pacific.

10. Reflections on *A Remarkable Journey*

Carol Kidu

My autobiography *A Remarkable Journey* is not a political life story – it is a love story that intertwines with politics because it is about the challenges of learning to live in a culture that is very different from my culture of birth, and about my life story that provided a foundation for my entry into politics. It also superficially documents political events that prompted me to contest an election in spite of the fact that I knew very little about politics.

A Remarkable Journey was written as part of the grieving process after the death in January 1994 of my husband, Sir Buri Kidu, and as a tribute to an extraordinary man who died too young. Buri's death from a sudden heart attack six months after his non-reappointment as Chief Justice of Papua New Guinea was attributed to the politics of the time by many commentators. At the cultural level, many family members attributed Buri's death to sorcery instigated and paid for by certain politicians who feared Buri. It was an extremely emotionally charged time in my life and that of my extended family. Thus I wrote as a release of emotions and wrote, from an emotional and very personal perspective, a story that I felt needed to be told. I wrote from the heart.

In reality, I did not write for publication completely of my own volition because a publisher I had met while writing social science textbooks for the curriculum unit of the Department for Education had been encouraging me for a long time to write my story. He eventually convinced me to continue the manuscript that I had started after Buri's death and which was planned to finish with his death. He and the publishers, Pearson Education, had to convince me to make it my story rather than Buri's story and to finish the story with my election into politics. My mother also repeatedly asked me if I was ever going to finish 'the book' and thus during December 2000, when visiting my mother for Christmas, I resumed what was to become an arduous task of researching, recording, rechecking, cross-referencing and acknowledging photographic materials to produce the final manuscript.

Thus my full political life story (as yet unwritten) started from a point of anger – extreme anger and frustration about politics and personalities. Other than the circumstances surrounding Sir Buri's non-reappointment as Chief Justice and the concluding chapter which covers my entry into politics and my first political campaign, my political life story remains untold – a task for the future perhaps – but a task that I know will not be easy because writing quite simply, although often pleasurable, is usually not easy and is very time-consuming.

Perhaps with a team of research assistants the task would not be so daunting, but it will still be difficult if it is to be a personal account rather than a documented political history of that 15 years of our nation's political history. A personal account can be exhausting and contentious, as was my experience with *A Remarkable Journey* – exhausting emotionally because it opens old wounds and because a personal account of historical events is, in essence, subjective and thus open to potential challenge.

Perhaps the hardest aspect of writing *A Remarkable Journey* was the issue of what to include and how to say it. It was an agonising process and I used one of my children as the initial 'editor' of content. Her advice was not necessarily useful regarding my early life in PNG and learning to live in Motu society: 'Say it as it was'; 'Don't avoid the hard stuff'; 'Take off the rose-tinted glasses'. My autobiography was very frank and personal but also cautious in content. I was fortunate in that there were no major issues when it came to editing and the publishers took a very flexible approach in the interactive editorial process. Only one issue was not to my liking but was insisted on by the editors, and that was the choice of title for the book.

My title choice was *Never Ask Me to Choose* because those were Buri's words when we discussed marriage. He said, 'Never ask me to choose between you and my people because I will not choose you, I will choose my people.' It was one of the most significant statements made to me in my whole adult life and in some ways the basis of all that was to follow. However, the editors insisted that it was not a marketable book title and gave me three choices, which eventually narrowed down to *A Remarkable Journey*. I still believe my title was a better one!

The launch of *A Remarkable Journey* was a low-key event bringing Buri's family together in the lead-up to the 2002 election to acknowledge their important role in my life.

The only open negative reaction to the book came in a letter from a grandson of one of the missionaries in Buri's early life who took offence to the way that section was written and felt it insulted his grandfather. It came as a surprise to me because definitely no insult had been intended. I simply wrote anecdotes that Buri had told me about his memories of his early life. In retrospect I realise that the particular anecdotes could be interpreted as negative reflections but I retold them because they illustrated Buri's leadership qualities and his courage to defend what he saw as right and wrong even in circumstances of authority.

10. Reflections on *A Remarkable Journey*

Undoubtedly there are people who do not accept my interpretation of the events surrounding Sir Buri's non-reappointment as Chief Justice but, if they have ever read the book, they have chosen not to comment.

One thing that has surprised me is that some young Papua New Guineans have thanked me for writing the book, saying that it helped them to understand and analyse the tensions in their own lives while growing up in two worlds. This is a reaction that I find particularly rewarding personally.

Similarly some non-Papua New Guineans have said that it has helped them to understand Papua New Guinea better. Other than that, there has been little reaction to the book which concluded with my election into Parliament.

'Geez, Mum, you've really got yourself into deep shit this time.'

'Shut up Basil,' I hissed between closed teeth.

Basil dozed beside me – slightly intoxicated after a sleepless night following the results with the tally team in the village. It was 1997, at the end of a very strategically planned and exhausting campaign, when word came to the village that the Returning Officer would declare the seat that morning. Basil had decided to accompany me to the counting room. Celebrations were already starting outside the family house in Pari village as we squeezed into the tiny Suzuki that had become my trademark during the campaign. The singing and dancing had begun as I left for the declaration. I forced myself to dance and smile with young Dadi who had diligently checked the Common Roll for the names of our supporters for weeks before the voting day. I was smiling on the outside but inside my heart was heavy – burdened by the enormity of what I had done and the implications carried with it.

'Geez, Mum, you've really got yourself into deep shit this time.' Basil roused beside me and continued like a broken record.

'Basil!!' I hissed again. 'Stop it or go outside.'

Only time would tell how deep that shit would be. But that's another story. These were the last two sentences of *A Remarkable Journey*. which acknowledged that the book was a task unfinished. Quite a number of people have asked me when I am going to write the next part of the story but, until now, it has remained a task on my 'to do one day' list.

On several occasions during my political career, a senior employee of Macmillan asked me to write my story. He first contacted me after the Australian Broadcasting Corporation (ABC) covered my life in a television documentary called *Australian Story*. I responded that I had already written a book, which he subsequently read, but he continued to encourage me to write the whole story starting from the beginning again and including my life in politics. It is something that I wanted to do but at that time, as a government minister, did not (and still do not) have the time to do, and I am not willing to work with a ghost writer on something so personal. I guess I may have missed the opportunity to have a publisher waiting for my manuscript but I explained to him when I met him that I am actually struggling not only with time but also with how to structure the book. He said just start at the beginning and write until the end. But I am still not comfortable with that.

Should I do a chronological autobiography? Or should I structure it around issues? Or should I write an autobiography that is a composite of many stand-alone stories within a total story? There is so much when I start thinking about it that it becomes overwhelming. What will interest people? Who is my main target audience? Why would I write another book? Certainly it would not be to make money. My returns from *A Remarkable Journey* soon made it clear to me that most writers struggle financially and it would not be a viable income option to meet my financial requirements if I continue to live with my large extended family.

I want to write again but then again …

I think of the workload involved: the content research, the searches for illustrations, the hours of drafting and redrafting as I agonise over the most appropriate way to express something, and becoming a self-appointed editor of my own work! Or should I do an autobiography that is also a biography and ask others such as my children and colleagues to contribute sections to make up the composite story?

I would not call myself a politician by choice but rather by circumstance. I knew nothing about politics – in fact I had never voted until I voted for myself as candidate. I was a teacher by profession and a village wife who had been widowed three years before I stood for my first election. I had met my husband when I was 16 years old – a grade 11 student. We met at a school holiday fitness camp. I was there with two girlfriends and he was there with a group of students from Papua New Guinea who were attending schools in Australia on colonial scholarships. Little did I realise where my first teenage romance would lead me – on a journey to the unexpected.

Was it worth it? That's a question sometimes asked of me. One positive personal outcome in each campaign was a dramatic loss in weight – no need for dieting. The adrenaline flow and constant pressure cooker campaigning – same messages but different delivery in different communities – setting up, packing up and moving on to another community undoubtedly led to the weight loss which was counterbalanced by more wrinkles and more grey hairs and complete and utter exhaustion. At the end of each day, late at night, I returned to sleep in the back room of the family village house with the 'golden girls' – the wonderful widows who had been inspired that a widow like them could challenge the norm and succeed. They sat around me talking in hushed whispers as I slept on the floor exhausted, rejuvenating myself for yet another day. They made it their personal duty to protect me from any possibility of evil sorcery invading my space in the darkness.

In the next room male elders kept vigil – and the young women served a constant supply of tea and flour cooked in a variety of ways. During my 2002 campaign, a campaign team leader complained that the elders were eating too much and should go to their own houses. I was horrified – no way would I let that happen. While the elders were there ensuring that all things were done properly to keep the spiritual world at peace I knew that I would win. They were my confidence and each day at least one elder travelled with me into different communities – *irutauna baine namo daini* (to maintain good karma and a good relationship with the spiritual world).

Was it worth it? I ensured that each campaign was an educational opportunity for people – a stocktake of what I had done and what I would try to do in the next five years. In 2007 I was very aware that two rival candidates were using a lot of money in communities while campaigning. How could I counteract the power of money in poor communities? I needed to put something into people's hands that could not be seen as bribery, so we produced a 'bag of knowledge' for each household in my base areas: thousands of colourful plastic bags from Chinese stores (except in my two major bases where women sewed the bags out of calico and youth screen-printed them) and thousands of leaflets about the work I had done – the new laws and policies, colouring books about malaria with coloured pencils, balloons etc. I wanted to put a condom into each bag because of my advocacy on HIV but the campaign team said no to that, not allowing me to push the barriers in conservative communities.

My rationale for the 'bags of knowledge' was that, even if I did lose, something worthwhile would have been achieved by my campaign. Was it worth it? I think so. But would I do it again? No way! As I watched my colleagues prepare for their 2012 campaigns, I felt such a relief that I had chosen not to stand again.

In 1997 I stood as an Independent. After declaration, winning candidates were being whisked away by political parties to gather the numbers into 'camps' to form government. I was declared early in the 109 seats so I chose to visit my mother to avoid all the horse-trading that is part of politics PNG style. When I returned, the winners were in two main camps with a few stragglers like me who were unwilling to be 'camped in'. All I could do was to look for people whom I thought I could identify with so I decided to join the Opposition and entered the Opposition caucus room.

I have never been conscious of my gender. I had married a man who was very proud of his Melanesian heritage but also a liberated man who had been educated in Australia in the era of the women's liberation movement. I did not anticipate the welcome I would receive when I entered the caucus room.

The Opposition Leader acknowledged me with the comment: 'People in this House wear pants not skirts.' He was a friend of my late husband but uncomfortable about my presence in the sacred modern men's house where there had not been a woman for 10 years before 1997. I smiled and sat down.

The next day, I dressed in a trouser suit and made sure that most men were already present before I entered the caucus room. With a cheeky smile, I stood to attract their attention then kicked one leg in the air to display my trousers. 'Am I welcome now?' I joked with the leader. My point was made. A small act of defiance but delivered with a smile – I knew that direct confrontation with my male colleagues would be counterproductive, a waste of energy. I had to learn how to operate in an environment that was uncomfortable about female participation. But, after 15 years, I felt that I had become like a piece of the furniture at Parliament. I had become comfortable with my male colleagues, and trust that the feeling was mutual.

Would readers be interested in this anecdotal approach to my political life story? Certainly it would probably seem superficial and frivolous to serious political commentators, but what size audience is there for a serious detailed political story? And in view of the fact that I have not kept detailed diaries of my political career, the research required for such an approach to writing would be enormous but certainly not impossible.

One definite reason to write again is that it would give me the opportunity to outline the policy and legislative reforms that I pursued as a Minister and why I pursued them. It would also provide the opportunity to highlight several other major changes in the social sector that were initiated by me; but as they evolved they became owned by my male colleagues for a variety of reasons, as is the case in politics. Would this be cynically viewed as self-promotion and retrospective justification? However, in a nation where there are still not enough women in politics and the role and even the capacity of women is still questioned, it is important to make sure that what women can achieve is documented and acknowledged. To write again would also give me the opportunity to correct some of the misperceptions about some of the work I initiated and issues that I pursued. But would people be interested in that or would it simply be writing for myself?

Would I write about the complexity of being a politician in Papua New Guinea, the political culture, the expectations of the general population, the frustrations of trying to negotiate through the system to make sustainable achievements and how those achievements inevitably lead to a whole new set of challenges? On top of all of this, a politician in PNG has to also be an ad hoc project supervisor in the electorate to ensure that their projects comply with guidelines to avoid allegations of corruption and investigation. The struggle to be an effective parliamentarian as well as an effective electorate representative is a constant struggle for politicians in Papua New Guinea. The workload for a conscientious person can be overwhelming, and thus the support systems for politicians are critical but not always available and appropriate. Would such issues be of interest to the general reader?

My decision to retire from politics by not contesting the 2012 election was actually made in 1997 when I told my supporters that if the people allowed me I would serve for three terms maximum. I knew that 15 years would take me into my early 60s and I also knew that I did not want to finish my working life as a politician.

In fact, to serve more than one term in politics in Papua New Guinea is not the norm with over 50 per cent turnover in every election since independence. To serve three terms has been a great privilege but definitely enough. Yes, I left some tasks I had set myself unfinished, but I had made varied inroads on other issues that were not part of my original agenda. Yes, I left politics at a time when I was becoming more efficient at achieving my parliamentary goals, but balancing one's parliamentary agenda with the electorate's expectations is a constant and exhausting juggling act. There are simply not enough hours in the day.

After my first successful campaign in 1997, my daughter gave me a Bird of Paradise ring. My wedding ring had been lost (stolen?) several years earlier so I symbolically put the Bird of Paradise on my marriage ring finger. I was well aware of the fact that my choice to enter politics was a huge commitment and that I was basically marrying myself to the nation. Unfortunately, however, my choice also had a huge impact on my children. I did not have a wife to ensure that all the domestic chores were done and extended family obligations observed. The fact is that politics did affect the lives of my children and I could not have managed without them to attend to all the family matters.

In addition to having to take on many family tasks to support me, they also had to contend with the fact that often the general public assume that the children of politicians live a privileged life with unlimited access to money. They often had to contend with anger from people who asked for, then demanded money from them. The girls also had to make endless pots of tea and refreshments to feed people who visited unannounced in the hope that I could solve their problems for them. And then the boys would be expected to drive the unexpected visitors back to their community because we live on traditional land away from any bus routes. They were patient with my politics but also very glad when the time for my retirement came close, making it very clear that enough was enough when people began urging me to stand again.

When the swearing in of the new government occurred, I felt a surge of pleasure when the public gallery and the other MPs clapped for each of the three women when they were sworn in. At last, the image of one white woman in parliament had been broken and the nation was proud to have three Melanesian women in the Chamber of Parliament. It was time to take off the Bird of Paradise ring! But what would replace it?

I had the replacement ring ready – a butterfly ring. After 20 years as a teacher and 15 years as a politician – a total of 35 years in public service earning a regular fortnightly income – I was now entering into new territory. I wanted to enter the world of consulting; I also wanted to transform my family home on traditional land at the beach into an income-generating business to help support the family; I wanted to perhaps continue being part of the regional and global lobby for human rights, equity, justice and peace at all levels of society; and I wanted to perhaps work to facilitate transformative change at community level. I wanted to …

Goodness, where is the space for retirement? So I have set a new target of five more years' hard work to be followed by the luxury of retirement. But that five years will require reinventing myself to some degree – a period of transformation as I learn the ways of life outside the public sector.

And thus I now wear the butterfly ring (a little too tight) to remind myself that during the process of metamorphosis that I have now entered I will face many challenges that I will have to manage. Clearly, at my age, I cannot transform into a beautiful butterfly but the imagery and fantasy will hopefully help me weather the storms still to come in my life.

Will I write another book? I think so. I want to. But I still feel the need for reflective distance before I am ready to begin the task and I definitely need some quiet space in my life – a luxury that I have not yet achieved. But that is another story.

11. Solomon Islands' Biography

Editors, co-authors, and ghost writers

Clive Moore

Solomon Islands' biography

Editing the autobiographies of leading Pacific politicians and statesmen is an unusual exercise which involves maintaining the integrity of the editor while encouraging the personal expression and beliefs of the autobiographer. I came to Pacific biography and autobiography late in my academic career when between 2006 and 2008 I edited the autobiography of Sir Peter Kenilorea, the first Prime Minister of the Solomon Islands.[1] I am also undertaking a similar task for Sir Nathaniel Waena, an ex-public servant, Cabinet Minister and Governor-General. As well, in the course of preparing a *Solomon Islands Historical Encyclopaedia, 1893–1978*, I have written 395 short biographical entries on Solomon Islanders, Europeans and Chinese associated with the Solomons. I have also published reflections on the creative process involved.[2] Although this chapter concentrates on my work with Sir Nathaniel Waena, I will also cover some issues raised by my participation in the other work. I will reflect on the need to build personal relationships with the autobiographers and on the thin lines that differentiate an editor from a co-author and a ghost writer.

I must say that I feel a little uncomfortable even writing this paper. I don't want to appear to compare Sir Peter with Sir Nathaniel, or to be critical of either. And I have been dealing with the Solomon Islands' elite long enough to know that a modern 'Big Man syndrome' exists that is exacerbated by the expectations of ex-prime ministers, cabinet ministers and governors-general. Presumably this is not just a Solomon Islands characteristic and applies to dealing with other statesmen and leaders of renown. They are used to being looked after by 'minders' and, no matter how polite they may be, they have expectations that the rest of us are there to do their bidding. However, academic editors with professorial status are afflicted by their own version of the 'Big Man syndrome'

---

1 P. Kenilorea, *Tell It As It Is: Autobiography of Rt. Hon. Sir Peter Kenilorea, KBE, PC, Solomon Islands' First Prime Minister* (Taipei 2008).
2 C. Moore, 'Biography of a Nation: Compiling a Historical Dictionary of the Solomon Islands', in B. Lal and V. Luker (eds), *Telling Pacific Lives: Prisms of Process* (Canberra 2011), 277–292; C. Moore, 'Pacific Islands Autobiography: Personal History, History and Diplomacy in Solomon Islands', *Journal of Historical Biography*, 10 (2011), 1–33.

and expect to be treated with the level of respect they receive in their own institutions. I see myself as an editor, and expect in other circumstances to become a co-author if the amount of work involved warrants the change in status. I certainly do not expect to be a ghost writer. The modern university system has no place for such acts of self-abasement and, anyway, most ghost writers get well paid to maintain their anonymity. The whole exercise of being an editor to Big Men in the Pacific is a financial drain on my institution and does not receive adequate recognition in academic circles. While I subscribe to the dictums of Ron Crocombe and Jim Davidson about responsibilities to assist Pacific Islanders to write their own histories, they both operated in a different era when universities were less corporate and funding oriented.

Solomon Islands' biographical entries for an historical encyclopaedia

Since the mid-2000s I have been chipping away at a *Solomon Islands Historical Encyclopaedia* based mainly on the Protectorate years, 1893–1978. When published as a website, it will have 284,350 words and 1,042 images. Of the 1,117 entries, 395 are biographical; the vast majority are of Solomon Islanders, along with the more important of the outsiders who shaped the history of the British Solomon Islands Protectorate. The entries vary in size, from fragments to quite substantial lengths. The standard practice in similar national biographical publications is to include entries only on the dead, which is not possible in a young nation where many of the leaders who steered the Solomon Islands to independence are still alive. One of my aims was to restore as many Solomon Islanders to the historical record as possible and the website will encourage their families to add background and update their entries.

Important individuals have substantial entries: Solomon Mamaloni (1,400 words), Peter Kenilorea (846 words), Gideon Zoloveke (530 words) and Lilly Ogatina Poznanski (341 words). Because of the nature of the sources, the large entries are on individuals involved in politics or the churches. Traditional leaders who were prominent in regions are largely missing as I have no way to access information on them and, as is usual given the nature of the sources, female leaders are seldom mentioned. Some people, once they emerged, usually through receiving a modern education, remain prominent, but I have been amazed by the number of Solomon Islanders who left their islands for education overseas in the 1950s and 1960s, travelled to far-flung places but then returned and left no further mark on the public record. I suspect that many of them did leave significant marks on the young nation, although the sources available to me left them unrecorded.

This exercise in writing biographical sketches is a preliminary exercise in historical retrieval, based on sources easily available. It is vastly different from another project in which I am involved: helping Solomon Islands' leaders to write their autobiographies.

Pacific Islands' autobiographies

My first experience was with Sir Peter Kenilorea's autobiography which, although not unique, is rare. There are many biographies of Pacific leaders, ranging from Christian hagiographies to academic treatises attempting to understand the motivations of colonial governors, to studies of politicians, missionaries, traders and wartime leaders. Many colonists have turned their hand to memoirs, often based on diaries from the time. Although several politicians have written autobiographical accounts, and several prime ministers have published biographic works, reflections by Pacific leaders about themselves and the political process are rare. Kenilorea's autobiography is the most substantial by any indigenous Pacific head of government.[3]

The Pacific autobiography process has involved many editors, co-authors and ghost writers. Ratu Sir Kamisese Mara, Prime Minister of Fiji (1970–1992) and President of the Republic of Fiji (1993–2000), published a memoir in 1997 which was ghosted unacknowledged by Sir Robert Saunders.[4] Sitiveni Rabuka, Fijian coup leader and Prime Minister (1992–1999) told his story to Eddie Dean and Stan Ritova.[5] At the time of Papua New Guinea's independence, Sir Michael Somare, Prime Minister during 1975–1980, 1982–1985 and 2007–2010, wrote an autobiography of his early years, heavily assisted by University of Papua New Guinea academic Ulli Beier.[6] Walter Lini, Vanuatu's founding Prime Minister, also wrote an early biography; and, recently, Pastor Sethy Regenvanu, ex-Deputy Prime Minister of Vanuatu, published an autobiography.[7] Two Papua New Guinea Governors-General, Sir Ignatius Kilage and Sir Paulias Matane, have published autobiographies, and others heads of governments have published speeches and writings.[8] The closest equivalent to Sir Peter's book is probably

---

3 I am indebted to my colleagues Michael Goldsmith, Robert Kiste, Brij V. Lal, Adrian Muckle, Doug Munro and Edward Wolfers for their advice on the references in this paragraph.
4 K. Mara, *The Pacific Way: A Memoir* (Honolulu 1997).
5 S. Rabuka, *Rabuka: No Other Way. His Own Story of the Fijian Coup as told to Eddie Dean and Stan Ritova* (Sydney 1988).
6 M.T. Somare, *Sana: An Autobiography* (Port Moresby 1975).
7 W. Lini, *Beyond Pandemonium: From the New Hebrides to Vanuatu* (Wellington 1980); S.J. Regenvanu, *Laef Blong Mi: From Village to Nation: An Autobiography* (Suva 2004), available online at editorrips@usp.ac.fj.
8 I. Kilage, *My Mother Calls Me Yaltep* (Port Moresby 2000); P. Matane, *My Childhood in New Guinea* (New York 1972); P. Matane, *To Serve With Love* (Mount Waverley 1992); 'T. Bavadra', in A. Bain and T. Baba (eds), *Bavadra, Prime Minister, Statesman, Man of the People: Selection of Speeches and Writings, 1985–1989* (Nadi 1990).

a memoir by Sir Tom Davis, Prime Minister of the Cook Islands between 1978 and 1987 (with a break of a few months in 1983) and later High Commissioner to New Zealand.[9] Several other Pacific politicians have published their speeches, journalism, and other writings and, recently, Ian Johnstone and Michael Powles published accounts of 19 Pacific leaders in the 1970s, accompanied by audio files of the interviews.[10] Most of these accounts have been edited, usually by male non-Pacific Islanders, area specialists who saw it as their duty to assist prominent citizens of the newly emerging Pacific nations to spread their message to the widest possible public. I suspect there are more ghosts and editors involved than the title pages indicate.

Sir Peter Kenilorea's autobiography also sits within the small number of biographies and autobiographies written by and about Solomon Islanders. Many Solomon Islands politicians and leaders have talked about writing autobiographies, but few have actually done so. Three biographies have been written – two by missionary George Carter, one a booklet on Ranongga Island missionary David Voeta, and another more substantial one on Reverend Belshazzar Gina. Guadalcanal academic Tarcisius Tara Kabutaulaka wrote a fine book on his grandfather Dominiko Alebua.[11] Sir Frederick Osifelo, senior public servant, Chairman of the Governing Council and Speaker of the Legislative Assembly, appears to be the only one who has written an autobiography unaided – or at least there is no acknowledgement of an editor. All other autobiographies have been written with the assistance of academic editors. Dr Gideon Zoleveke wrote with the help of political scientist John Chick. Anthropologist Roger Keesing assisted 'Elota and Jonathan Fifi'i from Kwaio in Malaita, and Noel Fatnowna, an Australian Solomon Islander, to write autobiographies.[12] Historians Judith Bennett and Khyla Russell assisted Sir Lloyd Maepeza Gina, first Speaker of the National Parliament, in the same way and anthropologist Ben Burt has similarly

---

9   T. Davis, *Island Boy: An Autobiography* (Suva 1954). Sir Tom and Lydia Davis also wrote *Doctor to the Islands*, Boston.
10   J. Cazaumayou and T. De Dekker (eds), *Gabriel Païta: Témoignage Kanak. D'Opao au Pays de la Nouvelle-Calédonie, 1929–1999* (Paris 2000); V.R. Singh, *Speaking Out: Commentary on Political, Social and Economic Issues in Fiji during the Decade 1995–2005* (Brisbane 2006); T.R. Vakatora, *From the Mangrove Swamps* (Suva 1998); A. Siaguru, *In-house in Papua New Guinea with Anthony Siaguru* (Canberra 2001); I. Johnstone and M. Powles (eds), *New Flags Flying: Pacific Leadership* (Wellington 2012).
11   G.G. Carter, 'David Voeta: The Story of a Pioneer Missionary', *Proceedings of the Wesley Historical Society, New Zealand*, 28: 5 (Auckland 1973); G.G. Carter, in E. Tuza (ed.), *Yours in Service: A Reflection on the Life and Times of Reverend Belshazzar Gina of Solomon Islands* (Honiara 1990); T.T. Kabutaulaka, *Footprints in the Tasimauri Sea: A Biography of Dominiko Alebua* (Suva 2002).
12   M. Moore, 'Noel Fatnowna and His Book: The Making of Fragments of a Lost Heritage', *Journal of Pacific Studies*, 18 (1994/95), 137–150.

helped Samuel Alasa`a and Michael Kwa`ioloa to write autobiographies.[13] Two more biographies are under preparation: one on Solomon Mamaloni by Christopher Chevalier and one of Francis Aqorau Talasasa by his son Transform Aqorau.

I knew how much work had been involved when Bennett and Russell laboriously taped interviews with Sir Lloyd Maepeza Gina and turned them into a book. The same occurred when Keesing edited self-recorded tapes by Noel Fatnowna in the 1980s. Kenilorea was different: he taught himself to type for the occasion and produced the most substantial and genuinely self-authored book ever written by a Pacific Islands' head of government or state. Sir Peter's contribution is unique because he is the father of the modern nation and because he prepared the draft himself. He is immensely proud of his book, which is readily available in the Solomons and has entered the local literature. Copies can be found in many Solomon Islands' homes because the book was distributed free or at low cost, courtesy of the Embassy of the Republic of Taiwan.

Nathaniel Rahumaea Waena

This brings us to my latest project, the autobiography of Nathaniel Rahumaea Waena. He was born on 1 November 1945 at Su`utaluhia on Ulawa Island, son of Joseph Talo and Matilda Tahalata. He attended Ripo village elementary school (1954–1955) until January 1956 when, at the age of eleven, his parents sent him to St Barnabas' Primary School at Alangaula on Ugi Island, which he attended until 1959. From 1960 to 1964 he completed his upper primary and secondary education at All Hallows' School at Pawa, also on Ugi Island. In January 1965 the BSIP Chamber of Commerce sponsored him to attend a year-long course in commercial training at Lae Technical Institute in Papua New Guinea. When he returned to the Solomons he worked at the Mobil Oil Company from January 1966 until 1971, when he joined the public service.

His first posting, on 15 September 1971, was at Kirakira on Makira as Executive Officer to the District Commissioner. In 1972 he served with the first Solomon Islander District Commissioner, Frederick Osifelo, and in 1973 he moved to Santa Cruz sub-headquarters. He returned to Kirakira in 1974 to serve under

---

13 F. Osifelo, *Kanaka Boy: An Autobiography* (Suva 1985); G. Zoleveke, in J. Chick (ed.), *Zoleveke: A Man from Choiseul* (Suva 1980); Elota, in R.M. Keesing (ed.), `Elota's Story: The Life and Times of a Solomon Islands Big Man* (Brisbane 1978); J. Fifi`i, in R.M. Keesing (trans and ed.), *From Pig-Theft to Parliament: My Life Between Two Worlds* (Suva 1989); N. Fatnowna, in R.M. Keesing (ed.), *Fragments of a Lost Heritage* (Sydney 1989); B. Burt and M. Kwa`ioloa (eds), *A Solomon Islands Chronicle: As Told by Samuel Alasa`a* (London 2001); L.M. Gina, in J.A. Bennett and K.J. Russell (eds), *Journeys in a Small Canoe: The Life and Times of a Solomon Islander* (Canberra 2003); M. Kwa`ioloa and B. Burt, *The Chief's Country: Leadership and Politics in Honiara, Solomon Islands* (St Lucia 2012).

District Commissioners Francis Talasasa and Peter Kenilorea. Waena became Deputy Clerk to the Makira Local Council under the Clerk (later Prime Minister) Francis Billy Hilly. During these years he was involved in the amalgamation of local councils. In 1975 he qualified as a lay magistrate and was posted to the Guadalcanal Local Council as Deputy Clerk. The next year he moved again, this time to Isabel, as Clerk to the Local Council. In 1977 he was posted back to the Eastern Outer Islands District as Clerk to the Local Council there, and in 1980 he returned to Guadalcanal as Provincial Secretary (1980–1982). Next Waena was based in Honiara as Chief Administrative Officer in the Ministry of Transport, Works and Utilities (1983–1984). He then returned to his home area as Permanent Secretary with the Makira-Ulawa and Temotu Provincial Affairs Ministry, and subsequently served a term as Permanent Secretary of Western Province, during which he helped establish Choiseul Province. He also held Permanent Secretary positions in the ministries of Provincial Government and Rural Development; Natural Resources; Transport, Works and Utilities; and Agriculture, Lands and Surveys. At the direction of Prime Minister Solomon Mamaloni, Weana was responsible for the capture in the 1980s of the vessel *Jeanette Diana*, which was illegally fishing in Solomon Islands waters. The ship's seizure sparked a major dispute with the United States, where the ship was registered.[14]

In 1970, Waena contested the election for the Makira constituency against Mamaloni (a former Pawa schoolmate) and Geoffrey Kuper, with Mamaloni the victor. In the 1973 election he stood for the West Makira electorate, receiving 446 votes against Mamaloni, who once again won, with 1,272 votes. Waena says that he did not campaign in either election. His maintained his interest in politics and in 1980 he joined Mamaloni's People's Alliance Party. In a by-election in December 1987, he entered National Parliament unopposed as the member for Ulawa-Uki constituency, serving until 6 July 2004. In 1989 he was appointed roving election manager for Mamaloni's People's Alliance Party. Both Waena and Mamaloni stood unopposed in that election. Wanea served as Minister for Provincial Government and Rural Development in Mamaloni's one-party Government in 1989–1990, but he was sacked along with four other Ministers for supporting the party's President, Sir David Kausimae, in a dispute with Mamaloni. Waena remained as leader of the parliamentary wing of the People's Alliance Party and took part in the negotiations to form the Ulufa`alu government (1997–2000). He served as Deputy Speaker from 1997 until June 2000, when the Ulufa`alu government was overthrown.

Between 1999 and 2002, Waena became the Executive Committee Representative of the Pacific Region (including New Zealand) for the Commonwealth Parliamentary Association, and travelled to Gibraltar, Jersey, London and

---

14 A.M. Kengalu, *Embargo: The Jeanette Diana Affair* (Bathurst 1988).

Edinburgh. In 2000 he became Minister for Provincial Government and Rural Development in the first Sogavare government, when he was responsible for brokering the ceasefire agreement with Harold Keke. He also served as Minister for National Unity, Peace and Reconciliation from 2001 to 2004 in Prime Minister Alan Kemakeza's government. Waena was elected as Governor-General on 7 July 2004 and remained in that position until 2009. He received a Cross of Solomon Islands in 2003 and was knighted in 2005 (GCMG and KStJ). In 2010 the Prime Minister appointed him as a member of the Eminent Persons Advisory Council within the Constitutional Congress to help develop a state government system. In the 2010 general elections he stood unsuccessfully for the Ulawa-Uki constituency. In 2011 he became Chairman of the College of Higher Education, tasked with converting the college into a national university. On Easter 1972 Waena married Alice Ole Unusu from Simbo, and over time they adopted six children: Reginald, Patricia, Raphael, Ian, Maureen and Alison.[15]

Sir Nathaniel Waena's autobiography: editor, co-author or ghost writer?

The Waena career should provide good material for life writing and I have been working with Sir Nathaniel since 2011, slowly turning his manuscript into a book. The manuscript arrived with its text in bold, with underlining of many sections and with a heavy border. I undid the 'shouting' and began to make the sentences read like a normal autobiography. None of the chapters were complete, all needed to be fleshed out and some were really just fragmentary notes. So far I have only completed editing his Ulawa and school years – the first 50 pages. The son of a typical Ulawa Anglican family, he was brought up by parents who were subsistence agriculturalists and his father sustained the family through his expertise in fishing. Anglicanism has pervaded Sir Nathaniel's life. He attended Anglican boarding schools and remains a staunch member of that denomination. I have been able to use sections of my *Solomon Islands Historical Encyclopaedia* to build up the early part of the Waena text. Much of the wider historical context for life on Ulawa, the introduction of Anglicanism in the Solomons, and the network of Anglican schools comes from the encyclopaedia and my own library. In this early section about half the writing is his and half is mine, although the style is his. Because the *Solomon Islands Historical Encyclopaedia* largely stops in 1978 I have less easily available supporting background to deal with the 1980s, 1990s and 2000s, meaning that the later sections of the books must be substantially his.

---

15 *British Solomon Islands News Sheet*, 30 November 1965, 21 December 1965, 22 June 1973; information from Sir Nathaniel Waena, 22 March 2012.

His public service career is fairly typical of the late colonial and early independence officials who had limited formal education and were plucked out of obscurity by British civil servants to be trained to serve their new nations. Having dealt with Sir Peter's public service years, I am aware of many issues that would be typical for any young public servant working on the cusp between the colonial and early independence eras. Clearly, he had a close relationship with Solomon Mamaloni, and there is much to say about this remarkable man, but Waena offers no depth or insight. Waena's public service and parliamentary career has interesting highlights as he was in charge of the early years of provincial government as a Permanent Secretary, and again in the 2000s as a Cabinet Minister when most provinces were threatening to secede. He says very little about his parliamentary career, nor the relationship between parliamentarians, political parties and constituents, or between ministers and public servants. He was in charge of the peace and reconciliation process at the most volatile time in the history of the nation,[16] yet once more he is guarded and not informative. He became Governor-General during the initial Regional Assistance Mission to Solomon Islands, or RAMSI years, which included the fascinating prime ministership of Manasseh Sogavare (2006–2007) and the 2006 Chinatown riots, yet there is no detail on this period.[17]

Initially I expected to be able to proceed at the same speed I managed with Sir Peter, but I have discovered that the process is quite different. There was a sense of urgency with Sir Peter's autobiography: 7 July 2008 was the 30th anniversary of Solomon Islands' independence and our absolute deadline, which we managed to meet with less than a week to spare. There is less urgency with Sir Nathaniel's manuscript and it is in far less of a final form. I also find myself in more of a predicament than I did with Sir Peter: am I an editor, or should I be a co-writer, or should I allow myself to become a ghost writer taking minimal credit?

With Sir Peter's manuscript I really was an editor. The manuscript was informative but far too long and my major task was to cut out repetition: with Sir Peter's permission I edited out about 60,000 words. This was not difficult as he combines the qualities of a Melanesian orator, a lay preacher and a modern politician: all rather verbose professions which use repetition to achieve their goals. I edited his sentences to make them flow better, a very usual exercise for any editor. I also suggested some alterations in the ordering of chapters, as

---

16   C. Moore, *Happy Isles In Crisis: The Historical Causes for a Failing State in Solomon Islands, 1998–2004* (Canberra 2004).
17   C. Moore, 'Uncharted Pacific Waters: The Solomon Islands Constitution and the Government of Prime Minister Manasseh Sogavare, 2006–2007', *History Compass*, 6: 2 (2008), 488–509; C. Moore, 'Pacific View: The Meaning of Governance and Politics in the Solomon Islands', *Australian Journal of International Affairs*, 62: 3 (2008), 386–407; C. Moore, 'No More Walkabout Long Chinatown: Asian Involvement in the Solomon Islands Economic and Political Processes', in S. Dinnen and S. Firth (eds), *Politics and State Building in Solomon Islands* (Canberra 2008), 64–95.

well as lifting out family genealogy into an appendix. However, the final book is closely based on the original manuscript. I am not at all sure that the Waena book will be said to be the same.

Most of the Waena manuscript often has no more than a few pages for each chapter. It lacks bulk and consistency and is far too formal; some sections are put together from a scrapbook of invitations. To give some examples, during his years as Governor-General Sir Nathaniel made trips to Australia, New Zealand, England, Singapore, Italy and Israel. In Singapore he made a formal visit to the President, S.R. Nathan, but overall Singapore rates only one paragraph. In Israel he visited the President (unnamed) and the Minister for Foreign Affairs and 'his dear wife', but neither is named. Often all that is recorded is a diary list of places visited: for instance, the Lake of Galilee, Nazareth, Mount of Transfiguration, Jerusalem etc., with no accompanying details. Sir Nathaniel and Lady Waena also visited the tomb of King David, the room of the Last Supper, and the Wailing Wall etc. I have tried to elicit from Sir Nathaniel his feelings as a strong Christian when visiting these holy places, with little success. Do I take over and provide descriptive information, easily gained from reference books and the Internet, thus fleshing out his brief notes, using my own imagination? Although I have never been to Israel I could create an interesting chapter, but do I ghost write for him and accept that he does not have the literary skills to describe what he saw?

In Italy he had a private audience with the Pope, something few of us will ever accomplish. He was impressed by the direct representative of St Peter and by the Papal Basilica of St Peter, but there is no detail provided. Do I read travel books and create a moving word picture, using my own experience of visiting the Vatican? The lack of depth is frustrating but not an insurmountable problem.

The historian versus the author and politician

Some of Sir Nathaniel's beliefs are at odds with my own academic understanding of historical events. The beginnings of my academic career were in research about the labour trade and I think it is fair to say that I have a reasonable understanding of the process. In a second draft of his manuscript Sir Nathaniel has used some statistics I provided, but then went ahead to describe the labour trade as slavery. I have modified his words so that there is a meeting of minds, but am I interfering in a Melanesian interpretation of events that is valuable in its own right? Significantly, perhaps, he has made no comment about my editing of the slave/recruit issue.

The original text

Two major changes occurred on Ulawa, in the second half of the nineteenth century. Ulawan men began recruiting on labour trade ships to Queensland and Fiji, and when the Anglican missionaries arrived. Before that, Ulawa had only been visited by passing vessels, such as the one in 1869 which passed on dysentery. The overseas labour trade began in the early 1870s and continued until the 1910s, by which time Ulawans were also recruiting to work as labourers within the Protectorate. Statistics from colonial records suggest that Queensland ships 'recruited' 147 Ulawans, mainly males between 1870 and 1904, and Fiji ships carried away another nineteen. In such a small population, these were significant numbers, and others left Ulawa through the Anglican Melanesian Mission.

I first visited Bundaberg, in Queensland State, Australia, in 2005 on a State Visit to Australia, on the invitation by the Governor General of Australia, and again in 2008, on the invitation of the South Sea Evangelical Church of Solomon Islands, when the Church commemorated the founding of the Mission by Miss Florence Young, among the Kanakas in the Sugarcane Farms at Bundaberg, in Queensland, Australia. I was able to see the historic sites, where South Sea Islanders worked as slave recruiters, and were kept as Slave-labourers on the Sugarcane Plantations. The remains of the old jetty, along the Bundaberg River, where the slave-Recruits were off-loaded, and the dormitory-like shelters in which the labourers lived, still remained when I went there again in 2008.

My edited version

I first visited Bundaberg, in Queensland, Australia, in 2005 on a State Visit on the invitation by the Governor-General of Australia, and again in 2008, on the invitation of the South Sea Evangelical Church of Solomon Islands, when the Church commemorated the founding of the Mission by Miss Florence Young among the Kanakas on the sugarcane plantations at Bundaberg. I was able to see the historic sites where South Sea Islanders worked as labourers, and were kept in what I would describe as slave-like conditions on the sugarcane plantations. I was shown the remains of the old jetty along the Bundaberg River, where my kinsmen were off-loaded and the dormitory-like shelters in which the labourers lived. Others left Ulawa through the Anglican Melanesian Mission, taken to Norfolk Island to become Christian missionaries in a process very similar to the taking of indentured labour.

This relatively small issue also points to another problem I am facing: communications. I travel to the Solomons about once every 12 months, usually only for a week. Sir Nathaniel does not use email and Solomons' international telephone calls are among the most expensive in the world. While editing Sir Peter's manuscript I was able to send emails to one of his daughters who dutifully printed them out, consulted her father and got back to me the next day. I also stayed with the Keniloreas while I was in Honiara working on the book. The Waena home is always full of Ulawans and there is, to speak, no room at the inn. A couple of days spent visiting him every year are not enough to push along editing of the manuscript. There is no way to discuss small issues as they arise.

Premonitions, dreams and interpretation

One thing that I have not edited out, and have encouraged, is an unusual feature of the manuscript: the inclusion of dreams and premonitions, and their analysis. Sir Nathaniel is more forthcoming with his dreams and strange experiences than with his public life. His explanation of their importance is in terms of a Christian context and their effect on his own personal decision making. He attributes most important decisions in his life to guidance from dreams.

> God has graciously revealed in my dreams certain important future events to which he wanted me to bear witness in my public and private life. Some of my dreams have related to important political leadership changes in the political affairs of the government of the Solomon Islands nation, which determined certain major political events of historic significance. Others of my dreams have related to significant events and leadership changes, in the Anglican Church of the Province of Melanesia. Yet others have revealed matters related to particular members of my own extended family, whose sad future misfortunes or impending disappointment and sorrow became real when the time set in the dreams unfolded. There were other dreams which related to my own personal and community leadership responsibilities and authority. These affected me as a national, island and family leader within my own extended family circle.

My favourite incident is not actually a dream at all but an unusual experience in 1971, which he entitled 'A Quiet and Gentle Voice, Which Called Me, Over Ten Days'. His first job was at the Mobil Oil Depot in Honiara as a clerk. He recounts receiving anonymous phone calls over 10 days, which led, according to his analysis, to his first public service position.

> Each day I would receive such a call by a person, whose voice was very gentle, and which sounded as if it came from a far away distance.

> The voice said to me on the first day, upon my saying good morning: 'Ten more days'. The count-down then went to: Nine more days; Eight more days; Seven more days; Six more days; Five more days, and so forth, to the last day of the process. I asked the voice on a number of those calls, as to whom it was who was talking, but I would not be given an answer at all. When the count-down, however, reached 'Five more days' I became extremely trouble-minded with the whole matter.
>
> I had to ring the Dean of the Saint Barnabas Cathedral, who was then the Very Reverend Father Norman Kitchener Palmer. I made an appointment to see him, which he was readily available to meet with me at his Office. We then met as agreed. He then prayed, before I was able to tell him of the strange telephone calls, I was receiving daily, which involved a count-down. I told him that the count-down was now on the fifth day. He advised me that, if it was a human being who was ringing, then I should not worry, because God will surely protect me from any physical harm. If however, it was some other matter, then, I would know what that might otherwise be, in due course. He prayed over me and reassured me of my personal safety and security.
>
> The next morning, the count-down however still continued. When the count-down reached 'One more day', which was the Second to the last day, my sister Mrs Maria Talohoula, whom I was staying with at Vara Creek, sternly advised me to remain indoors. I readily accepted her advice for my safety. On the day which was the last day of the countdown, I have had to remain indoors at my sister's residence at Vara Creek for safety. The first day following the last day of the countdown, I returned to work, obviously with much uncertainty and fear. That day went by with no sign of any adverse situation and with no more strange telephone calls.

Perhaps the calls were from a practical joker, but Sir Nathaniel connects these strange phone calls to his first public service position, an offer made several weeks later, as Executive Officer of the Malaita District to be based at Auki. This never eventuated because the Mobil Oil Company persuaded him to stay by raising his salary. Then another public service vacancy arose at Kirakira on Makira, the main town in the central Solomons, which he accepted a few months later, glad to be in his home area. Not many of us would be as frank in revealing such a strange experience but why should it be a premonition about joining the public service?

His dreams are scattered through the text and I am unsure how to deal with them. I find them fascinating and insightful into the character of the man. They reach into a 'Pacific' core that most leaders prefer to ignore. Should they be boxed off or included in the text? I am not qualified to analyse them (nor should I) but I can discern certain Christian and Ulawan characteristics, and a political undertone. My favourite dream title is 'The Best Dream I Ever Had, In My Entire Life Time'. Here is Sir Nathaniel in his own words:

> Only once, in my life-time, have I had such a holy and pleasant dream, which may well have related most probably to my personal leadership. I dreamt on one occasion, that I was walking with one European friend, along the old Honiara Main road. We were at a scene which seemed somewhat, similar to that of the old Mendaña Avenue, and in the seeming vicinity of the now new main market, but in the old setting, although I could not be too sure, as to the precise location. While my friend and I were walking along the road, we saw above us certain floating objects which seemed like gabion baskets, full of stones, which were being loosened and were dropping to the ground, as the baskets were being let open, to allow the stones drop. Fortunately for us, although we were walking along the path of those falling stones, from the baskets, no single stone ever fell on us, as we walked along.
>
> When we got to the point where the present main market facilities are now located, a voice came from above us, which was, in Ulawa language. The voice said this: 'Uure-mwamwanoto', 'Uuwelenga'; which means in English: 'Stand still and Raise your Head'. As soon as my concentration was directed towards the advice of the voice, I noticed at that point, that I was then left on my own. My eyes were fixed to the sky, and as I looked, an object which seemed like the moon, was descending towards me. When it came sufficiently closer to me, I recognised it, to being the moon indeed.
>
> Upon it coming to a stop, an object came down the face of the moon, on completion of which, it formed into a Sword. As soon as the Sword became fully formed, it immediately turned into a Cross. There on that wonderful Cross, the Saviour of Mankind, hung crucified. The Holy Figure, which I dreamt of, was not a dead person. He was indeed real and alive, on the Cross, and had such most pleasant calmness and coolness on his face, as if without pain.
>
> I have never before seen such a wonderful depiction of the crucified Lord and Saviour, the Redeemer of Mankind, and Judge of all Sinners. That particular presentation, which I was especially given in that dream, was so unique. At that point of the dream, I awoke, and immediately woke up my wife Alice, from her sleep, to tell her about that most wonderful dream. Like me, she too was unsure of what the dream meant, and the message it carried. We said a prayer and then went back to sleep. May be

> the words of the psalmist which speak of: 'I will lift up mine eyes unto the hills: from whence cometh my help; My help cometh even from the Lord, who has made heaven and earth'. Psalm121.
>
> On numerous occasions thereafter, I earnestly sought an explanation to the meaning of my special dream, with a number of ordained Anglican Church leaders, whom I approached for their advice or opinion or interpretation, but they were so reluctant or unhelpful to share with me, any such interpretation, which could have helped my mind to settle. It was when I asked the Rev. Fr. George Tara from Uki, (before his death) for his opinion and an interpretation, that, he was able and kind, to give me an interpretation, which made my mind settle. He was an Anglican Priest, who was at the time, the Parish Priest of the Vura Parish. It was him who said to me: the dream was about 'my personal leadership'. He further said that, 'my political leadership was not going to be any easy'. He also said that: 'my own relatives', are going to be 'a difficulty to my leadership'. He then advised me to 'remain firm and closer to Christ', whose leadership quality is like that of the 'coolness of the moon'. He further advised me that, 'as long as I remained faithful to Christ, and solely depended on him: for guidance, inspiration and enlightenment, my leadership would be blessed and strengthened'. To God, be all the Glory and honour, forever and ever. Amen.

Sir Nathaniel then goes on to cite the problems he has had in his political career when his close relatives have stood against him as candidates. In 1993 one of his cousins stood against him, in 1997 four of his nephews stood against him, and in 2001 two of his nephews stood against him. Ulawa's population is quite small: in the 1999 census there were only 31,006 people in Makira-Ulawa Province, only 4,535 of them in the Ulawa-Ugi constituency.[18] It is not unusual for close relatives to stand against each other in the national and provincial electorates. However, clearly Sir Nathaniel feels that he has a prior right to the allegiance of his extended family. His dream, with its Christian overtones, seems to be a justification for his superior position. It is a statement that will be viewed with interest back on Ulawa. The political axe he has to grind has God-given sharpness as revealed his dreams.

> Of all the General Elections I ever contested, the 2001 General Elections were the most difficult of all, and in particular, the one, with most nasty prejudicial experience. That was intentionally filled with unethical encounters, and so many unfounded allegations made against my

---

18 Solomon Islands Government, *Report on the 1999 Population and Housing Census: Analysis* (Honiara 2002), 24; Solomon Islands Government, *Statistical Bulletin 06/2011, Report on the 2009 Population & Housing Census, Basic Tables and Census Description* (Honiara 2011), 7.

entire political career. Much of the things said by the Campaigners for Candidate Chief John Douglas Teaitala, were purely, prejudicial overtures, against my leadership. Although I had achieved strategic major infrastructure projects, such as the Ulawa Circuminsular Road; the Arona Airfield; the Su'umoli Wharf; many Church Buildings; the Primary Schools' Projects; the initiation of establishment of the Pirupiru Community High School; and, the facilitation of the Pirupiru E-Mail Station, all of which got funded: most people on Ulawa, during the 2001 General Elections, denied the existence of all those achievements, despite their physical presence on Ulawa Island. The supporters of Candidate Chief John Douglas Teaitala, who owned vehicles, made certain that, I and my campaign team-members do not have access to hiring of any of their vehicles.

We however did our peaceful campaigns throughout Ulawa on foot. There had sadly been no feelings of appreciation whatsoever by those concerned, for the level of effort I had put into securing the necessary funds needed for the construction of the Ulawa Road Project, which was made possible even under very stiff opposition by persons who did not see value in such pivotal major infrastructure projects, which now wonderfully serve both vehicle-owners together with the general public, who now enjoy riding around Ulawa.

Conclusion

Clearly, I am experiencing some frustration in dealing with Sir Nathaniel's manuscript, and I am uncertain of how to proceed. But I also need to stress that I am enjoying my dealings with Sir Nathaniel. There is something refreshing about his humour, his upfront Melanesianness and his complex justifications of his actions in what most of us would regard as off-beat ways. Both he and Sir Peter are strong Christians, from their quite different denominational perspectives. As a long-time lapsed Christian I am outside this tradition, although from my decades of involvement with Solomon Islanders I have learnt to respect the centrality of religion to Solomon Islanders' worldviews.

There is something very revealing and endearing about Sir Nathaniel's honesty over what many would regard as private experiences and his obscuration of what could be fascinating public political observations. The problem is how to make a book out of all this. In *The Chief's Country* Ben Burt shared authorship with Michael Kwa`iola, but distanced himself a little in explanatory footnotes. This style would not be appropriate for Sir Nathaniel's book. I will have to be more involved than the usual editor and to become an invisible guide, or should

I say ghost? I am reticent to become a co-author, which to me would mean that I accept his interpretations. I would prefer to be the editor, which allows me some level of separation and scepticism. And how do I find time to be his editor given the difficult communications and my other responsibilities? If I was living in Honiara it might be easier, but then I would not have all of the other back-ups provided from living in Australia.

I am sure that *From Ulawa to the Big House: The Life and Times of Sir Nathaniel Rahumaea Waena, GCMG, CSI, KStJ* will be published and become an important addition to the autobiographical literature on the Solomon Islands. Along the way it has made me think deeply about the process involved in turning Pacific Islanders' manuscripts into books. Although the editors of the existing corpus of literature have not been revealing about the editorial processes involved, I suspect that I am not the first to face such problems.

12. Biographies of Post-1900 New Zealand Prime Ministers[1]

Doug Munro

Biography has long had a mixed reputation, hailed by some as the essence of history and by others as an unsatisfactory prism through which to view the past. Despite persistent criticism, the output of political biography remains unabated. In Pacific Islands historiography, a flourishing genre of political auto/biography can be divided into three broad categories: academic biographies; conventional autobiographies; and autobiographies of a different sort, involving Islander author and academic facilitator.[2] The state of political biography in New Zealand, also healthy, is more varied.[3] At the top of the food chain are the prime ministers, many of whom are the subject of one or more book-length biographies (see Table 5). But a monograph is not the only way to do political biography. Prominent in the study of New Zealand prime ministers are edited collections; almost all such volumes originated as conferences involving politicians, public servants, academics, and often family members (see Table 6). There are also a handful of books, usually written for a broad audience, that provide accounts on the lives of various prime ministers,[4] as well as a smattering of journal articles.

---

1   For discussions relating to this chapter I am grateful to Rod Alley and David Grant, and especially to Michael Bassett and Barry Gustafson. I am likewise grateful to Christine O'Brien of Auckland University Press who readily responded to my emails. Although I live in Wellington, I have an adjunct position with the University of Queensland, which has greatly assisted my research and writing.

2   J. Corbett, '"Two Worlds"?: Interpreting Political Leadership Narratives in the 20th-century Pacific', *Journal of Pacific History*, 47: 1 (2012), 6–91; R.M. Keesing, 'Writing Kwaio Life Histories: Issues of Authorship and Politics', *Journal of Narrative and Life History*, 2: 1 (1992), 39–47; C. Moore, 'Noel Fatnowna and His Book: The Making of Fragments of a Lost Heritage', *Journal of Pacific Studies*, 18 (1994–5), 137–50; C. Moore, 'Pacific Islands Autobiography: Personal History and Diplomacy in the Solomon Islands', *Journal of Historical Biography*, 10 (2011), 1–33, available online at www.ufv.ca/jhb/Volume_10/Volume_10_Moore.pdf.

3   For comparable works to the present chapter, see G. Bolton, 'The Art of Australian Political Biography', in T. Arklay, J. Nethercote and J. Wanna (eds), *Australian Political Lives: Chronicling Political Careers* (Canberra, 2006), 1–12; L. Riall, 'The Shallow End of History?: The Substance and Future of Political Biography', *Journal of Interdisciplinary History*, 40:3 (2010), 375–97; R.A.W. Rhodes, 'Theory, Method and British Political Life History', *Political Studies Review*, 10:2 (2012), 161–76; D. MacKenzie, 'Where Character Meets Circumstance: Political Biography in Modern Canada', *Adaciensis*, 42:1 (2013), 182–94.

4   For example, N. McMillan, *Top of the Greasy Pole: New Zealand's Prime Ministers in Recent Times* (Dunedin 1993); K. Eunson, *Mirrors on the Hill: Reflections on New Zealand's Political Leaders* (North Palmerston 2001); I.F. Grant, *Public Lives: New Zealand's Premiers and Prime Ministers, 1856–2003* (Wellington 2003); R. Wolfe, *Battlers, Bluffers and Bully-Boys* (Auckland 2005).

Political biography is multifaceted but the present chapter is narrower in focus. Pragmatically, the constraints on space require a manageable topic so the discussion is confined to book-length biographies of New Zealand prime ministers. The temporal span has also been attenuated. There is certainly an element of approximation in commencing at 1900, especially since the then incumbent Prime Minister, Richard John Seddon (1892–1906), had been in office for seven years and would remain so for another six years. But the choice of date is not altogether arbitrary. Quite simply, a gradual evolution of representative institutions since British annexation in 1840 had solidified by 1900 into the structures and conventions that have largely persisted to this day. A Westminster system of parliamentary democracy, including votes of women, was firmly in place. Of particular importance, provinces were abolished in 1876 and the unstable parliamentary factions of the 1870s and 80s had crystallised into formal political parties that were willing and able to exercise effective party discipline over their MPs. National and international conditions were prone to change but the institutional contexts within which prime ministers operated were entrenched by the turn of the previous century. Subsequent developments, such as the reorganisation of the public service in 1912, with competitive entry and promotion by merit, confirmed the prevailing dispensation.

As might be expected, the earlier biographies of Prime Ministers were products of time and place. They were not works of scholarship, as the term is understood. In the early decades of the twentieth century, the four colleges of the University of New Zealand were small and threadbare. More history was written outside the academy than from within. The history departments comprised two or three members and the teaching centred on Britain and Europe, and resolutely avoided New Zealand history. There was no research culture, although some academics wrote books. When such works dealt with New Zealand, the focus was on political and constitutional history or else nineteenth-century New Zealand history.[5] There was certainly no thought of writing the biography of a prime minister.

---

5   For example, J. Hight and H.D. Bamford, *The Constitutional History and Laws of New Zealand* (Christchurch 1914); J.R. Elder (ed.), *The Letters and Journals of Samuel Marsden, 1765–1838* (Dunedin 1932). For the purpose of this exercise, I have consulted the *Calendars* of the four constituent Colleges of UNZ for the period.

Table 5: New Zealand prime ministers (since 1900) and their biographies

Name	Term in office	Party	Biographies
Richard Seddon†	1893–1906	Liberal	James Drummond, *The Life and Work of Richard John Seddon, Premier of New Zealand, 1893–1906: with a History of the Liberal Party in New Zealand* (Christchurch: Whitcombe & Tombs, 1906), 392. R.M. Burdon, *King Dick: a Biography of Richard John Seddon* (Christchurch: Whitcombe & Tombs, 1955), x, 338. Jean Nichol, *The Totara Tree: a Life of Richard John Seddon* (Nelson: the author, 2006), 109.
William Hall-Jones	1906	Liberal	F.G. Hall-Jones, *Sir William Hall-Jones: the Last of the Old Liberals* (Invercargill: Hall-Jones family, 1969), 152.
Joseph Ward	1906–1912, 1928–1930	Liberal Reform	R.A. Loughnan, *The Remarkable Life Story of Sir Joseph Ward: 40 Years a Liberal* (Wellington: New Century Press, 1929), 234. Michael Bassett, *Sir Joseph Ward: a Political Biography* (Auckland: Auckland University Press, 1993), xi, 330.
Thomas Mackenzie	1912	Liberal	Nil
William Ferguson Massey†	1912–1925	Reform	H.J. Constable, *From Ploughboy to Premier: a New Life of the Right Hon. William Ferguson Massey, PC* (London: John Marlow Savage & Co, 1925), 79. G.H. Scholefield, *The Right Honourable William Fergusson Massey, MP, PC, Prime Minister of New Zealand, 1912–1925: a Personal Biography* (Wellington: Harry H Tombs, 1925), 25. D. Christine Massey, *The Life of the Rt. Hon. WF Massey, PC, LLD: Prime Minister of New Zealand, 1912–1925* (Auckland: the author, 1996), 70. (Reissued 1999, 78.) Bruce Farland, *Farmer Bill: William Ferguson Massey and the Reform Party* (Wellington: the author, 2008), 603.
Francis Bell (stopgap)	1925	Reform	W. Downie Stewart, *The Right Honourable Sir Francis HD Bell: PC, GCMG, KC: his Life and Times* (Wellington: Butterworth, 1937), xviiii, 322.
Joseph Gordon Coates	1925–1928	Reform	Michael Bassett, *Coates of Kaipara* (Auckland: Auckland University Press, 1995), 325pp. Bruce Farland, *Coates' Tale: War Hero, Politician, Statesman, Joseph Gordon Coates, Prime Minister of New Zealand, 1925–1928* (Wellington: the author, 1995), vii, 200.
George Forbes	1930–1935	United	Nil

Name	Term in office	Party	Biographies
Micahel Joseph Savage†	1935–1940	Labour	Barry Gustafson, *From the Cradle to the Grave: a Biography of Michael Joseph Savage* (Auckland: Reed Methuen, 1986), 369. (Republished in Auckland by Penguin, 1988).
Peter Fraser	1940–1949	Labour	James Thorn, *Peter Fraser: New Zealand's Wartime Prime Minister* (London: Oldhams Press, 1952), 288. Michael Bassett with Michael King, *Tomorrow Comes The Song: a Life of Peter Fraser* (Auckland: Penguin, 2000), 445.
Sidney Holland	1949–1957	National	Nil
Keith Holyoake	1957, 1960–72	National	Ross Doughty, *The Holyoake Years* (Feilding: self published, 1977), 274. Barry Gustafson, *Kiwi Keith: a Biography of Keith Holyoake* (Auckland: Auckland University Press, 2007), 429.
Walter Nash	1957–1960	Labour	Keith Sinclair, *Walter Nash* (Auckland: Auckland University Press, 1974/ New York: Oxford University Press, 1974), vii, 439. Craig Mackenzie, *Walter Nash: Pioneer and Prophet* (Palmerston North: Dunmore Press, 1975), 176.
Jack Marshall	1972	National	Nil
Norman Kirk†	1972–1974	Labour	John Dunmore, *Norman Kirk: a Portrait* (Palmerston North: New Zealand Books, 1972), 116. Jim Eagles & Colin James, *The Making of a New Zealand Prime Minister* (Wellington: Cheshire, 1973), 231. David Grant, *The Mighty Totara: the life and times of Norman Kirk* (Auckland, 2014).
Hugh Watt (stopgap)	1974	Labour	Nil
Bill Rowling	1974	Labour	John Henderson, *Rowling: the Man and the Myth* (Auckland: Australia and New Zealand Books Co/ Wellington: Fraser Books, 1981), 210.
Robert Muldoon	1975–1984	National	Spiro Zavos, *The Real Muldoon* (Wellington: Fourth Estate Books, 1978), 234. Barry Gustafson, *His Way: a Biography of Robert Muldoon* (Auckland: Auckland University Press, 2000), x, 545.
David Lange	1984–1989	Labour	Vernon Wright, *David Lange, Prime Minister: a Profile* (Wellington: Port Nicholson Press, 1984), 146. Michael Bassett, *Working with David: Inside the Lange Cabinet* (Auckland: Hodder Moa, 2008), 616.

Name	Term in office	Party	Biographies
Geoffrey Palmer	1989 – 1990	Labour	Raymond Richards, *Palmer: the Parliamentary Years* (Christchurch: Canterbury University Press, 2010), 472.
Mike Moore	1990	Labour	Nil
Jim Bolger	1990 – 1997	National	Nil
Jenny Shipley	1997 – 1999	National	Nil
Helen Clark	1999 – 2008	Labour	Brian Edwards, *Helen: Portrait of a Prime Minister* (Auckland: Exisle, 2001), 352. Denis Welch, *Helen Clark: a Political Life* (Auckland: Penguin, 2009), 240.
John Key	2008 –	National	Nil

† died in office
Source: Author's compilation.

Where academics feared to tread, others were less timorous and the vacant spaces were occupied by journalists, personal friends, political associates and party retainers. The first such effort constitutes what would today be called 'instant history'[6] – a substantial biography of Richard John Seddon, New Zealand's longest serving prime minister by James Drummond, published the year of Seddon's death in 1906.[7] Drummond was a parliamentary reporter who had observed Seddon from the time he was elected in 1879.

Work on the book commenced two years earlier and Seddon had agreed to cooperate. Pressed by his publisher for the completed manuscript, Drummond hoped to accompany Seddon on a holiday voyage to Australia in order to elicit further information, but Seddon asked Drummond to defer until he got back to New Zealand. It was an opportunity lost, because Seddon died on the return voyage. Nonetheless, Drummond in short order produced a book approaching 400 pages of text.

---

6 D. Butler, 'Instant History', *New Zealand Journal of History*, 2: 2 (1968).
7 J. Drummond, *The Life and Work of Richard John Seddon, Premier of New Zealand, 1893–1906: with a History of the Liberal Party in New Zealand* (Christchurch 1906).

Table 6: Edited collections on New Zealand prime ministers

Clark, M. (ed.) 1997, *Sir Keith Holyoake: Towards a Political Biography*, Dunmore Press, Palmerston North.
—— (ed.) 1998, *Peter Fraser: Master Politician, Dunmore Press*, Palmerston North.
—— (ed.) 2001, *Three Labour Leaders: Nordmeyer, Kirk, Rowling*, Dunmore Press, Palmerston North.
—— (ed.) 2003, *Holyoake's Lieutenants, Dunmore Press*, Palmerston North.
—— (ed.) 2004, *Muldoon Revisited, Dunmore Press*, Palmerston North.
—— (ed) 2005, *For the Record: Lange and the Fourth Labour Government*, Dunmore Publishing, Wellington.
—— (ed.) 2008, *The Bolger Years, 1900–1997*, Dunmore Publishing, Wellington.
Watson, J. & Paterson, L. (eds) 2011, *A Great New Zealand Prime Minister?: Reappraising William Ferguson Massey*, University of Otago Press, Dunedin.

The seven volumes edited by Margaret Clark came out of the annual Parliamentary Conferences jointly organised by the Stout Research Centre (Victoria University of Wellington), the Department of Politics and International Relations of Victoria University (VUW), and the Association of Former Parliamentarians. The volume on WF Massey resulted from the Massey@Massey Conference, Massey University, Palmerston North, 2006.
Source: Author's compilation.

Drummond's biography of Seddon is deferential and compendious. In keeping with contemporary conventions, the subject is referred to as 'Mr. Seddon' throughout. Apart from an account of Seddon's childhood and early influences, the book is overwhelmingly a political biography, accounting for Seddon's rise through the ranks, his stock of ideas and, when premier, a running account of his government's legislative achievements and his part in the process. The Liberal Party was a reforming government and Drummond provides detailed chapters on the bursts of social and labour legislation, and the provisions for female suffrage and land tenure that transformed the landscape. It is largely descriptive political biography but there are thematic chapters on Seddon 'The Humanist' (meaning someone 'eager to do something for humanity's sake') and another on how Seddon was represented 'In Cartoon and Story'. Drummond does not pass over the crises and scandals that beset Seddon and his government but he does put the best possible complexion on them. In short, the book is hagiographic, as instanced by the description of Seddon's decision to continue the thrust of his predecessor's policies:

> His success completely changed him. From the day when he was sworn in as Premier he became another man. His mind had broadened when he became a Minister; it expanded further when he became Premier. He said he was no longer merely a party fighter, but the representative of the country as a whole. He recognised that he was the servant of the people, a phrase which he used frequently. At the same time he let it be known that he would not be dominated by any factions. As a private

member, he had denied the right of his leader to gag him in the House. In the same way as Prime Minister he denied the right of any collection of individuals to control his actions or dictate his policy.[8]

For all that, Drummond's *Seddon* is a serious and diligent work containing a good deal of useful and accurate information. It set a reasonable enough benchmark which the next two biographies did not live up to. They followed closely on the death, in 1925, of William Ferguson Massey, the leader of the Reform Party on the conservative side of politics (1912–25). Henry Constable's *From Ploughboy to Premier* has a 'from log cabin to White House' quality about it. The author had already written an equally slight 'romantic history' of New Zealand, and a more hagiographic account than his 10,000–12,000-word biography of Massey could scarcely be imagined:

> Of all the countries lined up for the great struggle which in 1914 and the succeeding years convulsed the world and shook it to its foundations, only one – New Zealand – has not seen a change of government. In a great measure this was due to the fact that the Dominion had been exceedingly fortunate in its choice of a leader, the Right Hon. William Ferguson Massey, P.C., Prime Minister since 1912.
>
> Mr. Massey's services were not confined to New Zealand, however. He was looked up to, honoured and respected throughout the British world. He was deservedly regarded as one of the most trustworthy and dependable statesmen of the Empire.[9]

The second short biography of Massey was published the year of his death. It was an oddly unbalanced short book – a mere 25 pages of closely printed text where much is said about Massey's family background, early parliamentary career and his rise to leader of the opposition of the conservative Reform Party. Less than three pages is devoted to his prime ministership on the less-than-plausible grounds that 'The history of the Massey administration [which commenced in 1912] is too recent to require recapitulation'. To Scholefield, Massey personified courage, loyalty and steadfastness: 'Solidity, staunchness, straightforwardness and honesty have recommended Mr. Massey to the British people wherever he has met them, and through him the Dominion has been represented by the characteristics which most appeal to British people'.[10]

---

8   Ibid., 176.
9   H.J. Constable, *From Ploughboy to Premier: a New Life of the Right Hon. William Ferguson Massey, PC*, (London 1925), 9, 12. See also Constable, *The Romantic History of New Zealand*, with an Introduction by W. F. Massey (London 1924).
10 G.H. Scholefield, *The Right Honourable William Fergusson Massey, MP, PC, Prime Minister of New Zealand, 1912–1925: a Personal Biography* (Wellington 1925), 23.

Scholefield was a journalist, archivist and librarian as well as a trained historian. He had already published the first general history of the Pacific Islands, an undistinguished treatise that originated as a doctoral thesis at the University of London.[11] He would go on, among other things, to publish a book of essays on 12 prime ministers, entitled *Notable New Zealand Statesmen*.[12] But despite an academic training, Scholefield was unable to achieve critical distance from his subjects, and neither did he attempt to. As one assessment has it, Scholefield 'was over-protective of his "notables" so as not to give offence to the living or the dead ... [T]he critical analysis, assessment and reassessment practised by a later generation of professional historians were not his tools of trade'.[13]

These same features are evident in the next three biographies of prime ministers. The first was by R.A. Loughnan, a journalist and former editor of the *New Zealand Times* (which was effectively a mouthpiece of the Liberal Party). His biography of Sir Joseph Ward, in 1929, contains not a whiff of the financial scandal that engulfed Ward during the mid 1890s.[14] William Downie Stewart's 1937 biography of Sir Francis Dillon Bell (who was stopgap Prime Minister in 1925) treats the subject as a secular saint.[15] It too is full of verbatim transcriptions of speeches, letters and parliamentary debates, often replete with vacuous pieties. Trade unionist and Labour Party functionary James Thorn largely avoided these faults but his 1952 informative biography of Peter Fraser suffered a double disability.[16] First, many of the people who could have talked about Fraser's earlier years had died. Second, the biography was written too soon after Fraser's death to be other than devoutly respectful. Although Fraser (1940–49) does not appear in the one-dimensional vein that Massey and Ward did at the hands of their respective biographers, Thorn's study nonetheless tends toward veneration.

---

11 G.H. Scholefield, *The Pacific: its Past and Future, and the Policy of the Great Powers from the Eighteenth Century* (London 1919). See also D. Shineberg, 'The Early Years of Pacific History', *Journal of Pacific Studies*, 20 (1996), 3–4.

12 G. Scholefield, *Notable New Zealand Statesmen: Twelve Prime Ministers* (Christchurch 1946).

13 F. Porter, 'Scholefield, Guy Hardy, 1877–1963', *Dictionary of New Zealand Biography. Te Ara – the Encyclopedia of New Zealand*, available online at www.TeAra.govt.nz/mi/biographies/4s12/scholefield-guy-hardy. All the Prime Ministers and many other individuals named in this chapter can be looked up online in the *Dictionary of New Zealand Biography*. Scholefield destroyed what was left of his reputation in the early 1960s when it came to light that his edited publication of the correspondence between two prominent New Zealand families was marred by numerous errors of transcription and, worse, that he had defaced the originals with annotations in ink and deletions in crayon. W.H. Oliver, 'The Richmond-Atkinson Papers', *Landfall*, 17: 2 (1963), 177–87.

14 R.A. Loughnan, *The Remarkable Life Story of Sir Joseph Ward: 40 Years a Liberal* (Wellington 1929).

15 W. Downie Stewart, *The Right Honourable Sir Francis H.D. Bell: P.C., G.C.M.G., K.C: his Life and Times* (Wellington 1937).

16 J. Thorn, *Peter Fraser: New Zealand's Wartime Prime Minister* (London 1952).

Until the early 1950s, the biographies of New Zealand prime ministers were characteristically works of piety. These tactful and decorous accounts were typified in the original *Dictionary of New Zealand Biography* (1940), which was mostly written by Scholefield. As another historian said that 'our Dr Scholefield is not the man to soil a tomb with ambiguous flowers; he lays the pure lily; no weed of criticism enters into his wealth; our Great it seems are all Good, or if not good then Misunderstood'.[17] In this they mirrored the national and regional histories of the times which, with little exception, were cheerleading narratives of progress and virtue.[18] They were also based on inadequate research. It was only in 1955, with the publication of Randall Burdon's biography of Seddon, that the first such biography with a semblance of academic rigour appeared.[19] Burdon was a lawyer by training but had taken up full-time historical research. He had already, inter alia, written a biography of Sir Julius Vogel, a nineteenth-century prime minister, and would go on to publish a history of New Zealand between the world wars, his *magnum opus*.[20] Where Burdon departed from his predecessors – with the ironic exception of James Drummond – was that he attempted to come to grips with the political processes and to discuss the mechanics of policy-making as well as the ensuing legislation, and to recognise the importance of leadership rather than simply taking it for granted.

As mentioned, the high-minded panegyrics that had passed for political biography prior to Burdon's *King Dick* were, in part, a reflection of the times: tactful and decorous biographies were the order of the day. They are also a reflection of the state of the historical profession in New Zealand where relatively few historians were university trained – although this was no guarantee of quality, as Scholefield demonstrates. To compound existing problems, the sources for political biography were difficult of access thanks to the dishevelled, dispersed and under-resourced state of the National Archives.[21] As Burdon complained, researchers 'were not encouraged' to consult the records kept at Government House.[22] Change was already afoot, however. An expansion of university enrolments from the late 1940s resulted from ex-servicemen receiving rehabilitation scholarships to embark on, or complete, tertiary study. This, in turn, resulted in the growth of the history departments, and the greater numbers of qualified teaching staff led to the increasing professionalisation of New Zealand

---

17 Quoted in T. Beaglehole, *A Life of J.C. Beaglehole: the New Zealand Scholar* (Wellington 2006), 276.
18 An exception is J.C. Beaglehole, *New Zealand: a Short History* (London 1936).
19 R.M. Burdon, *King Dick: a Biography of Richard John Seddon* (Christchurch 1955). See the reviews by P.J. O'Farrell, *Landfall*, 9:1 (1956), 48–52; Michael Turnbull, *Political Science*, 8:1 (1956), 85–89.
20 R.M. Burdon, *Sir Julius Vogel* (Christchurch 1948); R.M. Burdon, *The New Dominion: a Social and Political History of New Zealand, 1918–39*, (Wellington 1965).
21 See J.C. Beaglehole, 'Why Archives?', *New Zealand Journal of Public Administration*, 15: 1 (1952), 9–16; A.G. Bagnall, 'The Historical Perspective', *Archifacts*, 7: 8 (1978), 5–11.
22 Burdon, *King Dick*, 322.

historiography.²³ In an associated development, hard-nosed professionals were urging more rigorous approaches to the study of history involving detailed archival research, a critical evaluation of sources and the proper preservation and management of archives.²⁴ This conjunction of influences saw a burgeoning of scholarly historical monographs and decent general histories from the early 1950s.²⁵ A related, although delayed, development was the establishment of political science departments in the universities. For many years, the only such department was at Victoria University College but after 1964 the three other universities took political science on board. The country's only specialist journal (*Political Science*) was established in 1947 and until the 1970s published many articles by historians on themes relating to political and labour history.²⁶

The scene was thus set for scholarly political biography to emerge, as it did in the 1960s with biographies of William Pember Reeves (Minister of Labour in the Seddon government and Agent-General in London), Harry Holland (Labour Party leader in opposition in the 1920s and early 1930s), and John A. Lee (Labour Party maverick).²⁷ The emergence of scholarly works by academics did nothing to prevent others from writing political biography. Limiting the discussion to Prime Ministers, family members wrote slight biographies of William Hall-Jones and W.F. Massey, both privately published, that recalled the hagiographic 'men of achievement' type works of a bygone age.²⁸ In one case a neighbour wrote a touching homily of the Labour Prime Minister Walter Nash.²⁹ Enterprising journalists and freelance writers added their might with hurriedly written works, usually of reasonable quality in the circumstances, timed for the

---

23 The changing face of New Zealand historiography can be traced in C. Hilliard, *Island Shores: the Writing of New Zealand History, 1920–1940*, M.A. thesis (Auckland 1997); G. Young, *The War of Intellectual Independence: New Zealand Historians and Their History*, M.A. thesis (Auckland 1998).
24 For example, K. Sinclair, *The Maori Land League: an Examination into the Source of a Historical Myth*, (Auckland 1950), 3; J.C. Beaglehole, 'The New Zealand Scholar', in P. Munz (ed.), *The Feel of Truth* (Wellington 1969), 51.
25 For contemporary assessments of New Zealand historiography, see T.G. Wilson, 'The Writing of New Zealand History', *Landfall*, 8: 4 (1957), 213–33; K. Sinclair, 'New Zealand', in R.W. Winks (ed.),*The Historiography of the British Empire-Commonwealth: Trends, Interpretations, Resources* (Durham 1966), 174–96.
26 W.J. Gardner, 'The Rise of W. F. Massey, 1891–1912', *Political Science*, 13: 1 (1961), 3–30; W.J. Gardner, 'W. F. Massey in Power, 1912–1925', *Political Science*, 13: 2 (1961), 3–30; P.S. O'Connor, 'Some Political Preoccupations of Mr Massey, 1918–20', *Political Science*, 18: 2 (1966), 16–38; P.S. O'Connor, 'The Stout-Sedden Precedence Controversy', *Political Science*, 22: 2 (1970), 2-22.
27 K. Sinclair, *William Pember Reeves: New Zealand Fabian* (Oxford 1965); P.J. O'Farrell, *Harry Holland: Militant Socialist* (Canberra 1964); E. Olssen, *John A. Lee* (Dunedin 1977). The latter was originally presented as an MA thesis in 1965.
28 F.G. Hall-Jones, *Sir William Hall-Jones: the Last of the Old Liberals*, privately published (Invercargill 1969); D.C. Massey, *The Life of the Rt. Hon. W.F. Massey P.C., L.L.D: Prime Minster of New Zealand, 1912–1925*, privately published (Auckland 1996).
29 C. Mackenzie, *Walter Nash: Pioneer and Prophet* (Palmerston North 1975). A neighbourly biography is not as surprising as it might sound in this particular case. As Nash's principal biographer has pointed out, '[he] had few, if any, intimates who were in politics, after he became a minister. (His closest friends were neighbours.)' Keith Sinclair, *Walter Nash* (Auckland 1976), 257–58.

aftermath of a general election.³⁰ One of them, however – a biography of Helen Clark (1999–2008) – takes verbal slapstick to new levels with passages such as: 'Labour staggered away from the 1990 election like a groggy boxer who's been too long on the ropes'.³¹ A little later we read:

> Whatever the mission statement, Labour wasn't so much a party for the first half of 1990 as a permanent political identity crisis; no matter how hard it tried to mow its front lawn and look respectable to the neighbours, there was the dreadful pong in the back yard from the decaying corpse of Rogernomics [the package by which the Fourth Labour Government restructured the economic, named after its chief architect Roger Douglas]. At the next annual conference, in September 1991, Moore [Mike Moore, former Prime Minister] tried to bury it once and for all by declaring 'Rogernomics has had its day' and 'New Zealand must move on'; but it came across like Dracula saying he'd lost his taste for necks.³²

This particular work, by a journalist who had twice stood for Parliament, is based on interviews, newspaper sources and a smattering of secondary sources. It cannot be described as scholarly or having academic merit. But the boundaries between academic and non-academic work are blurred, as demonstrated by an earlier biography of Helen Clark, published in 1991, in Clark's first term as Prime Minister.³³ The biographer, Brian Edwards, had made a career in television journalism but had a doctorate in German literature and was originally a lecturer at the University of Canterbury.³⁴ He had close links with the Labour Party and used his contacts to good effect in his interviews for the book. Although writing a sympathetic account for a popular audience and, despite consulting a limited range of written sources, the academic in Edwards unobtrusively emerges. The academic/non-academic dichotomy is also blurred by the works of Bruce Farland, a former secondary school teacher with a Master's degree in history.³⁵ His substantial biography of W.F. Massey takes issue with the stereotypes of Massey as a mindless imperialist and bigoted Protestant but is relentlessly descriptive and concludes with full-throated diatribes against

---

30 J. Eagles and C. James, *The Making of a New Zealand Prime Minister* (Wellington 1973); V. Wright, *David Lange, Prime Minister: a Profile* (Wellington 1984).
31 D. Welch, *Helen Clark: a Political Life* (Auckland 2009), 125.
32 Ibid, 127.
33 B. Edwards, *Helen: Portrait of a Prime Minister* (Auckland 2001).
34 B. Edwards, *Public Eye* (Wellington 1971).
35 Published in 1995 as *Coates' Tale: War Hero, Politician, Statesman, Joseph Gordon Coates, Prime Minister of New Zealand, 1925–1928*, the author, Wellington.

historians who have given Massey a bad press.[36] It is not that Farland is a hard-pressed journalist facing a deadline. Rather, he had time at his disposal and, despite a dearth of personal papers, nonetheless confined his research to newspapers, the *Parliamentary Debates*, and to a lesser extent parliamentary papers (the *Appendix to the Journals of the House of Representatives*).

The academic/non-academic dichotomy also breaks down in the cases of the shorter biographies of Norman Kirk (1972–74), Bill Rowling (1974–75) and Robert Muldoon (1975–84) that were written during their subjects' lifetimes. In the lead-up to the 1972 election, which returned the Labour Party to power after a 12-year wilderness, John Dunmore, an academic who was active in the Labour Party organisation, wrote a brief biography of Norman Kirk that could be unkindly, although not altogether inaccurately, described as an extended election brochure. The hagiographic tone is set by the opening statement: 'The first full-length [sic] biography of the man who, within eight years of entering Parliament, became Leader of the Opposition and the youngest leader of the Labour Party since its foundation in 1916'.[37] By contrast, in 1978, Spiro Zavos published *The Real Muldoon*, after Robert Muldoon returned the National Party to power in 1975. Although marred by numerous factual errors, it is a penetrating work by a venturesome journalist with postgraduate degrees to his name. No one was neutral about the abrasive and divisive Muldoon, and Zavos was hardly a supporter. Muldoon's appearance, together with his belligerent political style, earned him the nickname 'Piggy Muldoon', or sometimes just 'The Pig'. On one occasion, although severely provoked, he punched a demonstrator and then chased a group of them 'down the street allegedly calling out to them "one at a time and you're welcome"'.[38] Muldoon was into the third year of his reign when Zavos was writing his 'instant history'. Assisted by the research of fellow journalist Denis Wederell (who abandoned a biography of Muldoon), and not overlooking the less attractive side of his subject, Zavos countered the unrelenting (and often justified) criticisms of Muldoon's political opponents to provide what a later biographer described as 'astute overall assessment'.[39]

---

36   B. Farland, *Farmer Bill: William Ferguson Massey and the Reform Party*, privately published (Wellington 2008). Compare the nuanced discussion by Eric Olssen, 'Towards a Reassessment of W.F. Massey: One of New Zealand's Greatest Prime Ministers (arguably)', in James Watson and Lachy Paterson (eds), *A Great New Zealand Prime Minister?: Reappraising William Ferguson Massey* (Dunedin, 2011), 15–30.
37   J. Dunmore, *Norman Kirk: a Portrait* (Palmerston North 1972), 1. See also Dunmore, *I Remember Tomorrow: an Autobiography* (Waikanae, 1998), 149. Dunmore was Professor of French at Massey University and the historian of French exploration in the Pacific Islands.
38   B. Gustafson, *His Way: a Biography of Robert Muldoon* (Auckland 2000), 148 and photo opposite, 182.
39   S. Zavos, *The Real Muldoon* (Wellington 1978); Gustafson, *His Way*, 153–55, 528.

Of a somewhat different order is John Henderson's short biography of Bill Rowling. Rowling had the misfortune of stepping into the prime ministerial shoes upon the untimely death of Norman Kirk in 1974.[40] No one could have replaced a man of Kirk's stature and the diminutive Rowling was the butt of unfavourable comparisons, in particular that he was a weak and ineffectual leader. Muldoon, at that point the Leader of the Opposition, was vocal in his denigrating of Rowling's political standing but it transpires that the individual who led the charge from behind the scenes was the former Prime Minister Keith Holyoake (by then a member of the Muldoon cabinet), who insisted that:

> the Labour leader, although 'a nice little bloke', should be dismissed as 'not impressive' and as a 'schoolboy in a man's job'. He repeatedly urged his colleagues to 'laugh at Rowling. We've got to brand him as an inoffensive and ineffectual Prime Minister'. He demanded that … National MPs remember that … 'Rowling is a disaster'.[41]

The smears stuck. The immediate upshot was the formation of Citizens for Rowling, a campaign mounted in the lead-up to the 1975 election that sought both to bolster Rowling's public image and to attack Muldoon's leadership style.[42] But to no avail: Labour was defeated at the election and Rowling had a prolonged and disheartening time as Leader of the Opposition until being ignominiously replaced by David Lange in 1983. Henderson was very loyal to Rowling, as he later was to Lange. His biography of the former is unabashedly affectionate and avowedly sets out to rehabilitate a fallen reputation. He does so not as a Labour Party functionary but '[a]s a political scientist with a particular interest in political leadership'. When dealing with political biography, in other words, it is better to simply assess the product than to be influenced by such labels as 'academic' and 'non-academic'.

The question of motivation explains why some prime ministers and not others receive the accolade of a biography. Clearly, an individual's perceived stature will have a bearing. It is also the case that very recent prime ministers are less likely to be the subject of a biography, although exceptions readily come to mind (Muldoon and Clark), and that the political left is more likely to attract biography than the political right. But it requires explanation why certain prime ministers have yet to find their biographer — why they are non-starters or have been consigned to a no-go zone. It could be argued that all the good ones have been snapped up and the example of George Forbes (1930–35) lends credence to this observation. Arguably the least distinguished of New Zealand's twentieth-century prime ministers, Forbes was described by one historian as the

---

40 J. Henderson, *Rowling: the Man and the Myth* (Wellington 1981).
41 Gustafson, *His Way*, 360.
42 K.P. Clements, 'Citizens for Rowling Campaign: an Insider's View', *Political Science*, 28: 2 (1976), 81–96.

'Canterbury farmer who had been successful in spending a lengthy period in Parliament without giving rise to the suspicion that he would one day lead it',[43] and his government stands condemned for heartlessly mismanaging the social impact of the Great Depression. It stands to reason that no aspiring political biographer wants to touch him. Less explicable is why Sidney Holland (1947–57) has yet to receive a biography. His significance in remaking the conservative side of politics can scarcely be overestimated. It was his drive and ambition during the 1940s that turned the National Party into the force that enabled it to govern New Zealand for most of the second half of the twentieth century. But his repellent personality and his destructive decline at the tail end of his prime ministership have resulted in him becoming an especially despised individual whom no one seemingly wants to touch.[44] It has been 'unkindly noted' of National Prime Minister Jenny Shipley (1997–99) 'that publishers have not exactly been clamouring for her memoirs, despite the fact that she still has a stash of official papers locked away in a container which, she mischievously hints, contain some interesting nuggets indeed'. Neither have biographers been queuing on her doorstep.[45]

What motivates a biographer to choose one prime minister rather than another – or to write political biography at all – is less a matter of the stature of a particular prime minister and more a function of the chance event that someone is prepared to sink the time and effort into such a venture. There is a definite element of serendipity as to why some prime ministers are chosen and others are not. It can be quite a pragmatic, even an aberrant decision, as in the case of Raymond Richards embarking on Geoffrey Palmer's biography. Richards was hired by his alma mater, the University of Waikato, as an Americanist, but was unable to get funding for research into American history. Very reluctantly he turned to New Zealand history and decided upon a biography of Palmer, whose 'fingerprints' were all over the fourth Labour Government.[46]

---

43 Beaglehole, *New Zealand*, 89. See also M. Bassett, *Coates of Kaipara* (Auckland 1995), 174–75, 232.
44 The historian Bill Oliver fondly recalls that he first considered giving his obituary on Holland the title 'Death of a Salesman', but he 'chickened out at the last moment'. W.H. Oliver, *Looking for the Phoenix: a Memoir* (Wellington 2001), 107; W.H. Oliver, 'Sir Sydney [sic] Holland', *Comment*, 9 (1961), 4–6. Holland's decline is recounted in B. Gustafson, *Kiwi Keith: a Biography of Keith Holyoake* (Auckland 2007), 89–92. Holland prepared notes as an *aide-memoire* for an intended autobiography, but his declining health stalled the project. See R. Doughty, *The Holyoake Years* (Feilding 1977), 4–5. Had the memoirs been written they would have been the first autobiography by a New Zealand Prime Minister.
45 K. Scherer, 'The Prime of Mrs Jenny Shipley', *New Zealand Herald*, 4 February 2008.
46 D. Munro, 'Writing the Biography of Geoffrey Palmer: Interview with Raymond Richards', *History Now*, 8: 4 (2002), 2–4; R. Richards, *Palmer: the Parliamentary Years* (Christchurch 2010).

More commonly the decision to write a particular prime minister's biography is more purposeful, as in the cases of Barry Gustafson and Michael Bassett, the two most prolific biographers of New Zealand prime ministers.[47] Both were students at the University of Auckland in the late 1950s/early 60s, and both were politically active. Gustafson was a Labour Party activist before switching to the National Party; Bassett was a member of the Third Labour Government (1972–75). Re-elected to Parliament in 1978, and a Cabinet Minister in the fourth Labour Government (1984–90), he was a wholehearted supporter of the neo-liberal economic restructuring and he too subsequently shifted to the political right.

Neither Bassett nor Gustafson set out to be political biographers but early inklings were there, particularly with Bassett, who recalls taking an interest in the 1946 election at the age of eight. He was always interested in politics and the only history taught at university level in the 1950s was political history. He had suggested a biography of J.G. Ward (1906–12, 1928–30) for his M.A. thesis. Told that the Ward Papers had been destroyed, he settled to write about the 1951 waterfront dispute.[48] Becoming a Member of Parliament in 1972, Bassett was fascinated in the ways that political leaders 'controlled the scene, how they were successful and what caused problems'. This, in turn, aroused a fascination 'in how people got to the top, how they stayed there, and what they achieved'. The initial impetus to write political biography, however, was quite accidental. The 1981 cliffhanger election resulted in National being returned with a majority of one, thanks to support from the Social Credit Party. The Leader of the Opposition (Rowling), thinking that this was unprecedented, thus prompted Bassett to write a small book showing that political uncertainty of this kind was common enough in New Zealand political history.[49] This led Bassett back to Ward, his original proposal for an M.A. thesis topic. There may have been a dearth of personal papers but he now knew where official records were and he located material in the keeping of the Ward family. An added motivation for choosing Ward was, like Palmer, the prevalence of his 'fingerprints' – or as Bassett puts it:

> He was [quite apart from his contribution to Liberal Government policies] the one constant factor in New Zealand's political life in the period 1890-1921, where his irrepressible ambition obliged every other

---

47 The following discussion is largely based on telephone interviews with Michael Bassett (25 February 2013) and Barry Gustafson (4 March 2013).
48 Published in 1972 as *Confrontation '51: the 1951 Waterfront Dispute*, Wellington. See also M. Bassett, 'In Search of Sir Joseph Ward', *New Zealand Journal of History*, 21: 1 (1987), 112–24.
49 M. Bassett, *Three Party Politics in New Zealand, 1911–31* (Auckland 1982).

major player to keep a wary eye on his movements .... Ward's continuing presence on stage [was] like a piece of sturdy antique furniture around which the rest of the cast were forced to shuffle.[50]

Ward led on to a biography of Gordon Coates (1925–28). Bassett's interest in political leadership and his respect for strong leadership are apparent: 'My book is certainly no work of devotion. Coates had many personal strengths, but lacked that ruthless streak without which Prime Ministers seldom succeed'.[51]

Bassett did not confine his scholarly writing to biography but his next biographical assignment came as a result of his previous biographical work. Sir Alister McIntosh, the former head of the Prime Minister's Department, intended to write Peter Fraser's biography as a retirement project, but by then his health was not up to the task. He enlisted Michael King's assistance in the late 1970s but a few years later King suffered a lengthy illness and the project went into abeyance. Bassett was eventually asked to take over and the book was published in 2000.[52] Most recently, Bassett has written about David Lange. Although not strictly speaking a biography – it is as much about the fourth Labour Government and contains considerable autobiographical material – but it may be regarded as a biography for the purposes of this exercise.[53]

Gustafson's trajectory moved along broadly similar lines to Bassett's. When discussing a M.A. thesis topic, Gustafson suggested the first Labour Prime Minister Michael Savage (1935–40) as one possibility, but his advisers declined. Their attitude was that it was a non-topic on the grounds that Savage was simply the front man for Peter Fraser, who provided all the ideas, and Walter Nash, who did all the work. He settled instead for a thesis on the foundation of the Labour Party[54] and discovered that Savage was more significant than his advisers realised. After writing a booklet for secondary school use on Savage in 1968,[55] and once other projects were completed, Gustafson proceeded on a full-scale biography of Savage, published in 1986.[56] He did not intend to write another political biography but when he switched allegiances to the National Party

---

50 M. Bassett, *Sir Joseph Ward: a Political Biography* (Auckland 1993), vii–viii.
51 Bassett, *Coates of Kaipara*, 4. The prominent public servant W.B. Sutch, who was a member of Coates's 'brains trust' during the Depression years, embarked on a biography and had written six chapters by the time of his death in 1975. Sutch's research material and the chapters are in the Sutch Papers, 93-244-14, Alexander Turnbull Library, Wellington.
52 M. Bassett and M. King, *Tomorrow Comes The Song: a Life of Peter Fraser*, (Auckland 2000). The early start enabled King to interview Fraser's surviving contemporaries and family members. Most of these interviews would not have been possible by the time Bassett entered the scene. Moreover, the paucity of personal papers meant that the interviews were crucial to the eventual biography.
53 M. Bassett, *Working with David: Inside the Lange Cabinet* (Auckland 2008).
54 Published in 1980 as *Labour's Path to Political Independence: the Origins and Establishment of the New Zealand Labour Party*.
55 B. Gustafson, *Michael Joseph Savage* (Wellington 1968).
56 B. Gustafson, *From the Cradle to the Grave: a Biography of Michael Joseph Savage* (Auckland 1986).

and wrote its silver jubilee history, the interest in people as historical subjects returned. For one thing, he had formed views on Holyoake and Muldoon that were different from public perceptions. For another, there were biographies of Labour leaders, the most recent being a biography of Walter Nash (1957–60),[57] but nothing at that point on the National prime ministers. He was therefore receptive to Muldoon's invitation to write his biography on a 'warts-and-all' basis with complete access to Muldoon's personal archive.[58] One thing led to another: Gustafson then had thrust upon him the mantle of de facto National Party biographer-in-residence, was urged by senior party members 'to get on to Holyoake', and an invitation from the family was forthcoming.

The foregoing discussion might give the impression that the academic biographies of prime ministers effortlessly rolled out in majestic sequence. The reality is different. Surprise was expressed in 1997 that there was no sign on the horizon of a 'full and authoritative biography' of Holyoake: 'the family are keen and co-operative and the archives extensive and accessible'.[59] First, someone had to be willing and able to undertake such a sizeable commitment, and Gustafson eventually took up the family's request that he embark on the project. In 1999 Michael Bassett said of Kirk, 'He is a complex figure worthy of a big study. If I was only fifty instead of sixty, I would be tempted to tackle him'.[60] Fifteen years later, justice was done with the appearance of David Grant's biography of Kirk, and David Welch is working on another one.[61] Bassett also mentioned in 1999 that there were 50 years of New Zealand twentieth-century political life without a substantial biography of the prime minister of the day.[62] The actual figure was closer to 65 years. By my count that figure has been reduced to 40 years, largely through the efforts of Gustafson and Bassett. New Zealand historical biography would be impoverished but for the chance happening of these two individuals committing themselves to multiple biographies.

But quantity is never sufficient in itself. What impresses about the academic biographies, first, is the sheer extent of the research – a far cry from the lazy days of the 1920s and 1930s. It is not altogether correct that real lives are lived going forwards, not knowing what will come next, while the process of biography works in reverse. If that were so, then there would be no need for research. To the contrary, while many things are known in advance, the lived life still has to be unravelled by the biographer and this requires close and detailed research. Gustafson going to Australia to research Savage's early life and Bassett diligently tracking down material on Ward are but two examples of the increasing

---

57 K. Sinclair, *Walter Nash* (Auckland 1976).
58 Gustafson, *His Way*, 1–3.
59 M. Clark (ed.), *Sir Keith Holyoake: Towards a Political Biography* (Palmerston North 1997), 10.
60 T. Burnard, 'Bassett Tackles the State: the Politician as Historian', *History Now*, 5: 1 (1999), 8.
61 David Grant, *The Mighty Totara: the life and times of Norman Kirk* (Auckland 2014).
62 Ibid.

intensity of such research. To the official government publications and the newspaper sources that satisfied a previous generation of biographers are now added personal papers, party records, the files of government departments and interviews. There is an enormous amount of material. Raymond Richards was given access to 235 linear metres of Geoffrey Palmer's papers.[63] In Gustafson's case, the interview material from previous biographies is often pressed into service for his current project. Improved technology has also meant that television and radio broadcasts are available in ways they were not before. Consequently, the biographies of New Zealand prime ministers are getting bigger, without yet attaining the stretch limousine proportions of the multi-volume biographies of Lyndon Johnson and some other United States presidents.[64]

The expanding conception of the biographer's task also results in more satisfying books. The biographies are no longer devotional but they are almost always written by party faithful and true believers. An exception is Richards. Although generally sympathetic, he is by no means uncritical of Palmer, pointing out his leadership limitations and the ruthlessness with which Palmer rushed through his legislative program, which contradicted his principled earlier stance against the excesses of executive authority.[65] The academic biographers would probably agree with Gustafson that the objective is to present the life 'as honestly and accurately as one can'.[66] Truth, of course, is that elusive beacon on the hill, and in this case the journey is more important than the destination – namely, fairness to people, to situations and to the evidence. That is evident in Bassett's biography-of-sorts of David Lange, which must have been difficult to write considering their eventual falling out. But Bassett does capture the thrills and spills of 'working with David' – his enormous talent, the egregious flaws, and the negative influence, eventually, of Margaret Pope who became Lange's wife.[67] Lange's accident-proneness was also captured by the head of his office, Gerald Hensley:

> As the months turned into years ... the suspicion grew that in some mysterious way David Lange contributed to the general uncertainty.

---

63   Richards, *Palmer*, 7.
64   The automobile imagery is taken from M. Kammen, 'Teach Us Our Recollections', *Reviews in American History*, 29: 2 (2001), 183–91.
65   Richards, *Palmer*, 382–401, (ch. 20: 'The Court of History').
66   Gustafson, *His Way*, 12. Few political biographers would innocently say: 'My philosophy of history is extremely simple: I am interested in finding out what happened, not in perpetuating theories, myths or party ideologies; I do not attempt to justify any preconceived personal theory; and whatever conclusions I might arrive at emerge from what I discovered during my researches. Historical truth is too important to be distorted by historians' stubbornly held personal or political opinions, and too much New Zealand historical writing, from William Pember Reeves to Keith Sinclair (and even beyond), has been devalued by them'. E. Bohan, *Burdon: a Man of our Time* (Christchurch 2004), 10–11. Burdon was a National Party cabinet minister in the 1990s.
67   Bassett, *Working with David*. Margaret Pope presents her side of the story in M. Pope, *At the Turning Point: My Political Life with David Lange* (Auckland 2011).

He was a sort of political poltergeist: a restless and perhaps unhappy spirit around whom strange things happened, the equivalent of pictures falling off walls and objects rising from the table.[68]

Gustafson also said that 'No biographer can be completely sure that he has captured the whole truth. Indeed I believe no one can'.[69] And he frankly admits that certain aspects of his biography of Muldoon would have been different had he known at the time what he discovered post-publication.[70] Although stressing how brutal and aggressive Muldoon could be, I do not believe that Gustafson quite managed to convey the menace of the man. On the other hand, I am not alone in feeling that *Kiwi Keith* 'completely changed my view of the man and the contribution he made to New Zealand's society, economy, and foreign policies during his 1960 to 1972 tenure as prime minister under a National Party government'.[71] Holyoake was *far* more than the pompous ass of legend.

For all that, Gustafson does not shy away from depicting Holyoake's ruthless streak. His maneouvering in 1940, as Gustafson puts it, was 'not entirely altruistic'. Holyoake had lost his marginal seat in the previous election and as a condition of standing for election once again he demanded a safe electorate, and, furthermore, that the party machine arrange for the funding for the purchase of a farm as his new place of abode. He was holding his party to ransom with the veiled threat that he had been offered the parliamentary leadership of the newly formed People's Movement, whose mobilisation would have split the right-wing vote.[72] Gustafson also deals with Holyoake's role as a partner in a property at Kinlock in the central North Island. Gustafson recognises that Holyoake exerted improper influence in having a road built to the property at government expense, the effect of which was to enable profitable subdivision. More recently it has been demonstrated that the construction of the access road and the alienation of adjoining Maori land involved far more serious breaches of propriety than depicted by Gustafson.[73] Holyoake's determination not to bow out of politics is also adversely commented on. He was reluctant to stand down as prime minister and only did so when it became apparently that the National Party was unlikely to win the 1972 election. In effect, his successor received a 'hospital pass', in the same way Holyoake had in 1957 when Holland's delayed retirement gave him too little time before the upcoming election. Even then Holyoake refused

---

68   G. Hensley, *Final Approaches: a Memoir* (Auckland 2006), 293–94.
69   Gustafson, *His Way*, 12.
70   B. Gustafson, 'A Postscript to *His Way*', *Political Science*, 53: 1 (2001), 48–55.
71   See reviews by L. Bryder, *Journal of Historical Biography*, 5 (2009), 128–31; D. Munro, *Journal of Pacific History*, 43: 3 (2008), 404–05.
72   Gustafson, *Kiwi Keith*, 36–41. Gustafson also provides a corrective. An earlier biographer asserted that Holyoake was asked by the party to stand for a different seat but had no idea about the party arranging for the purchase of the farm. Doughty, *The Holyoake Years*, 82–83.
73   Gustafson, *Kiwi Keith*, 36–41, 82–85; P. Hamer, 'Kiwi Keith at Kinloch: a Closer Look at Holyoake's "proudest achievement"', *New Zealand Journal of History*, 44:2 (2010), 157–73.

to retire from parliamentary life. Instead he became an uncomfortable presence in the shadow cabinet; and when he finally did retire from parliament he was controversially appointed, at his own request, as Governor-General. He hung around far too long.[74]

People have strong views on who makes the best sort of political biographer and when the time is right for a particular biography to be attempted is a moot point. Michael Bassett is adamant that political experience is a prerequisite and points out, with respect to his biography of Ward, that 'My … ministerial experience gave me insights that no backbencher can ever gain. *Ward* is a miles better book than the early drafts, due to my much greater appreciation by 1990 of the way the system works'.[75] There is also often a feeling that a certain (always unspecified) time should elapse before a biography is attempted. In the case of Muldoon, one reviewer of *His Way* felt that '[i]ts appearance [in 2000] is appropriate. The hate factor has died down. Moreover, Muldoon can be assessed in the broader context of what has followed him'.[76] Having contact with the subject and his or her family is certainly helpful to the biographer in providing information and insights but it can also create complications. Gustafson was berated post-publication by Dame Thea Muldoon for his comment that Muldoon had come from 'the wrong side of the tracks': this was described as 'an insult to the family'.[77] The help given by subject and family can certainly restrain and even compromise a biographer, but it can also work the other way. Richards had absolutely no obstruction from Palmer. Palmer expressed surprise when approached by Richards but made all his papers and asked for a warts-and-all biography. He did not ask to see chapter drafts and neither was he shown any. At the book launch in November 2010, two weeks after publication, Palmer still hadn't read the book, to the astonishment of those present that someone could be so remarkably unconcerned at what had been written about him. Biographers dream of such latitude and it speaks volumes for Geoffrey Palmer that he more or less said, 'Write your book as though I am not going to read it'.[78]

Another point is that the recent academic biographies are narrative rather than analytical, or should I say that the analysis is embedded in the narrative. It is an attraction and an advantage that political biography is actually readable while at the same time becoming increasingly academic in research and footnoting. What this means is that the language of political science is eschewed and, for example, while models and theories of political leadership might inform the narrative,

---

74 Gustafson, *Kiwi Keith*, chs. 17–18.
75 Burnard, 'Bassett Tackles the State', 6.
76 K.R. Howe, review (of *His Way*, by Barry Gustafson), in *New Zealand Journal of History*, 35: 2 (2001), 244.
77 Gustafson, 'A Postscript to *His* Way', 54.
78 In his subsequent autobiography, Palmer acknowledged the extent of Richards' research, but barely mentions his biography again, explaining that he wished to tell his own story. G. Palmer, *Reform: a Memoir* (Wellington 2013), 12, fn 466.

the jargon is avoided. Such discussions are better suited to specialised journal articles or to monographs dedicated to questions of leadership.[79] This is perhaps as well, given the need for a broad audience if the publishers are to remain in business. The sales figures for the political biographies published by Auckland University Press give no grounds for complacency (see Table 7).

Table 7: Sales figures for political biographies published by Auckland University Press[80]

Keith Sinclair	*Walter Nash* hardback edition: 7,950 (OP)
Keith Sinclair	*Walter Nash* paperback edition: 4,970 (OP)
Michael Bassett	*Sir Joseph Ward*: 968 (OP)
Michael Bassett	*Coates of the Kaipara*: 1,448 (almost OP)
Barry Gustafson	*His Way* hardback edition: 6,270 (some stock)
Barry Gustafson	*His Way* paperback edition: 3,285 (almost OP)
Barry Gustafson	*Kiwi Keith*: 2,793 (some stock)

Source: C. O'Brien (see footnote 79).

Noteworthy is the fact that sales of *Walter Nash* almost exceed those of the other biographies combined. *Walter Nash* won two major book awards but the sales were boosted by factors extraneous to quality. The author was a very prominent historian and public figure; and the subject divided public opinion and would have been very much alive in the memories of book buyers of the day. The book itself became famously controversial as the Security Intelligence Service tried to ban it as a security risk.[81]

Conclusion

Political biography has detractors and many of the criticisms are summed up thus:

> Biographies are, very often, a most unsatisfactory form from an historical and political point of view. The reason for this is quite simple — very few politicians are particularly interesting *per se*, though many may

---

79 For example, J. Henderson, 'Muldoon and Kirk: "active negative" Prime Ministers', *Political Science*. 30:2 (1978), 111–14; Henderson, 'Muldoon and Rowling: a Preliminary Analysis of Contrasting Leadership Styles', *Political Science*, 32:1 (1980), 26–46; J. Johansson (guest editor), Political Science (special issue on political leadership in New Zealand), 56:2 (2004); Johansson, Two Titans: Muldoon, Lange and Leadership. (Wellington, 2005).
80 C. O'Brien, email to author, 12 February 2013.
81 K. Sinclair, Halfway Round the *Harbour* (Auckland 1993), 210–16; R. Lilburn, 'Security Intelligence Records in New Zealand: a Case Study', Archifacts, April–October (2003), 5–7.

be interesting *sui generis*. And few indeed were sufficiently important, or so powerful in their time, that they had a really decisive impact, single-handedly, on their environment.

Thus frequently biographers have to face the problem that their subject was decisively important on one issue, or one event, maybe two, but that otherwise he was only one of a number of actors in a political drama, the scenario for which was written by others and was largely beyond his control, and in which most of the action was directed by someone else. To put this another way, political biographers usually have to try to maintain an uneasy balance between what the biographical subject thought and did and what the rest of the world was doing at the same time – the context within which he was operating.[82]

In sum, such criticisms equate with saying that political biography ought to transmute into political history per se. There is the obvious point that biography necessarily revolves around a person and, as Gustafson warns, a biography 'should not also be the history of a nation or of a government or of a political party', although it may contain elements of each.[83] The criticisms would be valid if monographic biography was the only way of approaching political history, but it is not. Rather, biography is just one path towards an understanding of political history, one which complements the other approaches but without any suggestion that it is capable of displacing them. Context has to be discussed but not to the point that it overwhelms the subject. The opportunities and constraints of the times and the environment in which prime ministers operated cannot be ignored, and the biographer needs to steer a course between these two competing claims. A successful biography will demonstrate that events are shaped by the interplay of impersonal forces and human action, as demonstrated in Tom Brooking's biography of the Liberal politician John McKenzie.[84] Emerging from the work on McKenzie is Brooking's recent biography of Richard John Seddon, but this might never have happened had David Hamer lived to complete a similar project – which in turn emerged out of Hamer's work on the Liberal Party.[85] Two more different approaches to political biography could scarcely be imagined. In keeping with his previous work, Hamer would likely have written a history of the times rather than a biography of the man: context would, in all likelihood, dominate the narrative. Brooking gave a foretaste of his contrasting approach to Seddon in a public lecture. He intends to portray 'a more complex

---

82   L. Watson, review of D. Aitkin, *The Colonel: a Political Biography of Sir Michael Bruxner*, in *Australian Journal of Politics and History*, 15: 3 (1969), 154.
83   Gustafson, *His Way*, 12.
84   See T. Brooking, *Lands for the People? The Highland Clearances and the Colonisation of New Zealand: a Biography of John McKenzie* (Dunedin 1996), 9–10.
85   D. Hamer, *The New Zealand Liberals: the Years in Power, 1891–1912* (Auckland 1988). See also D. Mackay, 'Obituary: David Hamer, 1938–1999', *New Zealand Journal of History*, 33:2 (1999), 243.

and multifaceted character than the often one-dimensional portraits within our historical literature which tend to caricature [Seddon] as an insensitive, anti-intellectual populist'. Brooking, in other words, will be offering a corrective – 'a post-revisionist account or a re-bunk' – to the 'presentist dismissal by enabling us to better understand why [Seddon] was so very popular with the majority of the New Zealand electorate and so despised by his opponents'.[86] Such an approach – where the personal is never far away from the political – combined with balancing the interplay of impersonal forces and human action is the dominant mode of political biography, as practiced in New Zealand. The journalistic quickies and the tracts of the party faithful will not go away. But the lengthy, detailed and heavily researched (and documented) political biography is the way of the future.

---

[86] Tom Brooking, 'Tall Tales: Richard John Seddon and the building of "God's Own Country"', Michael King Memorial Lecture, University of Otago, 14 October 2009 – the podcast can be downloaded from www.otago.ac.nz/news/itunesu/podcasts/index.rss?podcast=OTAGO007012&type=video. Tom Brooking, *Richard Seddon: King of God's Own: the life and times of New Zealand's longest-serving prime minister* (Auckland 2014).

www.ingramcontent.com/pod-product-compliance
Lightning Source LLC
Chambersburg PA
CBHW061140230426
43663CB00024B/2975